'A fascinating and useful exploration of the continuing development of psychoanalysis in relation to influences of disciplines outside it, including philosophy, shifting worldviews and science. The author brings out connections between different psychoanalytic sensibilities and impacts of evolving surrounding disciplines. I'm tempted to speak of multiple faces, roots and currents of the shifting philosophical zeitgeist of psychoanalysis.'

Michael Eigen, *PhD, author of* The Psychotic Core, Emotional Storm, The Psychoanalytic Mystic and Bits of Psyche

'In this provocative and intellectually stimulating volume, Aner Govrin takes us on a journey from Freud to the present, focused on the inextricable link between philosophy and psychoanalysis. Tracing the historical changes in philosophy, he illustrates how they are mirrored in analytic theory from classical analysis to the Postmodern Turn. He creatively argues that no new school of psychoanalytic thought has emerged since the 1980's, the focus now being on "not knowing," and creating "sensibilities" rather than complete theories. As a philosopher, as well as a psychoanalyst, he brings unique observations and informative anecdotes to this scholarly yet accessible book. I highly recommend it for its thought-provoking look at the history and current status of psychoanalytic thinking. And for the implicit challenge to create new theories that meet the standard of philosophical rigor.'

Karen J. Maroda, *PhD, ABPP, Assistant Professor of Psychiatry, Medical College of Wisconsin and private practice, Milwaukee, US*

'This book shows how psychoanalysis became less enamoured with the tenets of positivist science, just as positivist science became less enamoured with psychoanalysis. It is an engaging read, even for positivist scientists like me!'

Mark Solms, *editor of* Revised Standard Edition of the Complete Psychological Works of Sigmund Freud

How Philosophy Changed Psychoanalysis

From Naive Realism to Postmodernism

Through this book, philosopher and psychoanalyst Aner Govrin demonstrates how psychoanalysis' engagement with philosophy was crucial in the evolution of new psychoanalytic theories in three areas: perception of truth, developmental theories, and study of psychoanalytic treatment.

Beginning with a Freudian perspective, through ego psychology to the intersubjective and the relational approach, Govrin shows that philosophy seeps into psychoanalytic theory itself, becoming a constitutive factor. When we discuss psychoanalysis, we cannot do it without reference to philosophy, since virtually every sentence it has generated harks back to, and is embedded in philosophy. Moving onto the Post-psychoanalytic Schools Era in the second part, this seminal volume provides a model for understanding the evolution of psychoanalytic thought in the postmodern era, where "sensibilities" like the relational approach and infant research replaced the orthodox psychoanalytic schools. Govrin also explores whether psychoanalysis is a branch of philosophy, how psychoanalysis progresses, what a psychoanalytic innovation is, and why mainstream psychoanalysis rejects neuropsychoanalysis.

Exploring the intricate relationship between psychoanalysis and philosophy, this book will be of interest to clinicians, scholars, teachers, and students of contemporary psychoanalysis across a broad spectrum of theoretical orientations, as well as those in philosophy of science, epistemology, and neuropsychoanalysis.

Aner Govrin is a psychoanalyst, philosopher, and clinical psychologist. He is the director of a doctoral program, "Psychoanalysis and Hermeneutics," at The Program for Hermeneutics and Cultural Studies, Bar-Ilan University. He is a Tel-Aviv Institute for Contemporary Psychoanalysis (TAICP) member and Editor of the series *Routledge Introductions to Contemporary Psychoanalysis*.

Philosophy & Psychoanalysis Book Series
Jon Mills
Series Editor

Philosophy & Psychoanalysis is dedicated to current developments and cutting-edge research in the philosophical sciences, phenomenology, hermeneutics, existentialism, logic, semiotics, cultural studies, social criticism, and the humanities that engage and enrich psychoanalytic thought through philosophical rigor. With the philosophical turn in psychoanalysis comes a new era of theoretical research that revisits past paradigms while invigorating new approaches to theoretical, historical, contemporary, and applied psychoanalysis. No subject or discipline is immune from psychoanalytic reflection within a philosophical context including psychology, sociology, anthropology, politics, the arts, religion, science, culture, physics, and the nature of morality. Philosophical approaches to psychoanalysis may stimulate new areas of knowledge that have conceptual and applied value beyond the consulting room reflective of greater society at large. In the spirit of pluralism, *Philosophy & Psychoanalysis* is open to any theoretical school in philosophy and psychoanalysis that offers novel, scholarly, and important insights in the way we come to understand our world.

Titles in this series

For more information about this series, please visit: www.routledge.com/
Routledge-Handbooks-in-Religion/book-series

How Philosophy Changed Psychoanalysis

From Naïve Realism to Postmodernism

Aner Govrin

Routledge
Taylor & Francis Group

LONDON AND NEW YORK

Designed cover image: © Getty Images

First published 2025
by Routledge
4 Park Square, Milton Park, Abingdon, Oxon OX14 4RN

and by Routledge
605 Third Avenue, New York, NY 10158

Routledge is an imprint of the Taylor & Francis Group, an informa business

© 2025 Aner Govrin

British Library Cataloguing-in-Publication Data
A catalogue record for this book is available from the British
Library

ISBN: 978-1-032-80700-3 (hbk)
ISBN: 978-1-032-80699-0 (pbk)
ISBN: 978-1-003-49816-2 (ebk)

DOI: 10.4324/9781003498162

Typeset in Times New Roman
by ApexCoVantage, LLC

This book is dedicated to my mother, Nurit Govrin

Contents

Acknowledgments

The following copyright holders have generously given permission to quote or adapt material from these copyrighted works:

Taylor and Francis: Govrin, A. (2021). Center and Margin in Mainstream Psychoanalysis: The Case of Neuropsychoanalysis. *Neuropsychoanalysis*, 23, 3–13.

Routledge: Govrin, A. (2023). *Introduction to The Routledge International Handbook of Psychoanalysis and Philosophy*, ed. A. Govrin and T. Caspi, 2–19.

Frontiers in Psychology: Govrin, A. (2019). Facts and Sensibilities: What Is a Psychoanalytic Innovation? *Frontiers in Psychology*, 10, 1781. https://doi.org/10.3389/fpsyg.2019.01781.

Dvir Publishing House: Govrin, A. (2003). Between Abstinence and Seduction – The Epistemology of American Psychoanalysis (Hebrew).

Preface

Gillian Silverman recalled (The New Yorker July 15, 2023) how her father, Dr. Loyd Silverman, a psychoanalyst from New York, raised her and her sister in the 1970s and 80s. The father, a devout Freudian, used to interpret his daughter's dreams. When he saw Gillian and her sister were upset, he pulled out the Rorschach cards to understand the unconscious meaning of their distress. Gillian remembers that her father spent hours in self-hypnosis and self-analysis and was convinced that if he shared his insights with other people, he would make them happier and self-fulfilled. He would write letters to well-known athletes and politicians, sharing his insights on their failures and advising them on how they should behave or play better. In addition to being a psychoanalyst, Dr. Silverman was also a researcher who tried to test psychoanalytic theories in the laboratory through exposure to sub-threshold messages. When Gillian's sister began choking at tennis competitions, Loyd Silverman attributed it to unresolved Oedipal anxiety. To reduce her anxiety, he recorded a message on a tape recorder that would play in her sleep: "Beating dad is OK," "Beating mom is OK." It was not until years later that Gillian's sister discovered the recording. "As bizarre as my father's home experiments seem, they still resonate as acts of care," Gillian wrote.

Today, the situation seems peculiar. Although Loyd Silverman may appear somewhat eccentric, his belief in the validity of psychoanalytic theory reflects a deeper issue. A whole post-Freudian generation, primarily medical doctors, considered psychoanalysis as legitimate as medicine. They believed the Oedipus complex was embedded in our psyche just as our lungs are integral to our bodies. In other words, psychoanalysts, particularly in the United States, were naïve realists.

Naive realism is the belief that our perception of the world reflects it exactly as it is, unbiased and unfiltered. We do not think our feelings, history, or cultural factors affect how we perceive the world; thus, we believe others see it the same way we do. Indeed, psychoanalysts thought that psychoanalytic concepts are part of the material, objective world accessible to well-trained experts who have the tools to reveal the unconscious; that is, to psychoanalysts.

Today, this view looks naïve even childish. Postmodernism has taught us that theories do not mirror objective truths. Instead, they are influenced by the subjective perspectives of those who build them. Freud, Klein, Winnicott, and all the psychoanalytic school founders were personally rooted in the theories about which they theorized (Teicholz, 1999).

Even if one does not endorse postmodernism and thinks one can still "reliably infer certain truths about the patient's mind" (Eagle, 2009, 30), Loyd Silverman's conviction certainty looks ridiculous.

What drove many US psychoanalysts to such a transformation? How have current psychoanalysts replaced the importance of objective knowledge with the therapist's subjectivity as a critical factor in healing?

I propose that changes in psychoanalysts' worldviews – i.e., in their philosophy – formed a crucial factor in the evolution of new psychoanalytic theories. The book's central thesis is that a necessary and absolute interdependence can be said to exist between psychoanalysis and philosophy. Unable to generate a conceptual foundation of its own, psychoanalysis needs philosophy. When we discuss psychoanalysis, we cannot do it without reference to philosophy since virtually every sentence it has generated harks back to and is embedded in philosophy. Over and beyond serving as psychoanalysis's conceptual infrastructure and critically shaping its fundamental assumptions, philosophy also seeps into psychoanalytic theory itself, becoming a constitutive factor.

The book consists of two parts, each demonstrating this thesis.

In **Introduction: Is Psychoanalysis a Philosophy?**, I dwell on the points of contact and differences between psychoanalysis and philosophy and draw a broad frame of reference to accompany the reading of this book. Since so many philosophers described the human psyche in detail, I ask why psychoanalysis is not considered a branch of philosophy but part of psychology.

The first part of this book, **How Philosophy Changed American Psychoanalysis**, follows the fascinating change American psychoanalysis underwent from Freud to the relational approach as it moved from a positivist-scientific era to a postmodern, contemporary one.

The assumption is that major conceptual junctures in American psychoanalysis were always contemporaneous with changed philosophical perceptions. Thus, to understand the conceptual history of American psychoanalysis, we must form a notion of American psychoanalysts' worldviews and philosophical tendencies in the relevant periods. Many other reasons were responsible for the changed perceptions of development and therapy, like the sexual revolution of the 60s, new attitudes to child-rearing practices and authority in Western culture, the emergence of hundreds of competing psychotherapies and the decline of psychoanalysis' status in the psychiatric establishment. However, I will limit myself to the relationship between philosophy and psychoanalysis.

The present focus on psychoanalysis in America focuses on a somewhat artificial distinction between it and psychoanalysis as it evolved in Europe. There are mutual relations between these two constituencies. It was the scores of psychoanalysts who immigrated to the United States from Europe between 1933–1941, in the wake of Nazism's rise to power, fleeing persecution in the Second World

War, that very considerably contributed to the speed with which psychoanalysis struck root there. Psychoanalysts who remained in Europe also impacted American psychoanalysis, especially the relational approach. While I have mentioned the role of Ferenczi, Winnicott, and Fairbairn as sources of inspiration for relational psychoanalysis, I believe that psychoanalysis' scientism bore greater weight for the Americans than the British. The detached, neutral position of the British and American psychoanalysts was justified in different ways. Thus, the rough the theory of object relations, the British advocated neutrality in therapy to advance projection and allow regression. At the same time, the Americans did the same under the banner of maintaining a scientifically objective position.

It is important to emphasize that ego psychology, self-psychology, intersubjectivity, and the relational approach are distinctly American theories with no European counterparts. Hartmann's influence on American psychoanalysis has been significantly more significant than elsewhere, where his theory gained little traction. Therefore, despite the existing connections between these communities, it is justifiable to describe the conceptual development of each in its own context.

Changes in worldviews influence all psychoanalytic theories, but the Americans seem to be the first to assimilate these influences. More than most European countries, Americans are motivated to create new movements reflecting the influence of contemporary intellectual developments. Alongside mainstream orthodoxy in the 50s and 60s, new psychoanalytic schools flourished (such as the Interpersonal school of Harry Stuck Sullivan and the existential psychoanalysis of Rollo May). Today, postmodernism (and before that, hermeneutics), neuropsychoanalysis, postmodernism, post-structuralism, and a wide range of feminist theories have found a theoretical home in the US. The scientific ethos in the US was quite robust, so the change that psychoanalysis went from a scientific to a postmodern worldview within several decades is quite dramatic.

In **Chapter 1, Freud's Compromising Positivism**, I show that, despite Freud's commitment to positivism and scientism, he was, mainly for pragmatic reasons, both pluralist and dualist, and his writing is marked by a persistent dialectical tension between objectivity and subjectivity, between archeological and narrative truth. This complex and ambiguous positioning cost him dearly by way of the many contradictions and unresolved problems that riddle his writings. The deviations from positivism discussed in this chapter are replacing the seduction theory with intrapsychic fantasies, the superiority of the pleasure principle over the reality principle, and changing the therapeutic technique from the recovery of memories to transference.

From here, the following four chapters are dedicated to four major theories in American psychoanalysis: classical psychoanalysis, Heinz Kohut's self-psychology, and two current postmodern theories: the intersubjective theory and the relational approach.

Each theory is presented via three reference points: worldview, developmental theory, and therapeutic theory. Each chapter starts with a short vignette or a therapeutic analysis typical of the approach.

These chapters aim to show that American psychoanalysis passed through a three-stage development: classical psychoanalysis represents the positivist phase in the American history of thought; Kohut's self-psychology reflects an intermediate stage, neither postmodern nor positivist, which includes elements of both. The relational and intersubjective approaches incorporate the postmodern phase in American psychoanalysis.

Chapter 2, Classical Psychoanalysis: The Scientific Dream, describes how classical psychoanalysis tried to solve the tensions between the various poles typical of Freud's theory. It has aspired to transform psychoanalysis into a more systematic, uniform, non-contradictory theory that would meet the strict criteria of natural science. Conceptually, the main difference between them and Freud lay in their attempt to solve the contradiction between his theory's subjective and objective elements. Through prominent figures in American mainstream psychoanalysis, such as Heinz Hartmann, Kurt Eissler, Lawrence Kubie, and Thomas Szasz, the chapter demonstrates its thesis on classical psychoanalysis in terms of epistemology, developmental theory, and the theory of therapeutic relations. The chapter shows that the psychoanalytic thought of those who played a significant role in this era was far more intricate and sophisticated than their contemporaries portrayed.

Chapter 3, Heinz Kohut's Self-Psychology, demonstrates that, although Kohut's theory includes some significant deviations from positivist philosophy, paving the way for postmodern theories in psychoanalysis, Kohut himself does not offer an alternative philosophy to take the place of positivist epistemology and stays faithful in some essential ways to many of positivism's tenets. Kohut's radical and orthodox aspects in his theory are discussed through his perception of truth, developmental theory, and therapeutic relations.

Chapter 4, The Intersubjective Approach, analyzes the notion of truth, development, and therapy within the intersubjective approach of Stolorow, Atwood Orange, and others in the nineties and the first decade of the millennia. Stolorow's and Atwood's first ideas were formulated precisely when Kohut began publishing his papers. This analysis will lead us to question whether the contribution of the intersubjective approach amounts to a certain theoretical sensibility or has it generated a new theory. Does it exist apart from the classical psychoanalysis which it criticizes? I show how the intersubjective approach has given self-psychology what it lacked: a postmodern philosophy in harmony with its perception of humans and its views of therapeutic objectives.

Chapter 5, The Relational Approach, presents Irwin Hoffman's thinking as representing the relational group. I chose him because of his fascinating epistemological views and radical therapeutic approach. Hoffman, more than anyone else, represents the postmodern approach to psychoanalysis. One of my main conclusions is that Hoffman's writing, detached as it is from the existing psychoanalytic tradition and with its peculiarities, fits in well with the postmodern tendency not to make up one more link in the chain of theories and to constitute, instead, a different voice with an ironic and unblinkered view of the modernist chain.

The second part, **The Post-psychoanalytic Schools Era**, provides a framework for understanding the evolution of psychoanalytic thought from Freud till the present day.

Chapter 6, Back to Positivism: The Case of Neuropsychoanalysis If, until now, readers thought that psychoanalysis had abandoned positivist-scientific philosophy, in Chapter 6, they will discover how wrong they were. It is back; it is here, alive and kicking in the form of a new "sensibility" – neuropsychoanalysis. Neuropsychoanalysis seeks to connect the discoveries of brain research with psychoanalytic discoveries. In other words, it returns the objective scientific dimension to psychoanalytic discourse. Alongside the popularity that neuropsychoanalysis has gained, it has also encountered harsh criticism from the camp that was supposed to endorse it: Orthodox psychoanalysis that shares the scientific worldview. The chapter discusses ways neuropsychoanalysis can evolve by becoming more relevant to the daily practice of psychoanalysts.

Chapter 7, Facts and Sensibilities: What Is a Psychoanalytic Innovation?, complements the first part by showing how psychoanalytic knowledge develops and what criteria a new psychoanalytic conceptualization must meet in order for it to be considered novel and used by analysts. Psychoanalysis is not just about trying to incorporate fashionable philosophies. Its primary motivation is to solve clinical problems and conceptualize human phenomena using psychoanalytic tools.

Since the 80s of the twentieth century and under the influence of postmodernism, no new psychoanalytic school has emerged. But this does not mean that schools of thought have stagnated. On the contrary, they continue to evolve, shape, and change, with the worldview behind them essentially assuming the existence of mental structures, developmental pathways, and dynamics of transfer relationships. Thus, the psychoanalytic world largely rejected postmodernism and continued to work with the more conservative epistemology based on realism and the correspondence theory of truth. The rejection of positivism impacted the development of "sensibilities," which are not construed as alternatives to the old schools. Rather, they guide analysts working with these schools to develop a "sensibility" to the central focus that each "sensibility" developed. These sensibilities include the relational approach, neuropsychoanalysis, and mother-infant research.

References

Eagle, M. (2009). Chapter 1: Postmodern Influences on Contemporary Psychoanalysis. In R. Frie and D. Orange (Eds.) *Beyond Postmodernism New Dimensions in Clinical Theory and Practice*. London: Routledge, 27–51.

Silverman, G. (2023). Growing Up in the House of Freud. *The New Yorker*, July 15.

Teicholz, J.G. (1999). *Kohut, Loewald, & the Postmoderns – A Comparative Study of Self and Relationship*. Hillsdale, NJ: The Analytic Press.

Introduction

Is Psychoanalysis a Philosophy?

Any thinking about the relations between psychoanalysis and philosophy involves clashing ideas, emotions, and associations. In this short introduction, I will try to discuss some pre-existing opinions that might get in the way of enriching our sensibilities to the two disciplines' profound affinities. Taking into account the various branches of philosophy and the engagements between philosophy and other bodies of knowledge, we may want to think of these interrelations from two possible perspectives:

1. Psychoanalysis is an autonomous and separate science, and its relation with philosophy resembles the relations the latter entertains with other domains, like physics, chemistry, social science, or literary criticism.
2. Psychoanalysis is a branch of philosophy: each and every thought or statement it produces is replete with philosophical axioms; like other branches of philosophy, such as phenomenology, existentialism, or the complex philosophical theories of Hegel, Nietzsche, and others, it directs itself to such problems as the human mind, freedom of choice, motivation, ethics, consciousness, the unconscious, and so on.

I would like to suggest that neither of these possibilities, as such, is adequate and that a third possibility might be what we have to think of: While psychoanalysis and philosophy are essentially and mutually embedded, they exist, at the same time, somewhat apart. This is mainly due to how psychoanalysts' professional identities evolved and our mental inclination to discipline-based categorizations based on group identities.

On one view, indeed, philosophical discussions of any academic subject are an early phase in the scientific study of that subject. Philosophy, by this approach, features as a form of protoscience on the basis of which any science subsequently develops. Hence, William James defined philosophy as "a collective name for questions that have not yet been answered to the satisfaction of all by whom they have been asked" (1907/1979, 23). Elsewhere, James suggests how we may identify the point in a discipline's evolution when it becomes autonomous: "As fast as

DOI: 10.4324/9781003498162-1

questions got accurately answered, the answers were called 'scientific,' and what men call 'philosophy' today is but the residuum of questions still unanswered" (James 1979, 12).

It is not hard to see that this type of phenomenon – consisting of an early and immature stage of fusion followed by development and a separation process in the direction of autonomy – never took place in the case of philosophy and psychoanalysis. Psychoanalysis was conceived as a scientific discipline in its own right from the outset and never saw itself as part of philosophy. There was, therefore, nothing to split off from. But, in addition to the fact that what we are looking at is not the regular evolution of a scientific discipline from its philosophical beginnings, there are also indications that psychoanalysis never attained this kind of autonomy. When clearly demarcated intellectual domains are properly separated, experts in both fields will accept and respect each other's authority. Philosophers, for instance, will usually avoid solving problems in physics by using their own logical or other conceptual apparatus, ignoring the existence of experimental physics. Nor will physicists, from their side, trespass into philosophy without thoroughly informing themselves of the conceptual and methodological ABCs of philosophy. Such boundaries and distinctions are also observed in the softer social sciences – sociology, anthropology, and social work.

Psychology became an autonomous science in the 19th century, with the inception of psychological experiments. In time, cognition and memory grew into key psychological domains. Once computer science began to produce knowledge about the structure of concepts or cognitive processes, philosophy lost some of its critical areas to the new science.

But psychoanalysis and philosophy find themselves on rather a different footing. Psychoanalysis never appropriated or took over any intellectual territory, ousting philosophy. There is a rich philosophical oeuvre addressing the emotions, personality, the structure of the mind, consciousness, and knowledge, which neither relies on psychoanalysis nor refers to it. The same goes for psychoanalysis, some of whose core issues, like psychic conflict or sexual drives, remain completely foreign to mainstream philosophy.

One reason why psychoanalysis was never recognized as an autonomous branch or an independent science was that the body of knowledge it generated was never granted scientific status. This is illustrated by the pointed criticism it received during a symposium organized by Sidney Hook (Hook, 1958). Philosophers, on this occasion, made painstaking and systematic efforts to show that the claims of psychoanalysis could not be taken seriously and that it did not meet the minimal requirements for being, in the usual sense, a scientific theory. Freudian hypotheses were deemed too vague to be subjected to empirical testing, there were no criteria for evaluating evidence, and the therapeutic efficacy of the method was questionable.

In the wake of this symposium, the critique of psychoanalysis almost grew into a research domain in its own right within philosophy, with leading philosophers like Karl Popper and Adolf Grünbaum taking a prominent part. In the eyes of the philosophers, one of the greatest sins of psychoanalysis was that it lacked conceptual clarity and tightness. Often using the same philosophical terms for different concepts – or vice versa – as well as deploying a range of concepts that could only be validated within their own terms, psychoanalysis produced a virtual Babel. For Wittgenstein, psychoanalysis essentially *imposes* interpretations rather than unfolding them as it claims. According to Wittgenstein, a psychoanalytic interpretation essentially involves a mythlike (that is, predetermined) explanation imposed on a mental state that reduces it to something familiar and common. Nevertheless, the assent of the person involved is the criterion of correctness. There is a fundamental tension here; for, once the mental state has been identified, its correct explanation would seem to be given by the mythology applied; yet, the assent or non-assent of the patient is supposed to be dispositive. It would be fair to say of Wittgenstein that, for him, psychoanalysis is a kind of crude religion; one that does not even realize that that is what it is (Levy, 1996; Harcourt, 2023).

But paradoxically, this lack of clarity in its conceptual makeup only further bolsters the connection between psychoanalysis and philosophy. After all, the thinking of many philosophers is hard to understand, vague, and open to interpretation. The very quality of psychoanalysis that received such opprobrium from (positivist) philosophers is what is a major similarity and connection between it and philosophy (those branches, that is, which the positivists shrugged off as metaphysics).

Which leaves us with the second question: Why is psychoanalysis not considered a branch of philosophy?

Any attempt to answer this question runs into even more obstacles. First, it is hard to find anything philosophy addresses – ontology, reality, the soul, consciousness, truth, logic, ethics, free will, causality, knowledge, cognition, and language – that does not directly communicate with core issues in psychoanalysis. The two disciplines discuss the same topics to subject them to rational investigation. Philosophers' definitions of their discipline even tend to identify their main concerns as overlapping with psychoanalysis's. Theodore Lipps, for example, argued in the first half of the 19th century that "logic is a psychological discipline, as certain as the cognition occurs only in the psyche, and the thinking, which completes itself in the cognition, is a psychical event" (Dale, 2006, 88).

Lipps believed that philosophy is psychology or the science of inner experience, so philosophy should be considered part of the natural sciences. Other, more conventional definitions that identify between philosophy and science (Descartes, Hobbes, and Bacon) indicate the near absolute identity between the two disciplines. The same can be observed for approaches like Hegel's that consider philosophy the "science of principles." Many philosophers, moreover, like Nietzsche, Schopenhauer, Spinoza, Hegel, Kant, Heidegger, Husserl and Sartre, developed detailed theories of the psyche, covering all its functions: perception, memory, emotions, development, adults-children relations, the perception of time, consciousness of self and society, and so on. It is difficult to fully keep apart from their philosophical investigations from psychological theories of the human psyche and behavior.

However, Freud made his name as a psychoanalyst, not as a philosopher, like Nietzsche, Schopenhauer, or Heidegger.

One possible way of understanding this is that these disciplines have different aims, and they are achieved using different methods. Psychoanalysis, indeed, is not only about an account or mapping of the human mind or psyche but also offers a method that seeks to alleviate individual suffering. Freud's theory – and every other psychoanalytical approach – is mainly devoted to precisely that: psychoanalytic healing. But many philosophical doctrines, too, suggest ways to heal the psyche (Banicki, 2014; Carlisle and Ganeri, 2010; Peterman, 1992). Almost every philosopher brings together precisely these two pillars of psychoanalysis: a theory of the human psyche and a theory for the healing of that psyche; that is to say, a set of values and principles that hold out a more meaningful life (existentialism) or a more intensely lived life (Nietzsche) or, again, a life guided by reason and the regulation of the emotions (Spinoza, Kant).

To explain why psychoanalysis is not a branch of philosophy, we might have to consider their respective research methodologies.

Philosophy has traditionally employed specific methodologies, including the systematic use of counter-examples, precise definitions, and logical analysis of the validity of arguments.

While philosophy relies on these, we might suppose that psychoanalytic knowledge is based on Freud's and his followers' clinical observations. This criterion also soon proves to be knottier than it seems. First, we know how much any observation is determined by the observer's point of view, feelings, and needs. Second, the psychologies of thinkers like Nietzsche, Schopenhauer, or Hegel refer back to some research object in an act we may call "observation," even if this particular kind of observation does not occur in the clinic. Instead, it relies on empirical acquaintance with and perception of human beings; mainly themselves and people encountered. On this argument, every branch of "scientific" thinking is, in fact, philosophy.

Two additional explanations for the separate existence of the two disciplines appear more adequate. A discipline defines and demarcates itself once it outlines a domain within which it aims to exist and operate while simultaneously indicating the group(s) to which it does not belong. This act of mapping is crucial to the discipline's self-definition and the way it is publicly perceived. Now, what does and does not belong in the province of the discipline is clearly staked out. Freud and his followers determined these domains.

The first stage of a positive affirmation of identity emerged when psychoanalysis presented itself, early on, as a medical profession. Freud and his followers created a firm professional identity for the psychoanalyst as both physician and scientist. At the same time – and this is the negative corollary of the process of identification – Freud (1933) himself sharply criticizes philosophy as such pointing out its failures and limitations. He affirms very clearly that psychoanalysis is a science. Philosophy, he argues, has not succeeded in giving an account of the human psyche. Psychoanalysis, which he emphatically identifies as a science, produces, by contrast, more adequate and valid theoretical directions.

We can look at how these two reasons fatefully shaped the relations between psychoanalysis and philosophy.

Even though at the start of his studies at age 17, Freud took his initial steps in the direction of philosophy, mainly through the work of Ludwig Feuerbach (Levitt and Turgeon, 2009) and Franz Brentano (Domenjo, 2000) (taking no less than five university courses with the latter), he began his formal studies at the laboratory of Carl Claus, (Cornejo, 2018) one of Darwin's most influential proponents in the German language. Freud's first empirical work involved the sex glands of the eel. This helped Freud develop the patient and accurate examination of a research object into the focused attention that he later brought to bear so effectively when listening to his patients. For the time being, Freud was clearly preparing himself to become a scientist doing laboratory experiments. Next, he moved on to Ernst Brücke, his great mentor, whose laboratory he worked in for six years. Peter Gay (1988), his biographer, describes how happy Freud was when solving the mysteries of the nervous system – initially, that of simple fish, and next, of humans. He deeply enjoyed fulfilling his admired teacher's exacting expectations. In 1881, Freud left Brücke's laboratory to take up his medical studies. As part of these studies, he joined the staff of Vienna's General Hospital for three years. He experienced with various medical fields, like surgery, internal medicine, psychiatry, dermatology, neurological diseases, and ophthalmology. Freud was heading for a career in medicine rather than philosophy or the humanities. He considered himself a scientist and researcher whose job was to ground each assumption he made in proven evidence.

The fact that Freud departed from philosophy eventually greatly contributed to Freud's (and his followers') professional identity. For many years after Freud's death, this identity grew ever more solid and fixed. In the US, psychoanalysis was regarded as a branch of medicine for decades. Consequently, training institutes refused to admit candidates like psychologists or social workers without medical training. This limitation was only removed in the 1980s, in a step that required legal intervention. Starting in Freud's lifetime, the psychoanalytic community's debate around this issue was longstanding. Interestingly, Freud was adamant about enrolling non-medically trained candidates (see his remarks in the paper on lay psychoanalysis on this). It was one of the very few issues that many (mainly American) psychoanalysts disagreed with Freud.

This identification between medicine and psychoanalysis gave psychoanalysis prestige and respectability among the general public, specifically in the medical establishment. It seems doubtful whether such a reception would have been possible if psychoanalysis had considered and presented itself as an offshoot of philosophy.

There are some interesting cases of philosophers becoming psychiatrists, like Karl Jaspers (1883–1969) and Ludwig Binswanger (1881 – February). Both were major philosophers-psychiatrists affiliated with existentialism who developed their own theories, like psychoanalysis, including psychological theory and an account of the ethically good and meaningful life. However, despite being influential philosophers, neither gave rise to a community of followers. That two leading philosophers should have emerged from psychiatry suggests that if we want to know why psychoanalysis was not considered a branch of philosophy, we should look for a socially contingent component rather than expect to find some inherent feature of psychoanalysis.

Freud flirted with philosophy throughout his life, which inspired much of his thought. However, once he became interested in being a medical doctor, he stayed clear of pure medical research. Still, his lack of taste for certain aspects of philosophy, mainly metaphysics, together with his great admiration for scientific positivism, did not allow him to cross the lines. Freud's ambivalence about the disciplinary relations between psychoanalysis and medicine is reflected in his contribution for a symposium dedicated to the subject (Gay, 1995, 490).

Freud's writings also illustrate that the broad imbrication between psychoanalysis and philosophy was on his mind. He, too, believed psychoanalysis to occupy a place within philosophy, though it was admittedly idiosyncratic. In an early letter to his friend Wilhelm Fliess, Freud admits to "secretly nurs[ing] the hope of arriving by the . . . circuitous route of medicine . . . at my own original, objective philosophy" (Masson, 1985). In 1925, he wrote about how he viewed psychoanalysis as occupying an uneasy "middle position between medicine and philosophy" (1925, 217).

Freud's criticism of philosophy is the other reason psychoanalysis never evolved into a branch of philosophy. His efforts to separate the two disciplines were substantial (Freud, 1933) (while, as we saw, he was also averse to identification with medicine). However, we must remember that Freud's critique of philosophy aims more specifically at metaphysics.

Alfred Tauber (2010) argued that Freud rejected philosophy because of three weaknesses: Philosophy represents comprehensive knowledge unresponsive to new empirical findings, which reduces it to an armchair theory. Moreover, philosophy is hermetic and limited, and finally, it unduly relies on non-scientific knowledge.

For Freud, psychoanalysis contrasts with philosophy in the narrow sense of metaphysics. He considers dedicating himself, like religion, to offering humans the possibility to escape harsh and painful reality into illusion and soothing indifference. Like religion, metaphysics results from philosophers' desire to create a clean and coherent picture of the world far removed from a clear view of reality (Berthold-Bond, 1989). Psychoanalysis offers a more scientific and realistic perception of a life involving suffering, uncertainty, and the unknown. These are seen as phenomena to which human beings must reconcile themselves. Ironically, Freud's critique of metaphysics reproduces positivism's critique of psychoanalysis.

In "Inhibitions, Symptoms and Anxiety" (1926), Freud describes philosophers as in the business of "fabricating Weltanschauungen," driven by their inability "to make their journey through life without a Baedeker" or "Handbook of Life," which promises to give them answers to all of life's problems. The scathing satire continues to compare the philosopher to a traveler who "may sing aloud in the dark to deny his own fears" but who, for all his singing, "will not see an inch further beyond his nose" (96).

Freud was not alone in his critique of metaphysics – philosophers like Kant, Nietzsche, and Kierkegaard had also argued against it. Psychoanalytic theory is not a mere replacement of metaphysics; for analytic philosophers, empiricism is a replacement but a transformation and hence a recovery. As Kant did, Freud believes that metaphysical thinking is a natural human disposition. However, according to Berthold-Bond (1989), Freud seeks to account for this metaphysical disposition in terms of his remarkable theory of Freud's distinctive phylogenetic model of man's epistemological evolution. As such, metaphysics cannot simply be removed from the mental makeup of man but must be displaced or transferred or sublimated into a different mode of knowledge.

We have seen how psychoanalysis cannot be regarded as autonomous and should, in many respects, be considered a branch of philosophy. Its historical development, however, problematizes this. We may compare these intricacies with the nature of family relations: One of the children (i.e., psychoanalysis) has chosen to turn away from the family (i.e., philosophy) in order to find itself a new family (in the shape of medical and biological science). Perceived as a foreign body and a stepchild, the child does not really fit in with its chosen family.

Yet, still. This comparison only serves us some of the way. As we know, up until recently, many psychoanalysts like to see themselves as scientists, much as Freud did. However, recently, many have wished to see their close connection to poetry. Ogden, for example, describes the relationship between the way the analyst listens to a poem's language and the way the analyst and his patient speak with and listen to one another. Interestingly, finding an analyst that declares an affinity between his profession and philosophy is most unusual. Psychoanalysts gain their reputation from clinical work or poetic language, not philosophical disputes about truth, free will, and the nature of consciousness.

Like medical doctors, psychoanalysts have patients whom they receive in their clinics. Like the former, the latter see it as their task to alleviate patients' suffering, and to practice, both have to be certified by the health authorities. While philosophers read, write, and debate, psychoanalysts treat patients (as well as read, write, and debate).

This is the outcome of psychoanalysis leaving its original family, even though it never became fully part of its new family. Still, their strong ties endure.

A necessary and absolute interdependence can be said to exist between psychoanalysis and philosophy. Unable to generate a conceptual foundation of its own, psychoanalysis needs philosophy. When we discuss psychoanalysis, we cannot do it without reference to philosophy, since virtually every sentence it has generated harks back to and is embedded in philosophy. Over and beyond serving as psychoanalysis' conceptual infrastructure and critically shaping its key assumptions, philosophy also seeps into psychoanalytic theory itself, becoming a constitutive factor.

One illustration of this is positivism's crucial role in Freud's development theory. The infant's main developmental achievement is transitioning from the pleasure principle – absolute subjectivity – to the reality principle, which yields sensory-based understanding resulting from trial and error. Reality is distinct and separate from the subject. By contrast, theories like those of Winnicott or Kohut, who were not committed to positivism, generated a different developmental model. Here, the infant's most significant developmental achievements occur in a state of absolute subjectivity. The difference has nothing to do with the infants – they stayed the same – but it involves changes in the theoretical, philosophical approach.

Having teased out some of the family dynamics, historical and conceptual, between philosophy and psychoanalysis, it is high time to turn to witness the close connection between psychoanalysis and philosophy.

References

Banicki, K. (2014). Philosophy as Therapy: Towards a Conceptual Model. *Philosophical Papers*, 43(1), 7–31.

Berthold-Bond, D. (1989). Freud's Critique of Philosophy. *Metaphilosophy*, 20(3/4), 274–294.

Carlisle, C. and Ganeri, J. (Eds.) (2010). *Philosophy as Therapeia*. Cambridge: Cambridge University Press.

Cornejo, R. (2018). Origins of a Theory of Psychic Temporality in Freud: The Study of Eels and the Darwinist Infuence of Carl Claus. *International Journal of Psychoanalysis*, 99, 450–467.

Dale, J. (2006). *Philosophy, Psychology, and Psychologism: Critical and Historical Readings on the Psychological Turn in Philosophy*. Dordrecht: Springer Science & Business Media, 88, 89.

Domenjo, B.A. (2000). Thoughts on the Infuence of Brentano and Comte on Freud's Work. *Psychoanalysis and History*, 2, 110–118.

Freud, S. (1925). Resistances to Psycho-Analysis. In *The Standard Edition of the Complete Psychological Writings of Sigmund Freud*, Vol. 19. London: Hogarth Press.

Freud, S. (1926). Inhibitions, Symptoms and Anxiety. In *The Standard Edition of the Complete Psychological Writings of Sigmund Freud*, Vol. 20. London: Hogarth Press.

Freud, S. (1933). The Question of a Weltanschauung. In J. Strachey (Ed. and trans.) *The Standard Edition of the Complete Psychological Works of Sigmund Freud*. Vol. 22. London: Hogarth Press, 158–182.

Gay, P. (1988). *Freud: A Life for Our Time*. London: Papermac. ISBN 0-333-48638-2.

Harcourt, E. (2023). Wittgenstein Disciple of Freud? In A. Govron and T. Caspi (Eds.) *The Routledge International Handbook of Psychoanalysis and Philosophy*. London: Routledge.

James, W. (1979). *Some Problems of Philosophy: A Beginning of an Introduction to Philosophy*. Cambridge, MA: Harvard University Press, 12.

Levitt, C. and Turgeon, A. (2009). Sigmund Freud's Intensive Reading of Ludwig Feuerbach. *Canadian Journal of Psychoanalysis*, 17, 14–35.

Levy, D. (1996). *Freud Among the Philosophers: The Psychoanalytic Unconscious and Its Philosophical Critics*. New Haven and London: Yale University Press.

Masson, J.M. (Ed) (1985). *The Complete Letters of Sigmund Freud to Wilhelm Fliess, 1887–1904*. Cambridge, MA: Belknap Press of Harvard University Press.

Peterman, J.F. (1992). *Philosophy as Therapy – An Interpretation and Defense of Wittgenstein's Later Philosophical Project*. SUNY Series in Philosophy and Psychotherapy. New York: Suny Press.

Tauber, A.I. (2010). *Freud, the Reluctant Philosopher*. Kindle edn. Princeton: Princeton University Press.

Part 1

How Philosophy Changed American Psychoanalysis

Chapter 1

Freud's Compromising Positivism

There is no better way to show Freud's ambivalence to positivism than to demonstrate it through his treatment of his patients. Here is a description from one of his patients' memories, the American psychiatrist John Dorsey:

> At times, for all his seriousness and focus on the work, Freud could be funny and personable. He once leaned over the couch and sent Dorsey a few lines from Mozart's Don Giovanni, which was playing at the Vienna opera. Another time, when Dorsey had some remark about Freud's father fixation Freud said, "You may analyze me if you wish, but I shan't pay for it". For Christmas, Freud gave his patient a copy of his recently published New Introductory Lectures on Psychoanalysis.
>
> (Lohser and Newton, 1996, 113)

Reading this, one must wonder whether classical psychoanalysis (described in the next chapter) is a continuation of Freud's true nature or a distortion. But let us first explore Freud's inclination to positivism.

Ever since Freud first introduced psychoanalysis, alongside the enormous interest and following, it also elicited academics' contempt and ridicule. The criticism psychoanalysis attracted took extraordinary proportions – regarding the number of participants, the number of publications it spawned, and the conferences it occasioned. This buzz reached the popular media as well, which more than once rushed to announce its demise and publish its send-off. Psychoanalysis was criticized from various perspectives and confronted with different arguments. One critic claimed that Freud's case studies were made up, another said he was a charlatan, yet another argued that Freud, concerned about social responses to his findings, concealed them, while yet another revealed Freud had had an affair with his sister-in-law – thus seriously compromising his integrity.

However, most of the serious criticism – among them Karl Popper, Adolf Grunbaum, Frank Sulloway, and Ernest Gellner – focused on one issue: the doubtful scientific status of Freudian theory. While these critics of psychoanalysis did not explicitly subscribe to positivism and, at times, did not see eye to eye with it, they were, nevertheless, affected by its fundamental ideas.

DOI: 10.4324/9781003498162-3

Psychoanalysis' Scientific Status

What Is Positivism?

I will, in this book, refer to positivism in its broad and general sense as a philosophical movement of the second half of the 19th century and the first decades of the 20th, which adopted the general philosophical view on which science is the one type of valid knowledge, scientific facts are the only objective of knowledge, and it is philosophy's aim to unveil the laws common to all sciences. Positivism rejects any metaphysics and investigative methodology that does not rely on scientific principles. Science-based knowledge is perceived as the highest form of human achievement – the pinnacle of human reason (Kolakowski, 1972).

Modern versions of positivism such as logical positivism, come under the critical positivism that evolved toward the end of the 19th century in the work of Ernst Mach and Richard Avenarius. Logical positivism included philosophers like Moritz Schlick, Rudolph Carnap, Otto Neurath, Herbert Feigl, and others, all members of the Vienna Circle. Over and above many differences, most of these thinkers shared some common features. The logical positivists aimed for scientific agreement among philosophers. Supporting an inclusive empiricism that drew on modern logical theory, their action was underwritten by modern science, which they set great store by. Their rejection of metaphysics was not only grounded in logic: Not only did they consider it a false and worthless approach; they believed it lacked meaning (Ayer, 1966). They wanted to search for a natural and vital role for logic and mathematics and to find an understanding of philosophy, according to which it was part of the scientific project. They believed that experience could be disassembled into the basic components: the direct and irreplaceable sensory observations that make up the observer's world. Referring to Wittgenstein, they showed that the structure thus represented is reflected in language; that is, logical analysis can show that the sentences using which knowledge is expressed can be reduced in a way resembling simple statements by means of a one-to-one correspondence with the real or possible details of sensory experience (Kolakowski, 1972).

It is quite evident that psychoanalysis cannot win this battle. However, it did not lose without a fight (see Hook, 1958).

Frank (1959) described how the doctrines of logical positivism had come to be seen as uncompromising gate-keepers, blocking entry into the science of any but the most logically strict theories – those whose terms have met the rigorous semantic standards and proven themselves to be meaningful. Unlike many of those who later claimed to represent logical positivism, its early advocates comfortably accepted that the theoretical system of axioms that organize a field cannot, themselves, be subject to observational tests. Instead, the logical positivist says "that one theory is more practical or convenient than another one . . . hence, the truth of Freudian or similar theories must not be understood otherwise than pragmatically. It may be convenient or not to accept them" (Frank, 1959, 311).

Psychoanalysis: Science or Hermeneutics?

Karl Popper was one of psychoanalysis' most important critics. While never actually joining the phenomenalist approaches of the Vienna Circle, his thinking has general affinities to them. Thus, for instance, Popper (1965) discussed how to demarcate science from non-science. Naturally, this question also includes how to classify science into good and lousy science (Ayer, 1966).

Popper argues that only proof from the attempt to refute the theory can be considered supportive, as each theory is susceptible to several supportive proofs. Thus, only the outcome of an examination that can potentially be refuted can count as confirmation. For Popper, human thinking progresses steadily as a result of criticism. Criticism, in his perspective, is equivalent to rationalism. As an ongoing chain of problems, assumptions, tentative solutions, and refutations, science is a rational activity. The scientist's work always takes part in this chain.

One of the central axes in Popper's work is the struggle against Marxism and psychoanalysis (10). Popper argued that it is not difficult to find proof in favor of nearly any theory, and he thus holds that such "corroboration," as he terms it, should be regarded as science only if it is the positive outcome of an indeed "risky" prediction, which might plausibly have been false. For Popper, the problem is not with Freud's truth but a lack of falsification criterion. He thinks that psychoanalysis has more in common with primitive myths than with science. Popper argues that Freud's theory can explain more or less every occurrence in the domains to which it relates:

> I found that those of my friends who were admirers of Marx, Freud, and Adler, were impressed by a number of points common to these theories, and especially by their apparent *explanatory power*. These theories appeared to be able to explain practically everything that happened within the fields to which they referred. . . . It was precisely this fact – that they always fitted, that they were always confirmed – which in the eyes of their admirers constituted the strongest argument in favour of these theories. It began to dawn on me that this apparent strength was in fact their weakness.
>
> (88–89)

Adolf Grünbaum, a philosopher of science at the University of Pittsburgh, is considered Freud's most remarkable contemporary critic after Freud. Grünbaum (1984) confronts Popper, arguing that Freud often adjusted his theory when discovering that it did not correspond with his clinical findings. He believes psychoanalytic theory holds all the components required to make it a science. The problem is that it is a flawed science. Grünbaum claims that Popper wrongly assumed that Freud's theory cannot be tested. Freud stated, "After all, his [the patient's] conflicts will only be successfully solved, and his resistances overcome if the anticipatory ideas he is given [by the analyst] tally with what is real in him. Whatever in the doctor's conjectures is inaccurate drops out in the course of the analysis" (Freud,

1917a, 452). This has been called Freud's *tally argument* (Grünbaum, 1984). Grün-baum believes that Freud argued that 1. only through the method of psychoanalysis whereby accurate interpretation is given in the therapy can patients reach insight into their unconscious psychoneurotic conflicts; 2. patients' true insight, which touches on the etiology of their neurosis, is a necessary and causal condition for healing the neurosis.

One implication of the tally argument necessary condition thesis is that only psychoanalysis can heal neuroses. Grünbaum believes that the fact that psychoanalysis does not always lead to recovery does not prove the theory's failure. The existence, however, of other non-analytic psychotherapies that yield successes does testify, he argues, to the theory's defeat. The most notable illustration of this is behaviorist theory, which is more successful than psychoanalysis in treating phobias and other disorders.

This is, for Grünbaum, where the necessary condition thesis crashes, pulling along the whole of psychoanalytic theory. For him, therefore, there is one, single test to either confirm or refute psychoanalytic theory, and on this test, psychoanalysis fails (2).

Frank Sulloway (1979) tried to show that Freud failed in terms of his own method. In other words, while Freud had positivist pretensions, he did not manage to realize them. He does not regard Freud as the psychologist or mentalist his supporters wished to represent but rather, as an empiricist-positivist who was himself misguided and, in turn, misled others. Gellner, in his astute and entertaining book *The Psychoanalytic Movement: The Cunning of Unreason* (1985), argued that Freud created a system of false and falsified beliefs that was, at the same time, sophisticated and cunning. With this cunning, Freud managed to gather a large following. Psychoanalysts used this false system to persuade the public that psychoanalysis was a proper science and that its arguments were valid in just the same manner as the arguments of any natural science.

A wealth of arguments against psychoanalysis can be found in Robert Bornstein's incisive paper "The Impending Death of Psychoanalysis" (2001). Bornstein argues that psychoanalysts are arrogant, not in touch with what is going on around them, and tend to look away from the discoveries made by other disciplines. Most of Freudian theory's fundamental notions – like castration fear, penis envy, and repression – have not been scientifically confirmed. Their scientific status, he claims, is like that of the Monster of Loch Ness: everybody has heard about it, but no one has seen it. Bornstein also argues that psychoanalysis is inefficient and that the same or even better outcomes can be attained in less time. To avert "The Impending Death of Psychoanalysis," Bornstein raises three suggestions: (1) transplantation: transplanting into psychoanalysis' terminally ill body daring and creative research stipulations and replacing the entire theory with something scientific and tested; (2) organ donation: taking psychoanalytic concepts that have an existence outside the domain of psychoanalysis – like unconscious motivation, defensive self-deception, dynamic representations of self and other – and contributing them to other, scientifically sounder disciplines; (3) burial of the corpse: refuting psychoanalysis, relinquishing it all together, and waiting to see what psychological concepts will emerge – then to name and conceptualize them anew, this time as scientific concepts.

Critics hit psychoanalysis in its soft spot. For over a century, it had failed to develop empirical proof to its key assumptions, nor had it established any scientific superiority vis á vis other psychotherapies. From a positivist perspective, which puts its faith in the ability of science to produce valid arguments, Freud's failure was total. **However, it is important to note that the harsh critique against Freud and psychoanalysis always comes from scholars who share a positivist worldview. They all believe in an independent and objective existence of truth and that every description of the world should be tested systematically against collected data.**

Yes, psychoanalysis has lost play in the positivist scientism game. For Freud, it was a significant loss. As Roger Frie wrote (Frie and Orange, 2009):

> Freud hailed the methods of late nineteenth-century science, which spawned scientific rationality, and held forth the belief that, eventually, science would uncover the secrets of the mind. Not surprisingly, Freud retained the concept of objectivity as the cornerstone of classical psychoanalytic treatment. In his view, the analyst is an objective scientist who can observe and identify the constituents of the mental processes working within the patient. A crucial aspect of this process rests on the analyst's ability to bracket out distorting prejudices and thereby maintain a neutral stance that allows for objective, scientific observation.
>
> (5–6)

This successful defeat, however, paradoxically led to the rise of the hermeneutic turn: the attempt to replace positivism with hermeneutics as a better philosophical framework for psychoanalysis. It also led to the rise of the relational approach inspired by postmodernism. Rather than meeting the positivists on their own ground and continuing the search for proof of psychoanalysis' capacity to meet scientific criteria, they turned away from positivism, considering it an epistemology that had lost its relevance for psychoanalysis (Govrin, 2016).

Modern hermeneutics from the late 1970s and 1980s – became considered an epistemology more pertinent to psychoanalysis. This approach was represented by psychoanalysts like Donald Spence, Roy Schafer, and Merton Gill. It was a comprehensive and radical effort at shielding psychoanalysis from methodological attacks aimed to prove its failure to meet scientific criteria. Hermeneutics held that, since psychoanalysis deals with interpretation and the making of meaning rather than with causal explanations, the positivists' arguments are irrelevant. Supporters of the hermeneutic approach argued that psychoanalysis should avoid using mechanistic or physical notions like drives, forces, and processes and replace them with human terminology referring to people who perceive, love, defend, and so on. Here, the view was that human behavior is open to a plurality of interpretations, one of which is psychoanalysis.

I will not, here, go into hermeneutics (but for an in-depth discussion, see Moore, 1999; Strenger, 1991) – because it is not my point to discuss philosophies that remained extraneous to psychoanalysis – but rather, to show how philosophy affected psychoanalysis' internal structuring: its theories of infantile development and therapeutic approaches. The question of why hermeneutics remained extraneous to psychoanalysis rather than producing its own psychoanalytic theories (of development and therapy), is interesting and complex. Maybe non-positivist approaches, uninterested as they are in describing new facts about the world (see the final chapter of this book), are not particularly productive. Therefore, it does not come naturally to them to evolve developmental theories based on facts about the human infant or psychopathology. Possibly, too, the representatives of hermeneutics mainly invested in founding a new external philosophy that does not require a revision in clinical theory. For that reason, it stayed marginal to mainstream psychoanalysis and was restricted to a philosophical niche.

Over and beyond the question of whether psychoanalysis is science or **hermeneutics**, the more interesting issue seems: Was Freud, as his critics argue, loyal to positivism? Did he express one worldview only?

I want to show that Grünbaum, Popper, Gellner, and Sulloway erred in their critiques to the extent that they reduced Freud and referred to his principles from the perspective of one approach only – one type of explanation. This starkly contrasts with the dialectic nature of Freud's thinking, as it is reflected in nearly every topic he discusses. Indeed, on a different approach, Freud's ideas include both hermeneutic and scientific aspects. Accordingly, while Freud expresses a declared commitment to a positivist stance that falls back on realism, hints of more complex Kantian insights can also be identified, as well as hermeneutic observations. Though Freud was influenced by positivist philosophy (via his teacher Von Brücke, a staunch positivist), he was also exposed to different modes of thinking (through his teacher, the philosopher Franz Brentano, who argued that true knowledge was to be obtained using introspection only, not by sense perception). The tension between these directions was fruitful for Freud's writing and psychoanalysis. Rather than dismissing one of them in an attempt to represent Freud in a closed conceptual framework – whether hermeneutic or scientific – the present approach deems it more appropriate to understand him in the light of this dialectic.

The Superiority of the Pleasure Principle

To what extent does Freud faithfully represent a positivist position in his description of infant development?

It would appear that Freud expresses ambivalence about positivism and the correspondence theory of truth in his developmental theory. I will illustrate this by dwelling on the following aspects: the subjectivity behind the transition from the pleasure principle to the reality principle, Freud's view that a person cannot perceive reality as it is, and Freud's abandoning the seduction theory.

The Transition from the Pleasure Principle to the Reality Principle

There is nothing new in the idea that the ideal of positivism constitutes a peak in human development. According to the law of three stages as formulated by Auguste Comte, the founder of positivism in the 19th century, the general history of humanity, the history of the individual, and the history of all human knowledge passes through three stages (Comte, 1865/2009).

The first is the theological or fictive stage when humans consider natural phenomena to be the outcome of supernatural forces. The second is the metaphysical stage, where these supernatural forces are replaced by forces of a higher order of abstraction – which humans believe to be behind natural phenomena. Third and finally, there is the positive stage: Here, humans refuse to look for the final causes of phenomena and instead turn to discover the laws of phenomena through observation and explanation. Comte believed that science incorporates the positivist stage. He thinks science's main objective is predicting phenomena to use them to the advantage of humanity.

Freud's developmental theory, characterized by the transition from the pleasure principle to the reality principle, corresponds with Comte's three-stage theory. What Freud, the founder of psychoanalysis, and Comte, the founder of positivism, have in common is that both men consider a specific type of knowledge as superior and another type of knowledge as inferior. Both look at human development as a linear process: from deficient to evolved. Both think of factually grounded, rational consciousness based on observation outcomes as the culmination of human development. Subjectivity is felt to be an interference that gets in the way of taking cognizance of external reality.

Knowledge, Valid and Invalid

Much like positivism, Freud's developmental theory assumes an apparent dichotomy between consciousness that can lead to knowledge and consciousness that cannot. Like Comte, Freud is convinced that humanity moves ahead in a clearly linear fashion: from non-consciousness of reality (the pleasure principle) to consciousness of it (the reality principle). Initially, the infant wishes pleasure, which, in its primary form, does not recognize the existence of reality. Mental activity driven by the pleasure principle takes place on the hallucinatory plane, intending to reproduce pleasure-arousing mental events. So, for instance, the hungry infant hallucinates the breast, and thus gains satisfaction. At this stage of her or his life, the infant dwells in a state of total subjectivity. Knowledge about the world, at this point, based on a hallucination, does not correspond with external reality. Freud considers this phase in infantile life transitory. The infant must "pass" through it, and only by "moving out of it" can she or he grow. Within the confines of this phase, no developmental achievements are possible. Despite the non-achievement, it is necessary and cannot be skipped.

Like the empiricists, Freud considered sense perception as the critical factor in enabling the infant to get acquainted with reality:

> The increased significance of external reality also heightened the sense organs' importance toward the external world. Consciousness now learned to comprehend sensory qualities in addition to the qualities of pleasure and unpleasure which hitherto had alone been interested to it.
>
> (1911, 220)

From this empiricist position, Freud believed that anything infants know must come to them through experience. Much like scientific prediction, which can only be based on experience, infantile development is grounded in accumulated experience. Learning sets in the moment the infant fails to gain satisfaction through hallucination. That is, infants hallucinate the breast, but this leaves them frustrated when no satisfaction and satiety ensue. This failed attempt at need fulfillment through hallucination leads to the creation of a new mental principle: the reality principle. For the first time, infants discover that reality exists – an external world that cannot be managed merely by one's desires and hallucinations. Thus, through their experience, the infant comes into "true" knowledge about the world.

There are similarities between Freud's infant and the positivist scientist: Both explore the world; both start from within themselves and turn outward; both ground their observations in sense experience; both draw their conclusions from experience; and both eventually develop an impressive predictive ability.

And yet, infants and scientists are motivated by different objectives. While scientists use positivist methods of investigation to obtain valid knowledge about the world, infants use these methods to satisfy needs. Thus, in the transition from the pleasure principle to the reality principle, Freud's ambivalence about positivism finds expression. These two principles are equally dedicated to fulfilling one aim: satisfying needs. For Freud, gaining better knowledge about reality is not a goal in its own right: It allows the organism to attain satisfaction and modify tension. Freud's developmental approach is dialectical: The pleasure principle is not overtaken by the reality principle. The new stage includes or subsumes the previous one. Humans remain in thrall to their desires, wishes, and drives from birth to death. Through the interventions of the reality principle, what changes in the course of life is individuals' sophisticated, pragmatic ways of fulfilling them.

Can the Mind Know the Other as Such?

The issues concerning the status of and interrelations between subject and object is the central question of epistemology.

Epistemological questions, dealing as they do with the human individual's ability to know the world, run parallel to psychoanalytic ones, which address humans' ability to know the other and communicate with others. The core questions of these two disciplines resemble each other: How can humans know what is outside them (whether it is objects in nature or human objects)? To what extent does human subjectivity "color" perception? Is it possible to know things as they are – whether in nature or the social world? Can the "outside" be seen independently of the "inside"?

Freud mainly focused on humans' ability to know and relate to the other. Later, I will show how his writings imply that objective knowledge is impossible and inaccessible to human beings. A person's recognition of the other (and of the objective world) will always be tied to the perspective from which the former observes or relates to the latter, that is, her or his subjectivity. Freud distinguishes various degrees of subjectivity in recognizing the other.

When we assert that a person entertains relations with others through the course of his or her life, this may seem to suggest a "self" that interrelates with an "other" and that this "self" and "other" have typical features that are characteristic of each of them, separately and distinctly. This was not Freud's position, however. He believed that a subjective component prevails in the person's adult relations with others. Parts of the self with which the individual interrelates are projected onto the other (1914a).

The approach here is reminiscent of Kant: Recognizing the other is not simply a passive capacity but includes an active component. Individuals "construct" their perception of the other as a function of their interests and needs. According to Kant, humans construct concepts based on their unified experience, which constitutes the ability to know. For Freud, the other with whom the self communicates is not the other-as-such – the true other. It is the other as perceived through the lens of the one who perceives.

However, there is an essential difference between Kant and Freud: Kant made his peace with the notion that our objectivity is based on subjectivity and that, a priori, we recognize in things what we put into them. Freud, in contrast, thought that subjectivity is a human limitation. He identified with the positivist idea that subjectivity negatively affects our ability to know reality. His formulations of his developmental model show that he regarded successful development as a reduction in subjectivity. In cases of pathological development, subjectivity "imposes" itself on the individual.

This point is clarified in Freud's paper "On Narcissism" (1914a). Here, he describes two types of investment and relationality towards the other. A person's energy (or libido) may be invested in the self or the object. The object – the significant other – is real as well as internalized. In other words, the individual can invest energy either inside (in his or her self) or outside (in the world). For Freud, these two types of energy are mutually exclusive: The more energy is used for one of these purposes, the less energy will be available for the other. So, for instance, when one falls in love, there will be a drop in self-worth as the excessive libido, now invested in the other (outside), is removed from the self (inside). This might suggest that Freud believed inside and outside can be demarcated and that some perception of the world (or the other) is possible that stands apart from the perception of self and is more objective. Things, however, are more complicated than this: In certain cases, for Freud, **the investment in the other is equivalent to self-investment and wish fulfillment**. Let me explain this.

The first type of relationship with the other is the *anaclitic* relation. Here, the object of love is found in search of the same satisfaction the child's parents provided when they raised, loved, fed, and protected the child. Suppose the child successfully passed through all its stages. In that case, he or she will look, in adulthood, for a partner reminiscent of the lost "external" objects of early childhood, hoping. One may say this is the highest level of knowing the other "as he or she really is" – a knowledge involving the lowest possible level of subjectivity. When this happens, the person loves someone "outside" him or herself and has the (limited) possibility of knowing another.

However, there is another mode of attaching to the other, which Freud calls "narcissistic." People who attach to others narcissistically, rather than looking for the "external" parent to whom they would like to return, look for themselves in others.

When development unfolds properly, the person moves from narcissism to object love. This exactly describes the transition from the pleasure principle to the reality principle: from a closed, subjective system, lacking any natural ability to know reality (loving her or himself only, autoerotically and unable to identify the separateness of the object of love in so far as it is not part of them), the individual moves to another, less subjective, relation where the connection to a better-knowable reality consolidates (the individual looks for the external parental figure).

When the object choice is narcissistic, realistic perception of the other becomes distorted and colored by the individual's subjectivity. In such a case, the person did not receive the yearned-for care, and now, she looks for it in significant others. Sometimes, one sees oneself in the other and treats her as one would have liked to be treated. The other is little more than a reflection of oneself, a means of satisfying one's needs. Here, individuals who have a relationship with the other relate to themselves giving the other what they would have liked to have been given.

According to Freud, having made a narcissistic choice, one can love what one is, what one has been, what one would like to be, or someone who once was part of oneself. Following the pleasure principle, this type of love stays within the self, within subjectivity, never addressing itself outward. The anaclitic type, by contrast, can love the mother who nourished her and the father who protected her. Much like positivism's stipulation that subject and object be held distinct, Freud demarcates the two types of attitude to the other. As the subject is more separate from the object in the anaclitic relationship, Freud considers this relationship, compared to narcissistic love, the more developmentally advanced. The latter he associates with women, perverts, and homosexuals, while he links the former with men.

Another paper of his, "Mourning and Melancholia" (1917b), leads to the conclusion that the more powerfully subjectivity affects the perception of the other, the more perception of the other (outside) gets mixed up with and influenced by subjectivity (inside); or, in psychoanalytic terms: the less clear cut the distinction between self and other, the more severe the pathology.

In "Mourning and Melancholia" (1917b), Freud distinguishes between two types of grief. He tries to contrast a normal process of mourning, when the person mourns for a beloved, a relationship that ended, with a pathological reaction of mourning, a state of melancholia. The main difference between these states is in how the person positions herself vis-a-vis the lost object or how the subject projects herself onto the object.

Where mourning takes its non-pathological form, the individual, though finding it difficult to withdraw the libidinal investment from the lost object, nevertheless does so, forced by the reality principle. Reality requires one to come to terms with the loss. In a slow and painful process, the person relinquishes the libidinal energy attached to the loved one. When this work of mourning ends, the self is freed and in the position to become attached to another object.

A different process occurs in the case of melancholia, or pathological mourning. Then, the subject experiences, over and beyond the expected grief responses, a significant lowering in self-esteem. While the world appears void and insignificant to the person in mourning, the self seems like this to the melancholic person. Melancholic persons will state they are worthless and incompetent regarding both accomplishments and love. This is how Freud explains this complex process: From the outset, the pathologically mourned object was a narcissistic choice. Even as the investment in this object has come to an end (as it is lost), the same is not true in the investment in the self. The libido released from the object cannot free itself to be invested in a new object, as would be the case in normative mourning. Instead, the self identifies with the lost object and sticks to it. Moreover, this is how the loss of an object transmutes into loss of self.

The pathological melancholic reaction, then, is a result of the insufficient separation between the (melancholic) subject and object (the one to which the melancholic person became attached to). The individual's primary choice of the other was a narcissistic choice, where the individual relates to herself through the other. In this choice, the person, unable to stay separate from the object, involves their own subjectivity to a considerable extent. Loss of the object does not lead to loss of the relationship and does not interrupt the attachment: The person continues the relationship with her or himself.

This further shows how, for Freud, a lack of separation between subject and object is identified with pathology, while a relatively sound separation between them is related to mental health.

Ambivalence Regarding Subjective Experience

In the two papers mentioned previously, "Mourning and Melancholia" and "On Narcissism," one can also clearly notice Freud's ambivalence concerning subjective experience: Does subjective experience have to correspond to external reality – or indeed, can it do so? Freud wishes to describe both the subjective experience and the degree of its correspondence to reality. He aims to point out the reality distortions in the individual's subjective experience of himself and the other. One of the most basic examples of Freud's exploration of this subject is the role of subjectivity in parent-child relations.

Most parents believe that their children are perfect or, at least, endowed with special merits. Obviously, this belief does not correspond to reality (not all children can be perfect or special). In his paper "On Narcissism" (1914b), Freud acknowledges how important subjectivity is to development:

> If we look at the attitude of affectionate parents towards their children, we have to recognize that it is a revival and reproduction of their own narcissism, which they have long since abandoned. The trustworthy pointer constituted by over-valuation, which we have already recognized as a narcissistic stigma in the case of object-choice, dominates, as we all know, their emotional attitude. Thus they are under a compulsion to ascribe every perfection to the child – which sober observation would find no occasion to do – and to conceal and forget his short-comings. . . . The child shall have a better time than his parents . . . the laws of nature and of society shall be abrogated in his favor; he shall once more really be the center and core of creation – His Majesty the Baby, as we once fancied ourselves. . . . At the most touchy point in the narcissistic system, the immortal-ity of the ego, which is so hard pressed by reality, security is achieved by taking refuge in the child. Parental love, which is so moving and at bottom so childish, is nothing but the parent's narcissism born again, which, transformed into object love, unmistakably reveals its former nature.
>
> (91)

There is probably no better quotation than this one to illustrate Freud's ambivalent attitude to subjectivity. On the one hand, he understands that parents cannot take an objective perspective and see their children as they are. For parents to love their children, they cannot but "distort" reality, idealize them, worship them, and, in short, color their perception with their subjective perceptions, seeing in their children the reflection of their own selves. The obvious conclusion is that parents' subjectivity is a necessary condition for the practice of caregiving and, therefore, for preserving humanity. What else can cause a person to care for the other than the feeling that the latter is part of him or herself?

Throughout the text, however, one also senses Freud's ironic attitude toward this human weakness. For Freud, subjectivity, rather than a virtue, is a necessary shortcoming in ensuring parents' love for their children. Parental love comes at a price: Parents distort reality, ignore their children's weaknesses, and overdo their strengths.

Toward the end of his life, in 1939, Freud was disappointed with humans' inabil-ity to see the truth:

> It has not been possible to demonstrate . . . that the human intellect has a par-ticularly fine flair for the truth or that the human mind shows any special inclina-tion for recognizing the truth. We have found, on the contrary, that our human

intellect very easily goes astray without any warning, and that nothing is more easily believed by us than what, without reference to the truth – comes to meet our wishful illusions.

(129)

Another example of Freud's vacillation between the subjective and the objective is in a paragraph from "Mourning and Melancholia," (1917b), which discusses to what extent the depressed person's subjective experience fits external reality:

> He (the melancholic) must surely be right in some way and be describing something that is as it seems to him to be. Indeed, we must at once confirm some of his statements without reservation. He really is as lacking in interest and as incapable of love and achievement as he says. . . . He also seems to us justified in certain other self-accusations; It is merely that he has a keener eye for the truth than other people that are not melancholic. When in his heightened self-criticism he describes himself as petty, egoistic, dishonest, lacking in independence, one whose sole aim has been to hide the weaknesses of his own nature, it may be, so far as we know, that he has come pretty near to understanding himself; we only wonder why a man has to be ill before he can be accessible to a truth of this kind. For there can be no doubt that if anyone holds and expresses to others an opinion of himself such as this he is ill, whether he is speaking the truth or whether he is being more or less unfair to himself.

(246–247)

This part of the paper is entirely irrelevant to understanding melancholy. Freud seems unable to stop himself: He must ascertain the correspondence of experience of the melancholic to external reality.

An interesting reversal seems to have occurred here, which begs for an explanation: While the previous conclusion suggests that the greater the degree of subjectivity people bring to their knowledge of the other, the more distorted it is, the further removed they become from a realistic view of themselves of others – here, Freud states the opposite.

In the previously quoted passage, he argues that the melancholic, whose perceptions suffer from excess subjectivity, is more faithful to the truth in her self-perception. Normal persons, by contrast, who usually have a reasonable opinion of themselves, find themselves at a greater distance from this truth. As Freud comically puts it: Does a person have to be depressed to have a reality-based notion of him or herself?

This contradiction Freud settles elsewhere in the paper. After mulling over the question to what extent melancholics' self-perceptions agree with external reality, he concludes that this is not really what is important. Melancholic people are close to the truth in only one sense: They are faithful to their psychological reality.

Let us have a close look at Freud's thinking. Having argued that the melancholic is right in his self-blame, he then reaches the opposite conclusion: His severe self-criticism is unjustified. Praiseworthy and good melancholics, just as much those who are not, exercise the same type of self-criticism.

> There is no correspondence, so far as we can judge, between the degree of self-abasement and its real justification. A good, capable, conscientious woman will speak no better of herself after she develops melancholia than one who is worthless; indeed, the former is perhaps more likely to fall ill of the disease than the latter, of whom we too, have nothing good to say.
>
> (247)

Therefore, the conclusion is that, rather than corresponding to the external reality, the melancholic's experience reflects an internal, experiential reality:

> The essential thing, therefore, is not whether the melancholic's distressing self-denigration is correct, in the sense that his self-criticism agrees with the opinion of other people. The point must rather be that he is giving a correct description of his psychological situation.
>
> (247)

We observe, then, Freud's vacillations on the question of the fit between subjective experience and reality. When it comes to parents and their children, he thinks subjective experience distorting reality is necessary to ensure their love for them. In the case of the melancholic person, he reaches quite a revolutionary conclusion, by his own standards: Whether or not subjective experience reflects reality does not matter since its truth is not reflected by correspondence to reality. The melancholic person's self-descriptions are truthful not because they agree with external reality but because they fit internal reality. Alongside the external, objective truth, another meaningful truth is subjective and experiential. In time, this view was held by later psychoanalytic approaches, those of Kohut and Winnicott, who no longer ponder the fit between experiential versus external truth and instead focus their theoretical work on subjective experience.

From Seduction Theory to Drive Theory: "The Ground of Reality Has Been Lost"

Further proof of Freud's move away from an empiricist-positivist model is his relinquishing of the seduction theory in 1897. Until then, Freud believed that neurosis originated in sexual trauma patients had suffered in childhood. Freud also argued that analysis exposed "severe" and, at times, "truly despicable" childhood experiences. In most cases, the villains were family members, and sadly, also teachers and "innocent" siblings (Gay, 2006). Furthermore, neurosis is seen to be caused by a specific, concrete event in reality: seduction. It assumes that actual events taking place in external reality are the cause of mental disorders.

In abandoning the seduction theory, Freud shifted dramatically to a wholly different position. Now, he came to believe that his patients' seduction narratives were nothing but childhood fantasies, constituting an unsuccessful solution to sexual conflicts. He thought the events his patients mentioned had happened not in concrete but in internal reality. It was Freud's first acknowledgment that events and facts can be internal, subjective, the product of fantasy, and do not necessarily occur in objective external reality. Psychoanalysis, therefore, only started in September 1897, when Freud abandoned the seduction theory and, for the first time, recognized the existence of an intrapsychic, subjective reality. Here is how Peter Gay (2006) describes what this development meant for Freud:

> This renunciation opened a new chapter in the history of psychoanalysis. Freud claimed to be anything but "upset, confused, weary," and wondered prophetically "whether this doubt merely represents an episode in the advance toward further discoveries?" He acknowledged that it pained him to lose "the expectation of eternal renown." It had been "so beautiful," as was the hope for "certain wealth, complete independence, travels, lifting the children above the severe cares that deprived me of my youth." Recalling this turning point much later, Freud wrote that when the seduction theory, which had been "almost fatal to the young science," had broken down "under its own improbability," his first response had been "a stage of complete perplexity." The "ground of reality had been lost" he wrote to his friend Fliess. "He had been too enthusiastic and a little naïve."
>
> (155)

Sulloway (1979) mentions a few reasons for Freud's decision to abandon the seduction theory.

1. Therapies he conducted based on the seduction theory did not succeed; 2. Freud concluded that, if the seduction theory explained hysteria, then sexual exploitation within the family must be an unreasonably widespread phenomenon. However, one of Freud's sisters suffered from hysteria, and Freud was quite sure that his father did not sexually abuse her. 3. Freud relinquished the seduction theory because of the difficulty in distinguishing between "truth" and an emotionally charged unconscious illusion; 4. Freud did not fully overcome his female patients' unconscious resistance to making their childhood experiences accessible.

These scientific and logical conclusions go hand in hand with a correspondence theory of truth: The theory must be set aside because it does not fit the facts of objective, external reality.

Nevertheless, it is important to note that, for Freud, the Oedipal drama, which replaced the seduction theory, was a concrete, unconscious event occurring in every child's internal reality. Freud never considered the Oedipal drama through a metaphor or narrative but saw it as something real with far-reaching effects on the development of human personality. Therefore, abandoning the seduction theory in favor of the Oedipal drama does not mean abandoning the correspondence theory of truth. Intrapsychic events happen; they are part of intrapsychic reality.

He was, moreover, aware (Freud, 1917b) of the difficulty of persuading a patient to search after events that had happened in fantasy rather than reality:

> If we begin by telling him straight away that he is now engaged in bringing to light the phantasies with which he has disguised the history of his childhood (just as every nation disguises its forgotten prehistory by constructing legends), we observe that his interest in pursuing the subject further suddenly diminishes in an undesirable fashion. He too wants to experience realities and despises everything that is merely "imaginary." If, however, we leave him till this piece of work is finished, in the belief that we are occupied in investigating the real events of his childhood, we risk his later accusing us of being mistaken and laughing at us for our apparent credulity. It will be a long time before he can take in our proposal that we should equate phantasy and reality and not bother to begin with whether the childhood experiences under examination are the one or the other. Yet this is clearly the only correct attitude to adopt toward these mental productions. They too possess a reality of a sort. It remains a fact that the patient created these phantasies for himself, and this fact is of scarcely importance for his neurosis than if he had really experienced what phantasies contain. These phantasies possess psychical as contrasted with material reality, and we gradually learn to understand that in the world of the neurosis it is psychical reality which is the decisive kind.
>
> (368)

Like his patients, it seems that Freud had to decide between the objective and the subjective. In setting aside the seduction theory, he opted for emotion and subjectivity rather than objective fact and objectivity – a choice about which he remained in doubt for the rest of his life. However, this choice was made for pragmatic reasons, and in no way did it represent a shift in Freud's belief in positivism.

Freud as a Therapist: Breaking the Rules

In this section, I explore three questions: For Freud, is the aim of psychoanalysis to help the patient or to expand psychoanalytic knowledge? By what method should psychoanalytic treatment arrive at this truth? Did Freud use the method he described and advocated in his therapies?

Therapeutic Objectives: Healing or Scientific Exploration?

Freud was consistent about therapeutic objectives by maintaining a positivist position, according to which the aim of psychoanalytic therapy (1904) is making the unconscious conscious. This is a positivist stance, as it stresses the role in the healing process of discovering the truth, human knowledge, and the subject's more realistic knowledge of herself. In this sense, Freud stayed faithful to the correspondence theory of truth. He believed that therapy usually aims to reduce the patient's distortions of truth and to help in reaching a more truthful awareness of the self – an awareness that is closer to reality, in other words.

Freud believed that the therapist's role is to neutralize, as much as possible, the patient's subjectivity – which is in the grip of her or his neurotic complexes – and to help free the patient from resistance. Resistance in therapy defends the person and prevents suffering by avoiding psychic pain but simultaneously removes the individual from the truth of reality. In "Freud's Psychoanalytic Technique " (1904) Freud writes:

> The task which the psychoanalytic method seeks to perform may be formulated in different ways, which are, however, in their essence equivalent. It may, for instance, be stated thus: the task of the treatment is to remove the amnesias. . . . Or the formula may be expressed in this fashion: all repressions must be undone. The mental condition is then the same as one in which all amnesias have been removed. Another formulation reaches further: the task consists in making the unconscious accessible to consciousness, which is done by overcoming the resistances.
>
> (252–253)

Here, Freud expresses a position that prioritizes practical considerations:

> The aim of the treatment will never be anything else but the practical recovery of the patient, the restoration of his ability to lead an active life and of his capacity for enjoyment.
>
> (253)

However, in other places, Freud argued that psychoanalytic treatment has another important objective. Analysis is an objective research tool, with the analyst in the role of the scientist and the analysand in the role of the research object. Every psychoanalysis, that is, is a type of scientific observation and experiment aimed to gain a better understanding of unconscious processes.

Sandler and Dreher (1996) mention that one of Freud's quandaries regarding therapeutic objectives concerned the following question: What should be prioritized in psychoanalytic encounter: scientific research or the healing of symptoms and the alleviation of the patient's suffering?

The following excerpt from "The Question of Lay Analysis" (1927) demonstrates Freud's absolute commitment to positivism:

> In psychoanalysis there has been existed from the very first an inseparable bond between cure and research. Knowledge brought therapeutic success. It was

impossible to treat a patient without learning something new; it was impossible to gain fresh insight without perceiving its beneficent results. Our analytic procedure is the only one in which the precious conjunction is assured. It is only by carrying on our analytic pastoral work that we can deepen our dawning comprehension of the human mind.

(256)

In A Phobia in a Five-Year-Old Boy (1909a), Freud states that

Therapeutic success, however, is not our primary aim; we endeavor rather to enable the patient to obtain a conscious grasp of his unconscious wishes.

(120)

For Freud, the psychoanalyst's role is to conduct an analysis. The psychoanalytic process suffers when the analyst gets over-ambitious in terms of healing.

Three years further along, however, Freud came to a different conclusion, reflected in "Recommendations for Physicians on the Psychoanalytic Method of Treatment" (1912). Here, he claims there is a clash between the wish to gain valid and scientific knowledge about human beings and the desire to heal the patient. Freud oscillates between scientific and therapeutic objectives:

One of the claims of psychoanalysis to distinction is, no doubt, that in its execution research and treatment coincide; nevertheless, after a certain point, the technique required for the one opposes that required for the other. **It is not a good thing to work on a case scientifically while treatment is still proceeding** (italics mine). Cases which are devoted from the first to scientific purposes and are treated accordingly suffer in their outcome; while the most successful cases are those in which one proceeds, as it were, without any purpose in view, allows oneself to be taken by surprise by any new turn in them, and always meet them with an open mind, free from any presuppositions. The correct behavior for an analyst lies in swinging over according to need from one mental attitude to the other.

(114)

Freud does not explain to his readers why it is not right to approach work with the patient scientifically while therapeutic psychoanalysis is still going on. Some way into the text, he offers a partial explanation: If psychoanalysis could reach complete and satisfactory knowledge concerning the unconscious, the psychoanalyst would not have to keep the scientific position separate from the therapeutic position. This is a curious argument, for it is unclear what would replace the scientific position and why the absence of absolute knowledge would be a reason to resign from such a position. It seems, however, that Freud understands there is a conflict between therapeutic and scientific objectives and that the psychoanalyst cannot have both in tandem. It seems that, at different points in his professional life, however, he stressed various therapeutic objectives.

The Therapeutic Method

Freud did not write a great deal about the therapeutic method. Between 1895 and 1937, he devoted twenty papers (of the 300 scientific articles he published, not including his case descriptions) to what should guide therapists in their psycho-analytic work. Only a few of these texts describe the psychoanalytic method. The remainder consists of general reviews of ideas published in the past, as in *Introductory Lectures on Psychoanalysis* (1916–1917).

Catharsis, Hypnosis, Free Association, and Transference

In "Remembering, Repeating and Working-Through" (1914b), Freud describes four therapeutic methods in psychoanalysis. The first three of these – catharsis, hypnosis, and free association – aim to lay bare an actual, specific event that occurred in the past, either in an external reality or in the patient's fantasy. These methods all rely on the assumption that healing occurs through the recollection of an actual traumatic event in the patient's life and by raising it to consciousness. The objectives of the first two methods Freud designates using expressions like: "bringing directly into focus," "discovering," and "the moment at which the illness broke out" (147).

The fourth therapeutic method, which focuses on transference relations, differs from the other three. While past events, too, carry important meaning, this is not uncovered using direct recollection but only indirectly through transference relations. As a result, the relationship between patient and therapist becomes more central to understanding the patient's past. What counts is not what patients recollect but what they do. The patient does not remember what he or she forgot and repressed. Instead, the patient expresses memory in action. For instance, the patient will not say she used to have a critical and rebellious attitude toward parental authority. However, this is how she acts towards her therapist. The patient cannot escape the urge to repeat when she is in analysis.

Freud, the text suggests, is a very practical therapist with a profound understanding of human complexity. He lets go of the naïve notion that the therapist can cause the patient to faithfully reconstruct an event from the past, whether using recollection or through hypnosis. Hence, he replaces the concept of remembering with the concept of acting out. The attempt to reconstruct the past clears the field for here-and-now events within the transference relations now perceived as highly significant. Treatment of pathology, rather than addressing a past event, is now perceived as expressing itself in the present through the "playground" of transference relations.

It seems Freud knew that this fourth method moves away from the scientific ideal. In this text, he expresses his unease with realizing the scientific ideal in the clinic. While the features of the technique of recollecting resemble those of a laboratory experiment, reconstruction via transference relations consists of dealing with real life.

Based on this text, it is tempting to argue that when Freud set aside the three first therapeutic methods in favor of transference relations, it reflected his growing detachment from positivism and his shift to a more moderate stance, underlining the importance of subjective and interpersonal processes in the therapeutic method. It should be noted, however, that similar to the abandonment of the seduction theory, practical rather than epistemological reasons were decisive for his choice. In other words, these concessions on his positivist principles were not the outcome of any misgivings concerning the existence of truth and objective knowledge of reality. Freud was willing to compromise on the issue of reproducing objective truth because he believed that the ways of unveiling this truth were less effective therapeutically than other, more subjective methods. Freud's ideal was and remained the same: The therapist always seeks the truth and aims to attain more valid knowledge about the patient's unconscious.

However, in contrast with the scientific method, the direct, immediate, and straightforward discovery of the truth does not suffice for the therapist to heal the patient. In overcoming resistance, therapists must be more sophisticated and subtle than merely causing the patient to recollect the past. However, this should not detract from the fact that all methods, in the end, have this one objective: They come to fill up the gaps in memory, overcome the resistance caused by repression, and attain knowledge of the truth.

The therapeutic methods Freud presents illustrate his increasingly sophisticated perceptions. Freud's writings bear out not only that he lost hope of unveiling the past using memory but also that he realized that memories of the past keep changing and being molded by the present. In this sense, Freud was formulating a near-postmodern approach when, in Notes upon a case of obsessional neurosis (1909a), he writes:

If we do not wish to go astray in our judgement of their historical reality, we must above all bear in mind that people's 'childhood memories' are only consolidated at a later period, usually at the age of puberty; and that this involves a complicated process of remodelling, analogous in every way to the process by which a nation constructs legends about its early history. It at once becomes evident that in his phantasies about his infancy the individual as he grows up endeavors to efface the recollection of his auto-erotic activities; and this he does by exalting their memory-traces to the level of object love, just as a real historian will view the past in the light of the present.

(206)

Furthermore, Freud (1918) advises psychoanalysts not to be tempted to fill the gaps in a patient's memory by interviewing family relations as their narratives, too, are tendentious. He believes that anything that can be recollected will emerge during the analysis. This is a strange attitude from a scientist who believes in systematically collecting observations and facts. The only thing that explains it is that Freud understood how dynamic, deceptive, and constantly changing human memory is.

The Truth Values of Interpretation

Freud discusses another question in his "Constructions in Analysis" (1937): How can one tell whether an interpretation reflects a true or false argument? Here, too, Freud displays his ambivalence toward positivism and the correspondence theory of truth. On the face of it, Freud addresses a patently positivist question. His preoccupation with the question discloses Freud's commitment to a position that holds it essential to attribute truth values to statements about the world. Indeed, in this text, Freud engages some arguments that Karl Popper raised when he claimed it was impossible to confirm or refute psychoanalytic theory.

Freud opens the text by referring to a criticism against psychoanalysis to the effect that psychoanalytic interpretations cannot be contradicted and proven invalid. If the patient accepts the interpretation, that means the interpretation was correct, and if the patient does not, this implies he resists repressed materials – in which case, again, the interpretation was correct. By this circular argument, the analyst's interpretation is correct, no matter what!

Freud concludes that patients' responses, whether in agreement or disagreement, do not qualify to refute or confirm an interpretation and that they are neither necessary nor sufficient conditions for determining its validity. In fact, the patient's immediate response to the interpretation contributes nothing toward determining its validity. When the patient disagrees with the interpretation, it does not follow that it is incorrect. Such a response might result from resistance to an untimely interpretation that the patient, at this moment, cannot acknowledge. Nor should a patient's approval of an interpretation be taken too seriously: She may respond in this way because it is socially gratifying, or it may be a case of suggestion – i.e., the therapist has convinced her of the correctness of the interpretation.

How, then, can therapists know whether their interpretations are objectively valid – if the patient's responses are unreliable? Freud believes the most critical thing is to what extent the interpretation received further confirmation. These confirmations are indirect and unrelated to the patient's conscious response regarding the interpretation's validity. Without using these words, I believe that Freud argues that the patient's subjective, emotional response can confirm an interpretation – rather than the stated, overt response. In the case of a wrong interpretation, the patient might answer "Right" or "Wrong," but the emotional response will be indifferent. Correct interpretation will not leave the patient indifferent – something the therapist will pick up indirectly. According to Freud, the various routes this may take reveal how important he considered the patient's subjective, emotional response.

The first response that suggests correct interpretation is the patient's surprise: when the patient says, "I never thought of it like this," or "This would never have occurred to me." According to Freud, in responding this way, the patient says: "Yes, this time you are right about my unconscious."

An associative flow that resembles or parallels what was said in the interpretation may also indicate the reliability of the interpretation. A valid interpretation may worsen the patient's predicament, especially in resistance or negative thera-peutic response cases.

In this text, Freud captures his patients' complexity: Though he would like to attain the objective reality as it is, he understands that to ascertain whether he has achieved this, he cannot go by the patient's direct reactions – i.e., by the external, concrete facts that are visible on the surface. He must, instead, refer to the patient's subjective parts. Only by listening to the patient's emotional reactions can the ther-apist appraise the validity of his interpretation.

Freud as a Therapist

Freud's case studies represent his most significant departure from positivism. Time and again, Freud broke his own rules during his therapies. As is well known, Freud recommended that therapists maintain the surgeon's indifference, avoiding the human tendency to seek closeness with the patient. He considered the latter wish, alongside the wish for an "amazing" recovery, as psychoanalysis' main enemies. As a therapist, however, Freud did not entirely act according to this ideal. In their book *Unorthodox Freud*, Lohser and Newton (1996) describe Freud as a creative and intuitive therapist who was warm, emotional, spontaneous, and full of humor. Based on Freud's analysands' analytic journals, the authors conclude that the mir-roring method or the empty screen was not Freud's working method. Instead, he stands revealed as a highly authentic person who acted with authority and took a personal attitude. He talked with his patients about his love of art, literature, and psychoanalysis. His patients knew how fond he was of his dog and how much he disliked anything related to the USA. He never kept his love of gossip hid-den, either. His moods, too, were accessible to his patients. Sometimes, he looked bored; sometimes, he was friendly, moved, angry, or impatient. He freely discussed with them how he felt about books, people, and theories and did not keep his politi-cal and social views secret. Some of his patients were introduced to his family. For instance, Marie Bonaparte was a good friend who often visited the family during the periods during which she was in analysis.

Lipton (1977) and Gay (2006) offer further illustrations. Freud did not charge certain patients when they experienced financial problems. During the analytic hour, he allowed himself affectionate comments, became friends with patients he liked, and did not always restrict his work to the couch in the clinic. He treated Max Eitington, for instance, during their evening strolls in Vienna. Analysands' pub-lished memories – like, for instance, Doolittle (1956), Wortis (1954), and Blanton (1971) – as well as shorter descriptions of Riviere's analysis (in Ruitenbeek, 1973, 180–185) and Alix Strachey's (Khan, 1973) – show what a pleasant and friendly therapist Freud was, expressing his subjectivity in the clinic. Strachey, for instance, recounts (in Khan, 1973) Freud's reaction to a dream she told him. After interpret-ing the dream, he got up from his chair and lit a cigar.

"Such insights need celebrating." Alix Strachey mildly protested that she had not yet told the whole dream, to which the Professor replied: "Don't be greedy, that is enough insight for a week" (370).

More than once, Freud realized that his warm and personal attitude to his patients would likely affect the therapy negatively. He did not consider the affectionate and close relationships between himself and his patients irrelevant to the therapeutic situation. It seems, rather, that he took anything that occurred in the psychoanalytic session to carry therapeutic meaning. The therapist must reflect on this meaning, analyze it, and sometimes mention it in the treatment. The therapist's subjectivity, too, is subject to scientific study and scrutiny. For instance, Blanton (1971) writes how he once mentioned to Freud that he was saving money to buy his works. The next day, Freud gave him his *Selected Work* as a gift. In the following sessions, Blanton was unable to recollect his dreams. Freud interpreted this as a "change in the transference relations." He told Blanton that this change must have occurred due to the present he gave him. Furthermore, even though Freud anticipated this type of problem, it did not stop him from giving presents, expressing his subjectivity in the therapy, and persistently breaking the very rules he had formulated for therapists.

Freud's classical case study of the Rat Man is the most controversial and best-known instance of his kind and personal attitude toward his patients. The Rat Man, Ernst Lanzer (Freud, 1909a) started seeing Freud when he was 23. A lawyer by profession, he suffered from some vexing and strange obsessive symptoms. He was afraid some catastrophic event would happen to his father and to a young woman he loved; he felt murderous wishes toward people as well as an impulse to use a knife to slit his own throat. He suffered from compulsive behaviors, some of which were around unimportant trivialities, like, for instance, returning tiny debts. The Rat Man's case is included in Freud's collected case studies, and as Gay (2006) comments, it remains a classic description of compulsive neurosis. The case study is exceptionally detailed and consists of Freud's therapeutic notes every evening.

Here, we can witness one of Freud's most far-reaching departures from the therapeutic rules he had defined about the "indifferent surgeon" who is detached from his feelings.

On 28 December 1907, Freud invited Lanzer for a meal.

Here is what Gay writes:

To gratify a patient by permitting him access to his analyst's private life, and to mother him by providing food in a friendly and unprofessional setting violated all the austere technical precepts that Freud had been developing in recent years and was attempting to teach among his followers. But evidently, Freud saw nothing wrong in thus setting aside his own rules.

(264)

Even by today's standards, Freud's conduct is exceptional. In Lanzer's analysis, there were some further, less conspicuous exceptions: Freud laughed when Lanzer thought that Freud's brother was a murderer and proceeded to correct this factual error (Freud, 1909b). He sent Lanzer a postcard from a vacation, lent him a book, and made a lot of comments as though they were having an everyday conversation.

At times, these unusual behaviors came in for sharp criticism by those who considered themselves his successors – analysts who are now identified as classical psychoanalysts. Freud's expressions of subjectivity during therapy were often not well received. For instance, Mark Kanzer (1952) argued that Freud failed to understand how his gifts to the Rat Man affected the transference. Though Elizabeth Zetzel (1966) thought favorably about Freud's interventions, she believed that his method in this case differed from his later methods.

In a comprehensive and widely quoted paper, Lipton (1977) became one of the first scholars who attempted to subvert the hitherto unquestioned equation between Freud and the proponents of classical psychoanalysis. He shows how Freud's therapeutic methods differed radically from those used by American psychoanalysts working with ego psychology, like Ernst Kris, Kurt Eisler, and Heinz Hartmann. Lipton argues that it was difficult for these psychoanalysts to accept Freud's departure from the neutral therapeutic stance. He does not believe that Freud's behavior vis á vis the Rat Man was something he recognized as a divergence and subsequently changed with other patients – as classical analysts had tried to argue. There is no evidence whatsoever, Lipton argues, to indicate that Freud came to see his behavior as problematic. Elsewhere, when Freud thought he had made a theoretical error, he corrected himself (he abandoned the seduction theory, for instance). But he never changed his mind about how he worked with the Rat Man – or any other patients – Freud never referred to these gestures as mistaken, and he went on to treat patients similarly at different stages in his working life. Lipton argues that Freud's method, in the case of the Rat Man, was the classical method used throughout the four decades until Freud's death. Lipton's significant contribution is to show that the classical method originates later and does not represent Freud's way.

It is my opinion, nevertheless, that Lipton did not correctly interpret either Freud's behavior or the differences between his method and that of his successors. Lipton argued that classical theory broadly extended the concept of transference relations, embracing the therapist's human gestures like a meal, sending a postcard, clarifications of reality, and various comments by the therapist. Freud, by contrast, thought the personal relations between therapist and patient were outside the range of the analysis. Lipton seems to argue that the difference between Freud, who was expressive and emotional, and the American psychoanalysts who subscribed to ego psychology was merely technical, not essential. In his way of seeing treatment, there is no contradiction between Freud's exhortations to therapists to maintain neutrality and his actual warm and personal therapeutic style. Freud did not consider these gestures part of his therapeutic method. By attributing the differences between Freud and classical psychoanalysis to an issue of method, Lipton settles for a weak argument. It would seem, however, that the difference is not a merely technical one: These are two distinct approaches; namely, a radically positivist one (classical psychoanalysis in the USA), which takes a scientific perspective on transference relations, and a more pluralist one (Freud's approach) combining various, sometimes clashing, epistemologies without the need to choose to either one. Freud was quite aware that everything occurring in the transference had therapeutic significance. However, he did not think of the transference relations only in terms of the paradigm of the investigative scientist and his research objective.

Moreover, Lipton ignores that classical psychoanalysis did not invent a neutral, detached attitude. It only reproduced it from Freud's writings. Though Lipton's paper seems to be discussing the gap between Freud's and ego psychoanalysis methods, Freud was simultaneously espousing both of these positions – the position we could call Freud's pluralistic position and classical psychoanalytic – without trying to settle the clash between them. Freud decided not to explain this contradiction in his writings.

Conclusion

In Freud, we notice a complex, dual, and contradictory position. It stems not from cracks in his unequivocal belief in science and positivism. Quite the opposite, he repeatedly expressed his belief in this worldview in his writings throughout his life.

Duality must first be found in his way of thinking: Freud refused to examine a mental phenomenon from a single perspective. Second, and even more important, the purely scientific approach, expressed, for example, by the brain research he conducted at the beginning of his career, did not bring psychoanalysis to the places he believed in and did not advance his patients. Therefore, for pragmatic reasons, he was forced to retreat and compromise. For example, in his publication "Constructions in Analysis" (1937), Freud argued that "an assured conviction of the truth of the construction . . . achieves the same therapeutic result as a recaptured memory" (265).

Therefore, the construction of the past can be based on a coherent and pragmatic truth, not necessarily on the correspondence theory of truth. Reluctantly, Freud had to compromise.

A fragmented psychoanalytic world replaced the duality prevalent in Freud's writings. Different communities took ownership of different worldviews. The first were those who saw themselves as the successors of Freud – classical psychoanalysis. It sought to replace Freud's contradictory theory with a scientific, systematic theory that would embrace the natural sciences and biology.

References

Ayer, A.J. (1966). *Logical Positivism*. New York: Free Press.
Blanton, S. (1971). *Diary of My Analysis with Sigmund Freud*. New York: Hawthorne Books.
Bornstein, R.F. (2001). The Impending Death of Psychoanalysis. *Psychoanalytic Psychology*, 18, 3–20.
Comte, A. (1865/2009). *A General View of Positivism*. Cambridge: Cambridge University Press.
Doolittle, H. (1956). *Tribute to Freud*. New York: New Directions.
Frank, P. (1959). Psychoanalysis and Logical Positivism. In S. Hook (Ed.) *Psychoanalysis, Scientific Method, and Philosophy*. New York: NYU Press.
Freud, S. (1904). Freud's Psycho-Analytic Procedure. *Standard Edition*, 7, 249–254.

Freud, S. (1909a). A Phobia in a Five Year Old Boy. *Standard Edition*, 10, 3–147.
Freud, S. (1909b). Notes upon a Case of Obsessional Neurosis. *Standard Edition*, 10, 151–318.
Freud, S. (1911). Formulations on the Two Principles of Mental Functioning. *Standard Edition*, 12, 218–226.
Freud, S. (1912). Recommendations for Physicians on the Psychoanalytic Method of Treatment. *Standard Edition*, 2.
Freud, S. (1914a). On Narcissism: An Introduction. *Standard Edition*, 67–102.
Freud, S. (1914b). Remembering, Repeating, and Working Through (Further Recommendations on the Technique of Psychoanalysis 2). *Standard Edition*, 12, 145–156.
Freud, S. (1916–1917). Introductory Lectures on Psycho-Analysis. *Standard Edition*, 15–16.
Freud, S. (1917a). General Theory of the Neurosis. *Standard Edition*, 16, 241–477.
Freud, S. (1917b). Mourning and Melancholia. *Standard Edition*, 14, 237–258.
Freud, S. (1918). From a History of an Infantile Neurosis. *Standard Edition*, 17, 7–122.
Freud, S. (1927). The Question of Lay Analysis: Postscript. *Standard Edition*, 29, 179–250.
Freud, S. (1937). Constructions in Analysis. *Standard Edition*, 23, 255–270.
Freud, S. (1939). Moses and Monotheism. *Standard Edition*, 23, 1–138. London: Hogarth Press.
Frie, R. and Orange, D. (Eds.) (2009). *Beyond Postmodernism New Dimensions in Clinical Theory and Practice*. London: Routledge.
Gay, P. (2006). *"Freud" A Life of Our Time*. New York: W. W. Norton & Company.
Gellner, E. (1985). *The Psychoanalytic Movement – The Cunning of Unreason*. London: Paladin.
Govrin, A. (2016). *Conservative and Radical Perspectives on Psychoanalytic Knowledge: The Fascinated and the Disenchanted*. London: Routledge.
Grünbaum, A. (1984). *The Foundations of Psychoanalysis: A Philosophical Critique*. Berkely: University of California Press.
Hook, S. (Ed.) (1958). *Psychoanalysis Scientific Method and Philosophy*. New York: New York University Press, pp. 57–77.
Kanzer, M. (1952). The Transference Neurosis of the Rat Man. *Psychoanalytic Quarterly*, 21, 181–189.
Khan, M. (1973). Mrs. Alix Strachey: An Obituary. *International Journal of Psychoanalysis*, 54, 370.
Kolakowski, L. (1972). *Positivist Philosophy: From Hume to the Vienna Circle*. Harmondsworth: Penguin Books.
Lipton, S. (1977). The Advantages of Freud's Technique as Shown in His Analysis of the Rat Man. *International Journal of Psychoanalysis*, 58, 255–273.
Lohser, B. and Newton, P.M. (1996). *Unorthodox Freud: The View from the Couch*. New York: The Guilford Press.
Moore, R. (1999). *The Creation of Reality in Psychoanalysis – A View of the Contributions of Donald Spence, Roy Schafer, Robert Stolorow, Irwin Z. Hoffman and Beyond*. Hillsdale, NJ: The Analytic Press.
Popper, K.R. (1965). *Conjectures and Refutations: The Growth of Scientific Knowledge*. London: Routledge and Kegan Paul.
Ruitenbeek, H.M. (Ed.) (1973). *Freud as We Knew Him*. Detroit: Wayne State University Press.
Sandler, J. and Dreher, A.U. (1996). *What Do Psychoanalysts Want? The Problem of Aims in Psychoanalytic Therapy*. London: Routledge.
Strenger, C. (1991). *Between Hermeneutic and Science – An Essay on the Epistemology of Psychoanalysis*. Madison, Connecticut: International University Press.
Sulloway, F.J. (1979). *Freud: Biologist of the Mind. Beyond the Psychoanalytic Legend*. London: Burnett Books.
Wortis, J. (1954). *Fragments of an Analysis with Freud*. New York: Simon & Schuster.
Zetzel, E.R. (1966). 1965: Additional Notes Upon a Case of Obsession Neurosis, Freud 1909. *International Journal of Psychoanalysis*, 47, 123–129.

Chapter 2

Classical Psychoanalysis

The Scientific Dream

Try to imagine how American psychoanalysts formed their identities in the 1950s. These professionals received rigorous medical training and viewed psychoanalysis as a legitimate part of the medical profession. Their education was Spartan, emphasizing objectivity and discouraging the expression of personal subjectivity in therapeutic settings. Consequently, analysts were often reserved and emotionally withdrawn, investing significant effort in concealing their own emotions to maintain a sense of clinical detachment.

This portrayal is, of course, a stereotypical description of the classical analyst. It's important to acknowledge that many analysts of that era were warm and affectionate, and some did indeed express their subjectivity. However, the prevailing norms of mainstream psychoanalysis at the time did not encourage such openness.

In the 1950s, psychoanalysts operated under the influence of figures like Heinz Hartmann, who promoted ego psychology, focusing on the role of the ego in mediating between the id, superego, and external reality. This theoretical framework reinforced the importance of maintaining a neutral, objective stance in therapy.

Furthermore, the culture of the time, which was characterized by a high degree of conformity and conservatism, influenced psychoanalysts to adhere strictly to these norms. The societal emphasis on professionalism and authority in the medical field left little room for the personal nuances and emotional engagement that contemporary psychoanalysis often embraces.

Here is a short example how it sounds:

> A patient described how, during previous treatment, her therapist had taken extreme measures to avoid social contact with her. She interpreted these efforts as manifestations of the therapist's positive feelings for her. The author was able to confirm that the previous therapist had had a positive countertransference toward the patient, against which he employed as a defense the analytic rule of anonymity without being fully aware that he was doing so. The rules of analytic technique can be employed in the service of defense.
>
> (Freedman, 1957)

This chapter does not aim to summarize classical psychoanalysis in all its manifestations and richness nor to present its prominent representatives. Instead,

DOI: 10.4324/9781003498162-4

it reviews Heinz Hartmann's theory of development and his conception of psycho-pathology. Additionally, it examines different therapeutic attitudes that reflect the thinking of classical therapists of that era. Throughout this chapter, I will demon-strate that the attempt to make psychoanalysis scientific and objective encountered many difficulties, leading many classical psychoanalysts to adopt a more complex conception than their successors attributed to them.

Scientific Vision and Self-Confidence

Classical Psychoanalysis: A Definition

Classical psychoanalysis includes two main groups. The first is made up of Freud-ian psychoanalysts – those who perceived themselves as Freud's successors. The Freudians argued that, like the natural sciences, psychoanalysis observes – or at least can observe – exacting positivist principles. In addition to their two funda-mental loyalties –Freud and positivism – this group did not introduce any theo-retical changes that amounted to new intellectual movements. Prominent figures in this group are Kurt Eisler, Laurence Kubie, Leo Rangel, Otto Fenichel, and others. These analysts were at the helm of the American Association of Psychoanalysis (ApsaA), which was characterized by its blind adoration of Freud's theory (in fact, as I will explain later, only its "positivist" parts), its conservatism, and the way it closed itself off both to non-psychoanalytic methods and to other psychoanalytic schools in the USA.

The other group that formed under classical psychoanalysis was ego psychol-ogy, which, as we will see, emphasized ego functions and the individual's adjust-ment to her or his surroundings. Its most prominent supporters included Heinz Hartmann, David Rapaport, Ernst Kris, Rudolph Loewenstein, Margaret Mahler, and, at a later stage, Charles Brenner and Jacob Arlow.

In addition to sharing the two beliefs of the first group (considering themselves Freud's natural successors and adhering to positivism), the ego psychology ana-lysts also introduced significant changes to developmental, personality, and moti-vational theories. Ego psychology grew into a new intellectual approach in the Freudian movement.

This division between Freudians and ego-psychologists was not so manifest at the time. Though there were tensions between these two groups, they did not split off in the American Psychoanalytic Association. Eisler, the Freudian, for instance, was considerably influenced by Hartmann and ego psychology. In his description of the New York Psychoanalytic Institute after World War II, Douglas Kirsner (2000, 24) mentions that ego psychologists did not dominate the New York Insti-tute because the latter lacked political and institutional clout. Their ego psychology formed a kind of departure from Freudian orthodoxy, and many Freudians refused to accept it.

Before embarking on a description of ego psychology, it must be mentioned that psychoanalysis in the United States was never monolithic. Russell Jacoby

(1983) mentions the rupture between the interpersonal approach of Harry Sullivan, Erich Fromm, Karen Horney, and others, called "revisionists," and mainstream orthodox analysts. Kanzer and Blum (1967) also mention intergenerational differences. While older therapists considered psychoanalysis a revolutionary body of knowledge, the younger generation considered it an exciting profession and a field of activity. The younger psychoanalysts came from a scientific background, and unlike Freud, they cared little for the humanities.

Nor was there agreement about the scientificity of psychoanalysis among the classical psychoanalysts. Discussion around how crucial the classical psychoanalyst's "neutrality" and "abstention" appeared as early as the late 1950s (Glover, 1955).

However, such voices were usually the exception. Most psychoanalysts assume that therapeutic objectives, too, are derived from values like science, truth, and rationality. Beate Lohser and Peter Newton (1996) argued that the formalist theory of ego psychology was supported by Americans' admiration of scientific rationality and the intense preoccupation with scientific research in US medical schools.

The Scientific Position of Classical Psychoanalysis

Classical psychoanalysis, here represented by Hartmann (1939), Eissler (1965), and others, took on positivism's (and especially logical positivism's) distinction between scientific and non-scientific bodies of knowledge, viewing psychoanalysis as a science in every sense of the word. It preserved the ontological split between subject and object, physical and mental reality, and inner and outer worlds. It assumed that the laws to which humans are subject are identical to the laws of the physical world, and hence, they can be understood by deterministic principles. It was the prevailing, though not the only, perception that the therapeutic reality is given, with the therapist unveiling whatever it consisted of while making the utmost effort to affect the outcome as little as possible. This therapeutic reality is insular, lacking context, and clean of external influence, much like a medical examination. Classical psychoanalysis puts great weight in this objective dimension, considering subjectivity an obstacle from which any individual who wishes to see reality as it is should free himself.

However, things appear to be more complicated. Among some classical psychoanalysts – Eissler, for instance – one can observe, much like in Freud, a discrepancy between declared theoretical positions and therapeutic approaches, which left more room for subjectivity and were responsive to a distinction between therapeutic activity and scientific activity (see as follows).

By ridding itself of the tension between the various poles typical of Freud's theory, classical psychoanalysis aspired to transform psychoanalysis into a more systematic, uniform, non-contradictory theory that would meet the strict criteria of natural science. Conceptually, the main difference between them and Freud lay in their attempt to solve the contradiction between his theory's subjective and objective elements. They made a sincere and earnest effort to settle these contradictions in psychoanalysis, which was scientifically speaking in a deplorable state, and to fill the big holes and gaps in it.

Classical theory's preference for Freud's positivist side is not hard to explain: The scientific and positivist pole offered psychoanalysis scientific legitimacy, which was crucial to establishing it in the United States then. In this way, classical psychoanalysis could describe itself as scientific, as opposed to its unscientific detractors. The positivist mindset was in tune with the general atmosphere in the United States of this period, as Philip Cushman (1995, 162) puts it. Cushman argues that US culture, between the 1930s and 1950s, ignored the political and ethical dimensions and turned to technology; it avoided the humanities and turned to science. It preferred a capitalist psychotherapy to workers' needs.

Classical psychoanalysts did not have to make a special effort to prove they were Freud's successors. Freud's declared view, repeated frequently in his writing, was one of absolute faithfulness to a scientific position and the correspondence theory of truth (Freud, 1933). These psychoanalysts, however, looked away from the subjective and hermeneutic elements in Freud's theory, refusing to acknowledge them.

Classical theory's epistemological position and notion of truth are quite clear: Classical psychoanalytic thinking, both its research objects and methods, conceived of itself as fundamentally identical to the natural sciences. In this view, psychoanalytic premises can be assigned truth values. The events in a patient's development, as they come to be revealed during an analysis, are not a story, a metaphor, a reconstruction, or one version among several possible ones. They are actual events or the products of fantasy that happened in the patient's past. Classical theory thus expressed a reductionist position for it is only through a reduction that contradictions can be resolved.

Those who believe in classical theory do not deny psychoanalysis' limitations. They admit that psychoanalysis is far from being valid in the way natural science is. Nevertheless, they believe this gap will narrow down once the new science develops meticulous research methods thanks to future discoveries in cognitive research. As far as they are concerned, there is no significant difference in philosophical premises between physics and psychoanalysis. The main difference is in the limit of the current research methods.

In the psychoanalytical journals of this period, the link between psychoanalytic theory and physical, medical, bodily, and human-biological phenomena is much discussed. Here are the titles of some papers published in the *Journal of the American Psychoanalytic Association* in the years 1954–1955 alone:

Colors in Dream (Calef, 1954) Dreams and Perception (Fisher, 1954) Orality Displaced to the Uthera (Keiser, 1954), The Homeostatic Regulatory Function of the Ego (Menninger, 1954), Enuresis and Bisexual identification (Berezin, 1954), Towards the Biology of the Depressive Constellation (Benedek, 1956) The Symbolic Meaning of the Elbow (Loomis, (1955.

A good illustration of the positivist mindset and the wish to stay faithful to what was considered Freud's spirit can be found in Hendrick (1955, 568), the president of the American Psychoanalytic Association in those years. Hendrick mentions the central tenets of American psychoanalysis. The most important of these, he believes, is that psychoanalysis is a science that contributes significantly to the objective understanding of humans. Many people, he claims, confuse between psychoanalysis and dogma or philosophy. While dogma consists of a final and absolute answer, a scientific-psychoanalytic assumption immediately spawns infinite questions for future research.

Another principle Hendricks mentions is that psychoanalysis is "a basic science of psychiatry in America" (568). This is important if we want to understand the epistemological assumptions of classical psychoanalysis as practiced in the United States. Psychoanalysts in these years were almost exclusively trained psychiatrists. They believed no profound difference existed between their working assumptions and those held by other physicians (Hale, 1995). One widespread tendency in psychoanalytic research was explaining physical diseases such as asthma and ulcers through psychoanalytic models and offering patients suffering from different diseases psychoanalytic treatment.

Classical psychoanalysis presented a confidently modernist position, unclouded by doubt, very clear, and referring to a causal model of the mind. An illustration of its unambiguous rhetoric can be found in a classic work by Charles Brenner, *An Elementary Textbook of Psychoanalysis* (1955). Many generations of candidates at the New York Institute of Psychoanalysis and nationwide were trained using this book, in which Brenner discusses such major psychoanalytic concepts as drives, the psychic mechanism, dreams, and psychopathology. This is how the book starts:

> Psychoanalysis is a scientific discipline which was begun by Sigmund Freud and which is still indissolubly associated with his name.
>
> (11)

Brenner believed that some of psychoanalysis' assumptions "are so scientifically grounded that they appear so fundamental in their significance that we are inclined to view them as established laws of the mind" (2). One of the laws of the psyche proved incontrovertibly, according to Brenner, by psychoanalysis is the law concerning psychic determinism. Here, the assumption is that, like in the physical domain, in the domain of the psyche, nothing happens by accident. Prior events causally determine each mental event.

Epistemological conservatism is a prominent feature of classical American psychoanalysis. Most papers published by the American Psychoanalytic Association reproduce the official medical-scientific approach of the association. There is hardly any expression of theoretically or philosophically innovative opinions. One reason for this is the positivist drive toward scientific uniformity, toward a mono-lingual, universally intelligible discourse. Even ego psychology, which became the central approach of American psychoanalysis in the 1960s and 70s, was relatively late to occupy a prominent place in the journal. This conservative line was manifested in a lecture by Leo Rangell (1962, 235–236), twice president of the International Psychoanalytical Association and the American Psychoanalytic Association. Rangell complains that psychoanalysts have not preserved Freud's psychoanalysis. According to Rangell, rather than making slow and cautious progress in discovering further knowledge, psychoanalysts have tended to "run" too fast, in a too disorderly and unsystematic fashion. New ideas, concepts, and insights, initially not admitted by the young science, have entered too rapidly through open and unattended doors. Rangell believes that psychoanalysts tend to exaggerate the importance of new ideas. It seems to him that these new ideas get in the way of older, existing ones (Freud's ideas), diminishing the latter's value.

Philosophy of science directly influenced supporters of classical psychoanalysis: They took an interest in it, read it, and made an effort to prove that the rules and research methodology of positivist science were also obtained for them. Hartmann (1964) explicitly mentioned psychoanalysis' indebtedness to positivism and natural science research methods. Another prominent figure in ego psychology, David Rapaport, wrote his doctoral dissertation on the theory of association from Bacon to Kant, and even though he was looking for a systematic construction of psychoanalysis to turn it into a theory capable of confirmation, he was less stringent than other members of this group in his demand for scientificity (Knight, 1961).

Still, a review of psychoanalytic journals in the mid-20th century shows that psychoanalysts were not intensely preoccupied with philosophical questions. This is undoubtedly the case compared to current publications that dedicate many papers to philosophical questions relevant to psychoanalysis. Psychoanalysts in the 50s and 60s seem not to have been very keen on adopting new philosophical approaches that might undermine their tremendous effort to stick to their scientific principles.

Development without a Subject

Heinz Hartmann is the most prominent representative of ego psychology. From his arrival in the USA in 1941 until he died in 1970, Hartmann was the most significant figure in the American psychoanalytic movement. Hartmann's monograph, *Ego Psychology and the Problem of Adaptation* (1939), was one of the most influential publications on psychoanalysis since Freud (Young, 1989). Hardly any paper on relevant subjects published between 1945 and 1965 failed to quote his work.

A reading in Hartmann's publications reflects his impressive effort to get psychoanalysis grounded as a coherent science, not different from other sciences. **Hartmann makes a tremendous effort to smooth out the clashes in Freud's theory and to transform Freud's position from a pluralist, indecisive, and complex one, riddled with contradictions, into a one-dimensional, positivist one that is coherent and systematic.** It is surprising how psychoanalysts like Hartmann, who considered themselves loyal to psychoanalysis' founding father and committed to his heritage, were, in fact, very different from Freud, who had intricate explanations and thick descriptions on almost any subject.

Hartmann's rhetoric aims to present him and his supporters as Freud's successors: They developed what Freud intended to create but never got around to; what Freud was thinking but never wrote down, what Freud meant to do but did not manage. As they put it, in other words, they were carrying on Freud's vision and his spiritual inheritance. Eissler (in Bergmann, 2000) argued that Freud's career ended too soon: Had he lived some more years, he would undoubtedly have laid the founding stone of his theory and written papers on the ego and its functions.

More than any other theoretician, Hartmann systematically developed the concept of the ego, expanding it to a new psychoanalytic theory. He tried to elaborate on the complex meta-psychological dictionary Freud had started employing.

One of Hartmann's projects was to release psychoanalysis from its isolation and help it to join other sciences, like biology or sociology. Viewing psychological development as tied up with adjustment and evolution, he wished to refine those aspects of Freud's theory that explained how humans survive in their environment. In all his publications, Hartmann underlines that, rather than changing Freud's fundamental principles, he was merely expanding them. He embraced the biological and evolutionary elements in Freud's meta-psychology as the core of psychoanalysis. In his view, psychoanalysis had to be based on biology, assuming that the differences between humans and animals were only relative. The main characteristic of Hartmann's personality theory is his perception of humans as biological organisms. The ego, he believed, was mainly an organ of adjustment.

Hartmann thought that the study of the ego was where psychoanalysis and brain physiology intersected. The newborn is equipped with the tools needed to adjust to environmental conditions, or to what Hartmann called the "average expectable environment" (1927/1964, 29). **The subjective and unique relations between the infant and its father and mother are at a complete standstill in Hartmann's developmental theory**. Instead, the theory discusses how the parents successfully provide the conditions of the average surroundings. The infant's significant relations with its parents are linked to the former's survival needs and maintaining balance. The child's development and its relations with its mother are essentially biological. Hartmann argues that child-raising parallels other processes of natural adjustment:

> Is the child's relationship with his mother or the care of children, not a biological process? Do we have the right to exclude the processes of adaptation from biology? Biological functions and environmental relationships are not antithesis.
>
> (33)

As Shaw (1989) pointed out,

> with the concept of adaptation Hartmann attempted to elucidate that part of the mental apparatus which *successfully* negotiates an individual's existence, in

contrast to the prior historical emphasis on psychopathology and defense. Thus Hartmann asks us to look at those aspects of mental life which are not ordinarily the focus of analytic investigation.

(597)

Interestingly, despite the positivist and purely scientific method he used, Hartmann's discoveries are rather abstract and not based on scientific research methods such as experiments or observation of infants. Indeed, he rarely bolsters his statements using clinical illustrations.

Shaw writes that

> while Hartmann developed many important concepts which have far-ranging clinical utility even today, his attempt to extend psychoanalysis into a general psychology backfired because it separated psychoanalytic concepts from analytic data. Because of his lack of clinical material or anecdotal illustration, Hartmann's theoretical scaffolding has been frequently misunderstood and misapplied.
>
> (592)

Busch (2022) wrote that the concept of adaptation is "very relevant to how we think about and work within an analytic frame" (163) and that psychoanalysts today underestimate Hartmann's contributions. Busch writes,

> In my view, every symptom, conflict, defense, or unconscious fantasy is a result, in part, of an adaptation. For example, cumulative traumas from childhood aren't just traumatic but become part of an individual unconscious fantasy while potentially contributing to a way of living that can lead to certain satisfactions along with crippling inhibitions.
>
> (164)

However, at least some criticism regarding Hartmann's non-Freudian spirit is true. While Freud's developmental theory was characterized by a certain ambiguity that rendered the existence of various motivations, Hartmann's developmental theory aimed to free itself of this ambiguity. At the height of its development, Hartmann's infant adopts positivist principles. In developing, the infant acts like a scientist who investigates the world to understand it better, engaging in conscious activities free of emotion and conflict.

Hartmann's ego psychology appears to blend behaviorism and a socio-biological version of psychoanalysis. Like behaviorism, ego psychology does not devote much attention to unconscious aspects of human experience. At the center of development, it puts conscious principles of learning that are shorn of conflict, and it underlines the importance of functionality and action, arguing that the human infant's developmental principles resemble other living creatures. Much like the socio-biological approach, ego psychology zooms into the infant's adjustment to its surroundings and its natural possession of inborn structures that help it survive. Like behaviorism and socio-biology, ego psychology also strives for an objective, scientific position.

In the following section, I detail Hartmann's developmental principles to illustrate how Freud's ideas lost their intellectual depth.

A Conflict-Free Domain

According to Hartmann, not every adjustment to the environment or process of learning or development entails a conflict between ego, id, and superego. He argues (1958, 8) that mental processes like, for instance, perception, intentionality, understanding, thinking, language, memory, and motor development do not involve conflict. Learning is also free of drives and defenses. Nevertheless, the very notion of something being "conflict-free" is foreign to Freud's spirit. In using this concept, Hartmann annuls the complexity of Freud's approach to infantile development, reducing it to one conscious-rational dimension. Unlike Hartmann, Freud observed complexity, contradiction, and conflict in almost every human phenomenon (Brunner, 1994). In Freudian psychoanalysis, no process comes free of conflict. (82) Hartmann uses an illustration from the political sphere to describe the differences between conflict and conflict-free zones. He likens the human personality to a state that experiences periods of war and peace. The internal struggle between id, ego, and superego and the external struggle between the human individual and reality resemble a state of war. However, for Hartmann, a state cannot be described solely in terms of its conflicts with other states. The state includes borders, movements between borders, an economy, a social structure, governance, legislative institutions, and courts. These entertain mutual relations. For him, ego psychology aims to investigate the relations between conflictual parts (war) and conflict-free parts (peace).

This comparison of the human personality to a state at war or in peace clearly shows how Hartmann reduces psychoanalysis by situating conflict on a time axis. According to Hartmann, people go through different life phases: Some are "quiet" and "free of conflict," and some are dynamic and burdened by conflict. He does not perceive the human individual as a complex system in which, at any given moment, contradictory and clashing motivations and needs are at play, involving feeling, thought, and imagination. This approach contrasts with Freud's, according to which mental life is based on conflict and includes various defense mechanisms and sources of pressure, both internally and externally. Unlike Hartmann, Freud did not separate "quiet" conflict-free parts, the more rational and conscious ones, from people's more complex, turbulent, and subjective parts – quite the contrary. Freud noted "pathological" aspects of normal behavior (dreams, slips of the tongue, normal development) and "normal" aspects of pathological behavior (the depressive person has a more exact self-perception than the person who is not depressive).

Astonishingly, it was during the Second World War and the Holocaust that Hartmann was writing about quiet states and "conflict-free zones."

Bergman considers Hartmann's theory of adjustment an expression of his denial of the realities of his time (Bergmann, 2000). Hartmann, whose grandfather was Jewish, escaped from Vienna to Switzerland in 1938 and emigrated to the United States. He said he fled because he was afraid of getting conscripted into the German army, seeming to deny the real danger he was in.

Inversion of the Freudian View: The Supremacy of the Reality Principle

The Freudian infant featured in his paper "Formulations Regarding the Two Principles in Mental Functioning" (1911) learns through the experience of conflict, frustration, and disappointment. Since all infants desire to satisfy themselves, familiarity with their surroundings and laws are required for the best possible achievements. Though the pleasure principle grows more subtle, changing and becoming channeled to less impulse-driven aims, it stays central throughout a person's lifetime.

Hartmann wanted to remain faithful to Freud's approach, according to which the pleasure principle remains crucial through adult life while simultaneously adopting a positivist view. The assumption, however, that people are subject to the pleasure principle rather than to adjustment and a correct and rational way of understanding reality puts people's subjective-affective aspects in the center of things – and this was unpalatable to Hartmann.

To reconcile this contradiction, Hartmann, while accepting Freud's two principles of development – pleasure, and reality – unyokes the reality principles from the pleasure principle, turning the former into an independent entity. In the course of development, he believes, infants disengage themselves from the pleasure principle and become subject to other – rational and conscious – rules. Hartmann believes that the infant's ability to delay gratification for the sake of other, safer gratifications in the longer term cannot derive from the pleasure principle. For him, the infant's ability to predict and foresee the future is one of the most significant achievements of early development. In his opinion, this ability is autonomous and separate from the pleasure principle.

It is no coincidence that Hartmann chose predictive ability, one of the main criteria for scientific theories, as a characteristic of a crucial stage in infantile development. His is a positivist version of development that is closely reminiscent of the stages of development as Auguste Comte defined them: There is an irrational, subjective stage, which the infant quickly gets rid of, followed by a new phase, dominated by the ego, or the reality principle, which is rational and devoid of subjectivity. From this point – and here, we have a second departure from Freud – it is only a short way to conclude that ego development, which is responsible for rational development and bears no connection to the id and the gratification of drives. How does the ego achieve autonomy from the id? According to Hartmann, this is a matter of neutralizing the drives. The ego acquires a kind of reservoir of energies of its own and develops autonomous objectives: It charges these objectives with these energies (*cathexis*). These objectives are "neutralized"; that is to say, they are converted from impulse-driven objectives into objectives in the service of the ego, and thereby, they have become neutralized. Initially, the rational parts of the subject come into being by way of defense against impulsive desires. In time, they grow less tightly associated with their original purpose and independent. At this point, they can serve new additional purposes like adjustment and synthesis.

The concept of "conflict-free," much like "neutralization," is foreign to Freud's spirit. By neutralizing the drives, Hartmann can surmount the ambiguity that marks Freud's theory and build his own developmental theory on a pure positivist model.

Subjectivity in the Service of Objectivity

One of Hartmann's main moves is to "recruit" the subjective elements in the individual's development for better adjustment to reality. These subjective elements are not essential in their own right, but only in so far as they assist in improving one's adjustment to external reality. Here, Hartmann's reasoning is not very unlike that of the etiologists, who look for the survival value of every human and animal attribute. Hartmann, for instance, enquires about the positive components of fantasies that help children adjust to reality. This involves, it would seem, a contradiction inso far as fantasy, by definition, aims to remove one from reality, deny it, or create a better reality. Fantasy usually involves the distortion of reality. For Hartmann, however, fantasy prepares people for reality and allows them to control it more efficiently. Its function is synthetic and organizational. Rather than an intrapsychic, experiential component that expresses part of the internalized life of the imagination and emotion, it is a tool for better adjustment to reality.

Another indication of the reduced status of subjectivity in his theory was the limited significance Hartmann attached to the emotional component of human life. Ruth Stein (1991) mentions that Hartmann hardly refers to feelings and sensations. They appear only as factors that get in the way of ego functioning. Hartmann's far-reaching disregard for emotions in a psychoanalytic theory that is presumed to be a continuation of Freud's theory is surprising. One might want to ask: Can there be a psychoanalytic theory that does not make central space for feelings? One that gives hardly any room to consider the emotional component in the lives of both patient and therapist?

This negation of subjectivity may have led Hartmann to write a theory lacking a therapeutic method. Any implications concerning therapeutic method, patient-therapist relations, transference, and countertransference are absent from Hartmann's theory. Martin Bergmann (2000) writes that, in his later work, Hartmann never presented any clinical illustrations, and one cannot be sure whether he was actually familiar with the psychoanalytic therapeutic method. One of the relatively rare passages in which Hartmann refers to method suggests that the central therapeutic objective was to make the patient into a rational, logical person who thinks and acts like a scientist:

Interpretations not only help to regain the buried material but must also establish the correct casual relations.

(1939, 63)

Kris (1951) and Loewenstein (1951), Hartmann's colleagues, were the ones who tried to translate his theory into a therapeutic method.

Schafer (1976) notes that Hartmann's theory was based on an elaboration of Freud's economic model and only marginally referred to contents as such. Most of Freud's psychoanalytic material is subjective and touches, for instance, on negative or erotic transference, sexual perversions, hysteria, and other psychopathologies. Hartmann does not relate to these clinical phenomena – perhaps because they are sub-jective and human in character and get in the way of using a professional-technical language that is clear of any elements likely to "pollute" its scientific status. Thus, Hartmann objects, for instance, to the notion of "meaning" – an idea he believes is not clear enough. Instead, he thinks that the meta-psychological concepts of secondary and primary processes can address humans' sexual and non-sexual func-tioning that are free of sexual conflicts.

In fact, the subject is absent from Hartmann's theory. He discusses, for instance, how the child accumulates knowledge, and at the center of this process, he places the investment of energy. However, the subject who determines the importance and meaning of knowledge is absent from his thinking. Concepts of psychic economy replace concepts of meaning in Hartmann's theory – to the point that it might seem that "energy investment" rather than the subject is what remembers, attributes importance, and finds meaning.

The Patient in the Service of Science

In the context of the therapeutic approach, the typical positivist position grows more complicated and problematic than Hartmann's developmental theory. Thera-pists in the classical tradition were more sophisticated, ambivalent, and complex than their present-day postmodern colleagues tend to credit them for. As was the case with Freud, therapists practicing classical psychoanalysis, too, manifested a discrepancy between statement and actual therapy. In contrast with the philosophi-cal position – which stayed faithful to a positivist vision – and the developmental approach – which narrowed the subjective aspect of human life – the therapeutic approach showed a much greater degree of epistemological flexibility.

Despite this, there is no doubt that the desire for a neutral, objective position that leaves no room for the therapist's subjectivity has sometimes led to a distant and alienating attitude toward the patient. Consider the case study of Dickes (1967).

Dickes (1967) tells us of a patient who suddenly said the consulting room was too hot and asked his therapist to open the windows. The therapist thought that the room was quite comfortable and that one window was open. He made no immediate reply to the patient. After a short pause, the patient remarked angrily that he expected to be ignored by the therapist and that, even though the room was hot, he expected the therapist to behave spitefully and not allow him to cool off. Dickes writes:

> At this point the better type of analytic patient could and would continue to asso-ciate and the material referring to the transference, the heat, and the room, could

become clarified. Instead the patient experienced a series of physical reactions. He reported that he began to feel a plugging and unplugging of his ears. They felt stopped up. His head was stopped up. His complaints increased in force and he began to complain about pulsating eyeballs. The symptoms increased in severity and extent, gradually involving the whole body. He also began to attack me making remarks such as, "I can see you're going to say nothing and you're going to ruin this hour for me." He became vituperative and finally refused to continue talking.

(520)

From this example, we can see how much the objective analytic cold stance is distressing the patient and that the therapist's lack of empathy resulted in rage and difficulties in thinking. I do not believe Dickes was a cruel therapist. By the standard of his era, he simply believed that his involvement and subjectivity would likely undermine the therapeutic aim. This aim is to help the patient become more aware of his inner world. While the patient attributed the therapist's indifference to a malignant tendency, the therapist assumed he was working according to the correct therapeutic and scientific criteria. Not even an empathic response to the patient's rage was possible, being perceived as an infringement of the rules.

However, Dickes certainly does not represent all classical analysts. On the one hand, the therapeutic outlook of psychoanalysts with a positivist inclination portrayed the analyst as a scientist, the patient as a research object, and their interrelations as a kind of scientific experiment. Unlike Freud, who was not sure whether to use psychoanalysis as a scientific tool or for alleviating the patient's suffering, some classical theoreticians decidedly preferred the scientific objective (see the stance of Thomas Szasz, later).

On the other hand, some classical psychoanalysts also recognized the subjective side of therapist and patient, distinguished between psychoanalysis and other sciences, and were willing, unlike the logical positivists, to accept knowledge that was not scientific. Because most of them were not interested in epistemology and knew little about it, they could not back their deviations with a new epistemology.

I will present four philosophical approaches to classical psychoanalysis's aims: Lawrence Kubie's radical positivism, Thomas Sasz's and Kurt Eissler's instrumentalism, and the position of William Meisner in the late nineties which was an answer of a classical analyst to the criticism of the concept of neutrality.

The Radical Stance: Lawrence Kubie

Lawrence Kubie (1959) who presided over the New York Institute in 1939–1940) endorses a highly conservative positivist approach, even by the standards of classical psychoanalysis. For him, the scientific research objectives of psychoanalysis are more important than alleviating the patient's suffering. He believes that psychoanalysis' therapeutic aims have drawn it away from its primary mission, which is to function as a tool for scientific research. This is not the first time, he argues, that medicine uses scientific tools erroneously and ill-advisedly before they have been fully elaborated. The same happened in the case of X-rays and nuclear energy. What was crucial to the ascendancy of therapeutic objectives was the pressing need to help patients, together with the physician's optimistic and misguided assumption that they could actually do so (Kubie, 1959, 59).

Kubie describes some of psychoanalysis' limitations as a scientific research method: As opposed to other sciences, psychoanalysis relies exclusively on auditory input. As a result, information is distorted immediately upon absorption. The information will likely be skewed even when the psychoanalytic session is audio-recorded. There are other sciences, Kubie points out, that suffer from similar drawbacks: Both the microscope and the stethoscope produce distorted measurements, and the chemical composition of blood changes once it has been extracted from the human body and put into a test tube. The fact, moreover, that no control group is possible for psychoanalytic therapy also seriously impedes scientific conclusions. Like other sciences, psychoanalysis must ensure that these distortions are corrected or kept to a minimum. The only way he believes psychoanalysis can be studied is by using meticulous, detailed, minute-by-minute transcription. This method, too, however, can easily be compromised. Kubie predicted that, in the long run, the solution would seem to lie in many psychoanalysts observing many patients while using accurate protocols.

For Kubie, the ideal analyst can predict the patient's behavior – no different than in chemistry or physics. He is aware, however, that since not all of its phenomena can be described in terms of "more" or "less," psychoanalytic data are challenging to quantify. In addition to quantitative changes, there are also qualitative ones that are unmeasurable.

These limitations, mentioned by Kubie, bear out how far-reaching classical psychoanalysis' naïve aim of turning psychoanalysis into a science. Some psychoanalysts simply attempted to create a clinic like an insulated and hygienic laboratory.

It should be noted that Kubie does not attempt to excuse his focus on the therapist's objectivity and neutrality by claiming it has therapeutic value.

Even though Kubie does not represent the average American analyst of his time, he does seem to convey a vision that many analysts shared:

By remaining as ill-defined as is humanly possible, by masking his own emotional reactions, his esthetic tastes, his political and religious views, the details of communications, the analyst attempts to remain a blank about whom the patient can imagine anything he feels, and feel anything he must. As long as the analyst is not real to the patient, whatever the patient thinks, feels, and imagines about the analyst is not anchored to reality. Instead, the patient's fantasies and feelings are a product of his own imaginative and creative psychological potential. The unknown analyst remains a sample of humanity drawn from a grab bag; in this image of the analyst, the patient can drape his fantasies as one might drape a costume on a dummy in a store window. The study of this process gives the patient insight into the subtle ways in which similar process distort all of his daily human relationships; with the stranger he passes on the street, the man who greets him, a boss, an associate, a child. Gradually it becomes clear to him that none of these is a simon-pure reality; but that all are mixtures of reality plus projections of his own unconscious needs and conflicts and fantasies. . . . The more real the analyst becomes to the patient, the less helpful for the exploration of unconscious components in the patient's psychology are his transplanted feelings about the analyst.

(68–69)

It is not only concerning psychotherapy that Kubie presents a radically positivist approach but also to the entire human psyche. Patients do not see reality as it is (only science can do this). Distorting reality, the patient projects parts of herself onto it. People's subjectivity interferes with their ability to gain correct and truthful knowledge of reality. Reality exists as such, but it can only be reached if people get rid of projected subjective parts and adopt a strictly scientific view. Kubie believes that the therapist can perceive reality as it is – i.e., to almost absolutely separate herself from the research object, observing the patient just as one observes bacteria through the microscope.

The Instrumental Stance

Kurt Eissler's reputation as representing conservative rigidity seems not to be quite deserved. Compared to other classical psychoanalysts, Eissler was better able than others to contain Freud's complexity rather than solve it. In his therapeutic approach, too, Eissler is less one-dimensional and orthodox than he has tended to be perceived.

It was Eissler's (1965) basic view that **if laboratory conditions enable research obtained in psychoanalytic therapy, then this also serves the needs of the patients**. No logical distinction, he believes, is possible between research and therapy in the psychoanalytic situation.

Like science, psychoanalytic therapy aims to acquire valid knowledge about the patient's inner world. Eissler, however, is careful not to present therapists as omniscient scientists who merely pass knowledge to their patients.

Eissler describes four stages in therapy. In the first stage, the observer (the therapist) collects information. In the second stage, she passes this knowledge to the research object (the patient). In the third stage, the therapist tries to remove any obstacles that hinder the patient's integration of the new knowledge. The fourth stage involves discovering new knowledge about the research object's personality. **Eissler's therapeutic stance is far from being positivist**. In the process of acquiring knowledge, the patient and therapist are mutually dependent. Only when the research object agrees to collaborate can the observer gain knowledge. The therapeutic process fails when the therapist, while acquiring a great deal of knowledge about the patient, does not share this with the latter or when such knowledge is presented to the patient without integrating it with other components of the patient's personality. **Knowledge depends on two people's shared activity in the clinic**.

When he argues that knowledge can only be relevant when it is part of the therapist's and patient's joint process, Eissler implies a two-person psychology (a revolutionary and groundbreaking concept set forth much later by postmodern approaches, which rejected the one-person psychology of classical psychoanalysis).

Eissler faces a more challenging task than Kubie. As the latter is not committed to showing that the psychoanalytic scientific methods serve the patient's needs, he is not obliged to cope with the subjective elements of therapy, which makes it stand out from scientific research proper. Eissler, by contrast, must address these parts as well. Eissler mentions two differences between scientific facts and the type of facts unveiled by psychoanalytic therapy. Psychoanalytic knowledge, first, must relate to all conscious and pre-conscious systems (67). This knowledge must be represented in all three personality structures – ego, id, and superego – and in ways that are typical of each of these, respectively. Psychoanalytic knowledge, unlike scientific knowledge, requires a change in the patient.

The second difference between scientific and psychoanalytic knowledge is tied to the emotional implications knowledge has for the patient. The patient might love, hate, or feel wholly indifferent to some piece of information revealed in the course of the therapy. Knowledge, in psychoanalytic terms, is defined by reference to the emotional impact it has on the research object. In psychoanalysis, an indifferent attitude toward knowledge is tantamount to no knowledge (68), and knowledge must include the integration of the content's full emotional significance. For Eissler, the most essential interpretations are ones that the patient experiences as revelations, as the opening of a new horizon with new possibilities, casting a light on the patient's past. According to Eissler, the synthesis between knowledge and emotions it triggers is one of psychoanalysis's most complex and subtle endeavors. The absence of such a synthesis – rather than invalid interpretations – leads to the failure of many psychoanalytical therapies.

As far as the therapist's feelings (the countertransference) are concerned, Eissler has only this to say: The therapist must avoid emotional isolation as well as emotional over-investment. Admitting that putting one's finger on the therapist's appropriate attitude is hard, he argues that it should not be based on reason alone or one intellectual process.

Thus, Eissler understands the differences between intellectual, scientific activity and psychoanalytic therapy. These differences, however, do not cause him to assume there is a substantial difference between psychoanalysis and scientific activity. Having mentioned the most notable differences, he does not follow through by recognizing their importance or value. Eissler lacks a new philosophical perception that departs from positivism and makes available the epistemological basis for his distinctions between different kinds of knowledge. In this manner, he observes the subjectivity of therapy and, unlike Kubie, does not try to neutralize it. However, he lacks the philosophical-cultural context that might enable him to find an alternative to the positivist mindset.

Eissler's Parameters

In his famous paper, "The Effect of the Structure of the Ego on Psychoanalytic Technique" (1953), Eissler refers to the subjective components of psychoanalysis. Eissler intends, in this paper, to define interpretation as the major, "standard" tool of psychoanalysis and to indicate in which cases exceptions in technique are allowed. According to Eissler (1953), a parameter is

> the deviation, both quantitative and qualitative, from the basic model technique, that is to say, from a technique which requires interpretation as the exclusive tool. In the basic model technique the parameter is, of course, zero throughout the whole treatment. We therefore would say that the parameter of the technique necessary for the treatment of a phobia is zero in the initial phases as well as in the concluding phases; but to the extent that interpretation is replaced by advice or command in the middle phase, there is a parameter which may, as in the instance cited here, be considerable, though temporary.
>
> (109)

According to Schafer (1994)

> Eissler was attempting to establish what would, at that time, have been a sound, contemporary, ego-psychological Freudian theoretical base for those analysts engaged in therapeutic work with deeply traumatized or terrified patients. These are patients who, in order to salvage some psychic equilibrium, rely desperately on a pervasive and rigid network of defensive operations and transferences. For such patients it is as though life itself, in every casual as well as significant aspect, had come to seem perilous.
>
> (722)

Parameters needs to meet four conditions in order for a treatment to remain fundamentally psychoanalytic: (1) the introduction of a parameter only when necessary – i.e., when what he terms the "basic model technique" is not adequate; (2) minimal use of the parameter; (3) elimination of the parameter before the final phase of treatment; and (4) a temporary effect on transference that can be abolished by interpretation.

Such exceptions can be justified wherever patients cannot adjust to traditional psychoanalytic techniques. Clinical reality, he believes, is so heterogeneous and unpredictable that it is hard to come up with one criterion for all situations – as would be the case in medicine. In optimal conditions, the surgeon (Freud, as is well known, was fond of likening the psychoanalyst to the surgeon) closely follows the rules, and even though they are often not implemented, they are studied in medical schools.

Eissler's paper, to many readers, exemplifies classical psychoanalysis' rigidity and orthodoxy: Other than in emergencies, it leaves no room for deviations from its therapeutic (interpretative) method (Orgel, 1995; Schafer, 1994). In time, Bergmann (2000, 29) argues that the parameter concept came to be seen as morally tainted. It was unclear if the parameters were a legitimate exception or an infringement of the rules. In an influential marginal note, Eissler went as far as to warn therapists against the innocent act of passing the patient a cigarette just in case it might interfere with the therapeutic process (1953, 110).

However, the paper seems to be open to a different interpretation. When Eissler used the term "rules thrown aside" (105), he did not think of departures from psychoanalytic technique only but also from the scientific rules that must be observed to preserve psychoanalysis as a scientific therapy. As Garcia (2009) writes, "even treatments that are of necessity non-interpretive and almost entirely 'parametrical' derive from the most informed psychoanalytic understanding possible" (112). Schafer (1994) writes that "Eissler also followed Freud in noting that, even under ideal conditions, the analytic process is influenced by non-interpretive factors. He mentioned specifically the personality of the analyst, the necessary use of questions and nonverbal communication" (723).

Legitimizing exceptions proves that practical purposes carried more weight for him than scientific ones. Joseph Sandler and Anna Dreher (1996) observe that many psychoanalysts of this period considered using parameters to be a sign of the failure of the classical method.

Bergmann (2000), too, believes that there was a liberating side to Eissler's paper. Hitherto, the deviations reported by senior psychoanalysts to their students were told through anecdotes. Now it transpired that behind these deviations, there were rational considerations.

Psychoanalysis: A Game of Chess

Thomas Szasz, like Eissler, in his paper, "On the Theory of Psychoanalytic Treatment" (1957), thinks that sticking to a scientific position is for the best of the patient. Szasz, who would, in due time, gain fame as the US representative of the anti-psychiatric approach, had been trained psychoanalytically. Like Eissler, he, too, assumed an absolute identity between the objectives of psychoanalysis and science. Szasz, however, introduces an even more extreme position than Eissler's: **It is not upon therapists alone to adopt a scientific stance – patients, no less, must take this perspective, both as regards the therapy and as regards their life as such.** This is the fundamental objective of psychoanalytic treatment: To establish the patient's scientific position:

> According to this view, the final goal of psycho-analytic treatment is the establishment of a never-ending, ever-deepening *scientific attitude* in the patient towards those segments of his life which constitute the sphere of psychoanalysis.
>
> (1957, 176)

For Szasz, the ideal scientific position is devoid of emotion. The scientist has no desires, values, or moral judgments.

This total identity between therapy and science leads Szasz to draw two interesting conclusions. In the admission process for the Institute of Psychoanalysis, it is important to consider how much interest a candidate has in science. Second, psychoanalysis, like scientific activity, never comes to an end.

Another point of interest is a comparison Szasz draws – grasping back to Freud – between the aims and rules of psychoanalytic technique and those of chess. In both cases, he argues, participants play by existing rules. In both cases, these rules are clear and straightforward. Even though it would be irrelevant to apply notions of "rigidity" or "flexibility" when it comes to chess (since players have agreed to specific rules), it is irrelevant to use them in the context of psychoanalysis. The rules determine the occasion and the framework, while the players decide the complexity and richness of what emerges within that framework. The final objective in chess and psychoanalysis is set in advance rather than being a matter of choice or up for negotiation.

Yet, despite his firm position, one can find hints in Szasz's work that he, too, recognizes subjective components in the therapy – or at least the influence both therapist and patient have on the therapy. For instance, Szasz explains that the word "treatment" is less appropriate than "psychoanalytic effect." While in a "treatment," the therapist takes an active role vis á vis a passive patient – i.e., the therapist does something to the patient. Healing, in psychoanalysis, depends on the joint activity of the patient and analyst.

Therefore, Szasz distinguishes a fundamental difference between psychoanalysis and medical treatment. However, he does not elaborate on this idea.

There is one issue on which Kubie, Eissler, and Szasz think alike: They all believe that psychoanalysis' scientific objective is more critical than its therapeutic objective. For Kubie, **the scientific contribution remains essential even when the therapeutic activity is not effective.** For Eissler, this privileging of scientific activity necessarily serves patient's needs and helps them. Paradoxically, for him, therapists will best serve the patient's purposes when they no longer consider healing the primary motive, replacing it with acquiring knowledge. The therapist's intention to heal the symptom, Eissler believes, is a fundamental stumbling block to the healing process. This, he argues, is precisely the mistake of those who left the Psychoanalytic Institute, abandoning Freud's path. Rather than following Freud to discover new knowledge about the human individual, they preferred to achieve better therapeutic outcomes – and failed.

Why were Freud, Kubie, Eissler, and Szasz troubled by the possibility that the therapist's main motive might alleviate the patient's suffering? They seemed to have assumed that therapeutic enthusiasm would come at the expense of scientific research. They feared research would evolve into a mere tool rather than a goal in its own right. Pure, strict scientificity, which puts scientific discovery at the forefront, must put psychoanalytic research at the center of the scientist's interest. Any other impetus – religious, medical, or social – must play havoc with scientists' objectivity and affect their outcomes. In the natural sciences, scientists are interested in learning about new objects and the laws of the phenomenal world. Szasz (1957) put this very succinctly as follows:

> In Freud's day, though, much more than in our times, it was perfectly legitimate to be interested in trying to understand the world about us without any practical gains necessarily deriving from such ventures. Indeed, the men Freud admired most – Galileo, Copernicus, Darwin – and his own teachers in Vienna were characterized by this spirit of "pure science" . . . it is added that Freud was, after all, a physician, and he was forever trying to perfect his way of healing sick people. I personally think such a view may be nothing short of a sentiment rewriting the history of psychoanalysis. (168)

I do not wish to portray a false impression that all analysts in this era were strict positivists. One should not forget that there were always those, even in the classical period of psychoanalysis, who objected to the analyst's neutrality in the psychoanalytic situation (the most famous example is Hans Loewald, who was probably unaware of the profoundly radical nature of his writings).

Sacha Nacht (1965), a French psychoanalyst whose translated work influenced the American ego psychology tradition, challenges the neutral, cold, and detached therapist who wants to work like a scientist. The subjective factors that play a role in therapy occur in any scientific activity; hence, they are also legitimate in psychoanalysis. By way of an illustration, he refers to the physicist Niels Bohr, who argued that scientists in physics or chemistry change in the course of experiments and that the person who started the experiment is not the same as the one who concludes it. If reciprocal relations affect both scientists and research objects in the natural sciences, then this is all the more so in the case of psychoanalysis. In both situations, an intersubjective process takes place (10).

Before his time calling for therapists to avoid rigid neutrality, Nacht wrote his paper in a philosophical framework that idealized science. So, despite his exceptional ideas relative to his contemporaries, he could not present a new philosophy that could be an alternative to the scientific one. The one justification for allowing subjective elements into the psychoanalytic situation is that they are also to be found in scientific activity.

Meissner's Account

So far, I have been discussing the work of three psychoanalysts working during a period marked by adherence to positivist premises. However, at least in its extreme form, this tradition has long been replaced by other more contemporary philosophies such as Hermeneutics and postmodernism. So, another interesting question is how more current classical psychoanalysts justify the therapist's neutrality given the considerable loss of positivism's grip on the world of psychoanalysis, philosophy, and culture. Of course, it is unclear if any psychoanalysts today would agree to be called "classical." Still, several psychotherapists have remained faithful to ego psychology principles.

An expression of support for the neutral position is expressed in the paper "Neutrality, Abstinence, and the Therapeutic Alliance" by William Meissner (1998) several decades after the heyday of ego psychology. The paper illustrates how much the fundamental concepts of psychoanalysis and the values it cherishes have changed, even among those who uphold an approach that considers itself conservative and orthodox. One should remember that Kubie, Eissler, and others' advice to therapists to maintain a neutral stance was the result of their belief in the scientific positivist model, which separates between researcher and research object and which requires that the scientist/therapist rid her or himself from any subjective element that might compromise their neutrality. Meissner's paper remains faithful to the classical method as he calls on therapists to stay neutral. Still, where he justifies this stance, there is no trace of the positivist-scientific approach. First, he never mentions the word "science." Second, all the arguments in support of neutrality are practical and utilitarian: Neutrality boosts the therapeutic alliance, makes therapy more efficient, allows the therapist to focus on the patient, and helps the patient to take a more neutral position in her or his own life. Nothing has left from the position that psychoanalysis's uppermost objective is scientific, and the aim of healing the patient only takes second place.

The terms that the psychoanalysts of the 1950s had been using proudly – like "neutrality," "scientific investigation," "objectivity," and so on – had become a liability for the orthodox psychoanalysts of the 1990s. Meissner writes:

> The concept of neutrality is poorly served by its name. It is not synonymous with the negative connotations we have become accustomed to associate with it – impartiality, indifference, detachment, uninvolvement, anonymity, even objectivity.
>
> (1998, 1119)

Finally, one of the main advantages of neutrality for Meissner is that it can fortify the balance between subjective and objective components in psychoanalysis. Neutrality makes subjectivity possible, as well as empathic listening and emotional involvement while allowing therapists to hold on to their objectivity and special perspective. It even facilitates self-revelation without negatively affecting the therapist's responsibility and therapeutic stance (1119–1120).

Classical therapists like Victoria Hamilton (1993), Ronald Baker (2000), and Charles Hanly (1995), have argued that the objective stance and neutrality in therapy should be upheld using philosophical justifications. Currently, a philosophical approach favoring neutrality and objectivity is trying to articulate itself within the dialectics between the subjective and objective in psychoanalysis. Here, the neutral stance is justified rather than as a singular, isolated one that contrasts with an intersubjective position as complementary to that position. The relational approach, the argument goes, has gone too far by banishing objectivity and leaving therapy to lean on subjectivity alone. Psychoanalysis should be grounded in epistemology, which combines the objective and the subjective. As it strives to preserve certain aspects important to classical psychoanalysis, this position could be called a classical one. At the same time, it is extremely unlike the views and values of the old psychoanalysis. This type of psychoanalytical conservatism does include a recognition of the subjective elements of the therapy, even of the intersubjectivity between patient and therapist. However, it also wishes to preserve the objective sides of the therapeutic relations and include them in an intersubjective structure.

The search for truth in psychoanalysis has become less popular in recent years. Partly because this search has been replaced by another, much more common goal: Therapy is supposed to be a corrective emotional experience that heals the trauma of early relationships through a healthy and benign relationship. At the same time, the importance of the search for psychical truth in therapy has not entirely dissipated. But the search today is done much more sophisticatedly, with no connection to a scientific or positivist approach. The truth that is sought is not a truth of correspondence to reality, but experiential, emotional, and subjective.

The difference between past conceptions of truth and current perceptions was well expressed by Fred Busch (2016):

> Previous generations of analysts saw their role as telling the patient who the patient is, especially with regard to the patient's unconscious. . . . However, there were a number of problems with such an approach. First of all, it did not help the patient to experience analysis as a process in which one comes to understand *how to know*. The analyst presented interpretations as facts, rather than as something to reflect upon and play with in a variety of ways. The patient was left with only what he had learned from the analyst.
>
> (354)

He further writes (2016):

> In my early training as an analyst, as was typical at the time, there was a quality of "gotcha" to the kind of interpretations that were recommended – i.e., the analyst not only found something the patient was trying to hide, but it was often something not pleasant about the patient.
>
> (349)

Busch (2016) thinks that the quest for truths – instead of psychic truths – can falsely guide patients "to look for Answers with a capital A" (341), which often terminates thinking instead of encouraging the ability to think spontaneously at liberty about whatever comes to mind, observe it, and play with it.

According to Busch (2016), to help the patient, the analyst needs to be as accurate as possible in understanding what is going on in the patient's psyche. However, this is not the accuracy of classical psychoanalysis. Accuracy should be expressed in understanding emotional experience, not the connection between past and present or interpretation of the unconscious. Accurate intervention allows the patient to think about it without feeling anxious and defending against it. The discovery of mental truth in therapy allows the patient to create different ways of thinking, leading to emotional development and growth and the ability to live a fuller life.

If Busch is the contemporary vanguard of psychical truth, it seems that not much has been left of the "truth-seeking" of classical psychoanalysis. In fact, Busch attempts in many of his papers to differentiate between his psychical truth and interpretations that aim to reveal unconscious material.

Conclusion

One of the most interesting phenomena related to classical psychoanalysis and the prominent figures mentioned in this chapter is that their interest in empirical research was quite limited. The psychoanalytic institutes did not engage in laboratory research at all. The great interest in empirical research came only decades later with the vigorous work of Robert Wallerstein, Joseph Sander, Otto Kernberg, Peter Fonagi, and others. Perhaps more than anything else, classical analysts were interested in proving that the method of psychoanalytic therapy, which was based on interpretations and the discovery of the unconscious, was identical to scientific activity. In order to validate their method, they had to prove that the unconscious exists in the patient regardless of the therapist's presence and that it simply needs to be discovered using the tools that psychoanalysis makes available to therapists. Heinz Kohut, the founder of self-psychology, was the first to challenge this concept. He considered empathy a crucial component in our understanding of human beings.

References

Baker, R. (2000). Finding the Neutral Position: Patient and Analyst Perspectives. *Journal of the American Psychoanalytic Association*, 48(1), 129–154.

Benedek, T. (1956). Toward the Biology of the Depressive Constellation. *Journal of the American Psychoanalytic Association*, 4, 389–427.

Berezin, M.A. (1954). Enuresis and Bisexual Identification. *Journal of the American Psychoanalytic Association*, 2(3), 509–513.

Bergmann, M.S. (Ed.) (2000). *The Hartmann Era*. New York: The Other Press.

Brenner, C. (1955). *An Elementary Textbook of Psychoanalysis*. New York: International University Press.

Brunner, J. (1994). Every Path Will End in Darkness or: Why Psychoanalysis Needs Metapsychology. *Science in Context*, 7, 83–101.

Busch, F. (2016). The Search for Psychic Truths. *Psychoanalytic Quarterly*, 85, 339–360.

Busch, F. (2022). The Clinical Significance of Hartmann's Concept of Adaptation. *Psychoanalytic Inquiry*, 42, 163–172.

Calef, V. (1954). Color in Dreams. *Journal of the American Psychoanalytic Association*, 2, 453–483.

Cushman, P. (1995). *Constructing the Self, Constructing America – A Cultural History of Psychotherapy*. Boston: Adison-Wasley Publishing Company.

Dickes, R. (1967). Severe Regressive Disruptions of the Therapeutic Alliance. *Journal of the American Psychoanalytic Association*, 15, 508–533.

Eissler, K.R. (1953). The Effect of the Structure of the Ego on Psychoanalytic Technique. *Journal of the American Psychoanalytic Association*, 1, 104–143.

Eissler, K.R. (1965). *Medical Orthodoxy and the Future of Psychoanalysis*. Madison, CT: International University Press.

Fisher, C. (1954). Dreams and Perception: The Role of Pre-conscious and Primary Modes of Perception in Dream Formation. *Journal of the American Psychoanalytic Association*, 2(3), 389–445.

Freedman, A. (1957). The Bulletin of the Philadelphia Association for Psychoanalysis. VI, 1956: Countertransference Abuse of Analytic Rules. *Psychoanalytic Quarterly*, 26, 286.

Freud, S. (1911). Formulations on the Two Principles of Mental Functioning. *SE*, 12, 218–226.

Freud, S. (1933). *Standard Edition*, 22, 158–182. London, United Kingdom: Hogarth Press and Institute of Psycho-Analysis.

Garcia, E.E. (2009). Enduring Relevance: An Introduction to the Clinical Contributions of K.R. Eissler. *Psychoanalytic Quarterly*, 78, 1109–1126.

Glover, E. (1955). *The Technique of Psycho-Analysis*. New York: International Universities Press.

Hale, N.G. (1995). *The Rise and Crisis of Psychoanalysis in the United States – Freud and the Americans 1917–1985*. New York and Oxford: Oxford University Press.

Hamilton, V. (1993). Truth and Reality in Psychoanalytic Discourse. *International Journal of Psychoanalysis*, 74, 63–79.

Hanly, C. (1995). On Facts and Ideas in Psychoanalysis. *International Journal of Psychoanalysis*, 76, 901–908.

Hartmann, H. (1927/1964). Concept Formation in Psychoanalysis. *Psychoanalytic Study of the Child*, 19, 11–47.

Hartmann, H. (1939). *Ego Psychology and the Problem of Adaptation*. New York: International University Press.

Hartmann, H. (1958/1964). *Comments on the Scientific Aspects of Psychoanalysis, Essays on Ego Psychology*. New York: International University Press.

Hartmann, H. (1964). *Essays on Ego Psychology*. New York: International University Press.

Hendrick, I. (1955). Presidential Address: Professional Standards of the American Psychoanalytic Association. *Journal of the American Psychoanalytic Association*, 3(4), 561–600.

Jacoby, R. (1983). *The Repression of Psychoanalysis: Otto Fenichel and the Political Freudians*. New York: Basic Books.

Kanzer, M. and Blum, H.P. (1967). Classical Psychoanalysis since 1931. In B.B. Wolman (Ed.) *Psychoanalytic Techniques: A Handbook for the Practicing Psychoanalyst*. New York: Basic Books.

Keiser, S. (1954). Orality Displaced to the Urethra. *Journal of the American Psychoanalytic Association*, 2(2), 263–279.

Kirsner, D. (2000). *Unfree Associations: Inside Psychoanalytic Institutions*. London: Process Press.

Knight, R.P. (1961). David Rapaport—1911–1960. *Psychoanalytic Quarterly*, 30, 262–264.

Kris, E. (1951). Ego Psychology and Interpretation in Psychoanalytic Therapy. *Psychoanalytic Quarterly*, 20, 15–30.

Kubie, L. (1959). Psychoanalysis and Scientific Method. In S. Hook (Ed.) *Psychoanalysis Scientific Method and Philosophy*. New York: New York University Press, 57–77.

Loewenstein, R.M. (1951). The Problem of Interpretation. *Psychoanalytic Quarterly*, 19, 501–539.

Lohser, B. and Newton, P.M. (1996). *Unorthodox Freud: The View from the Couch*. New York: The Guilford Press.

Loomis, E.A. (1955). The Symbolic Meaning of the Elbow. *Journal of the American Psychoanalytic Association*, 3(4), 697–700.

Meissner, W.W.S.J. (1998). Neutrality, Abstinence, and the Therapeutic Alliance. *Journal of the American Psychoanalytic Association*, 46, 1089–1128.

Menninger, K. (1954). The Homeostatic Regulatory Function of the Ego. *Journal of the American Psychoanalytic Association*, 2(1), 67–106.

Nacht, S. (1965). Interference between Transference and Countertransference. In M. Schur (Ed.) *Drives, Affects, Behavior*. Vol. 2. Madison, CT: International University Press, 315–325.

Orgel, S. (1995). A Classic Revisited: K.R. Eissler's "The Effect of the Structure of the Ego on Psychoanalytic Technique". *The Psychoanalytic Quarterly*, 64(3), 551–567.

Rangell, L. (1962). Prospect and Retrospect – President's Interim Report. *Journal of the American Psychoanalytic Association*, 10(2), 227–257.

Sandler, J. and Dreher, A.U. (1996). *What Do Psychoanalysts Want? – The Problem of Aims in Psychoanalytic Therapy*. London: Routledge.

Schafer, R. (1976). *A New Language for Psychoanalysis*. New Haven: Yale University Press.

Schafer, R. (1994). A Classic Revisited: Kurt Eissler's "The Effect of the Structure of the Ego on Psychoanalytic Technique". *The International Journal of Psychoanalysis*, 75(4), 721–728.

Shaw, R.R. (1989). Hartmann on Adaptation: An Incomparable or Incomprehensible Legacy? *The Psychoanalytic Quarterly*, 58(4), 592–611. https://doi.org/10.1080/21674086.1989.11927254.

Stein, R. (1991). *Psychoanalytic Theories of Affect*. London: Karnac Books.

Szasz, T.S. (1957). On the Theory of Psychoanalytic Treatment. *International Journal of Psychoanalysis*, 38, 166–182.

Young, M. (1989). Heinz Hartmann, M.D.: An Introduction and Appreciation. *Psychoanalytic Quarterly*, 58, 521–525.

Chapter 3

Heinz Kohut's Self-Psychology

Most of the dramatic conceptual changes in psychoanalysis were made out of pragmatic considerations. A technique that did not prove itself and was based on an old theory was replaced by a new technique behind which stood a new theory. From this place also Kohut developed self-psychology, as can be seen from the following vignette:

> The patient could not tolerate the analyst's silence, but, at approximately the mid-point of the sessions, she would suddenly get violently angry at me for being silent. . . . I gradually learned, however, that she would immediately become calm and content when I, at these moments, simply summarized or repeated what she had in essence already said (such as, "You are again struggling to free yourself from becoming embroiled in your mother's suspiciousness against men." Or, "You have worked your way through to the understanding that the fantasies about the visiting Englishman are reflections of fantasies about me"). But if I went beyond what the patient herself had already said or discovered, even by a single step only (such as: "The fantasies about the visiting foreigner are reflections of fantasies about me and, in addition, I think that they are a revival of the dangerous stimulation to which you felt exposed by your father's fantasy-stories about you"), she would again get violently angry (regardless of the fact that what I had added might be known to her, too), and would furiously accuse me, in a tense, high-pitched voice, of undermining her, that with my remark I had destroyed everything she had built up, and that I was wrecking the analysis.
>
> (Kohut, 1968, 108–109)

However, as I will show throughout the chapter, the change in technique would not have occurred had Kohut not used a philosophical foundation that was new to his time. In many places in his books, Kohut corresponds with philosophers, quotes them, and even argues with them (Kohut, 1980a, 1984).

The Crux

Heinz Kohut (1913–1981) was born in Vienna, the only son of a wealthy Jewish family. When Heinz was a boy, his father died of cancer. Having completed his

DOI: 10.4324/9781003498162-5

medical studies in 1939, he immediately emigrated to the United States on the eve of the Second World War. His mother joined him there at a later stage. He became a member of the Chicago Institute, where he was influenced by ego psychology. Over time, he occupied many senior positions, such as Chairman of the American Psychoanalytical Association. While he only came to formulate self-psychology ideas when he reached his sixties, hints of what was to come can be found in his early writings. (On his disturbed and paranoid mother, his homosexual tendency, his concealing of his Jewish roots from his close friends in the United States, and his unstable relations with his colleagues – see Charles Strozier's fascinating biography, 2001.)

Kohut established self-psychology, the first branch of psychoanalysis within mainstream psychoanalysis that questioned some of the positivist assumptions of classical theory.

His self-psychology, I believe, includes some significant deviations from positivist philosophy, paving the way for postmodern theories in psychoanalysis. However, Kohut does not offer an alternative philosophy to replace positivist epistemology and stays faithful to many of positivism's tenets in some essential ways. On several epistemological issues – perception of the truth, theoretical validity, the similarity between psychoanalysis and natural science – Kohut, especially toward the end of his life, avoids settling the question and presents unresolved, ambivalent positions. While often critical of classical psychoanalysis's positivism, he hesitates to give it up altogether.

The Philosophical and Cultural Context

Kohut's writing occurs in a clearly philosophical context. Kohut often refers in his writings to many philosophers (especially in footnotes) such as: Koyre (1977, 36), Kuhn (1977, 299; 1984, 163, 224), Wittgenstein (1980, 492), Popper (1980, 492), Feyerabend (1984, 230), Lauden (1977, 231).

Kohut published his ideas during a time when dominant ways of thinking were undergoing a shift: This was when Thomas Kuhn published his *The Structure of Scientific Revolutions* (1962), Georg Gadamer published his important *Truth and Method* (1960), when Paul Ricoeur's (1970) and Jürgen Habermas' (1968) work on hermeneutics started to make waves, and positivism came under the severest attacks since the Frankfurt School.

As these changes in scientific views and the notion of truth occurred, the 1950s and 1960s saw the rise of new therapeutic approaches offering an alternative to psychoanalysis. Carl Rogers' humanist psychology was one of the most influential schools of thought on therapy. Both Rogers and Kohut – though they never actually met – were teaching at the University of Chicago between 1945 and 1957. Rogers was a professor of psychology while Kohut was teaching at the Department of Psychiatry and Neurology. Many scholars have noted similarities between the two approaches (Bohart, 1991; Kahn, 1985, 1989; Tobin, 1990). Both share an American perspective marked by optimism, a belief in self-realization, a core of authentic selfhood, and the individual's ability to change and be happy. Cushman

(1995) notes that the self Kohut found in the United States in the 1950s and 60s is very similar to that typically featured in humanistic psychology. The self of these theories was reflected in contemporary advertising and magazines, or as it appeared in the then-famous musical *Hair*: It is exhibitionistic, self-involved, idiosyncratic; it values emotional expressiveness, is personally, uninhibited, and oriented toward instant gratification.

Both humanistic psychology and self-psychology drew attention to the role of empathy in therapy and highlighted the therapeutic value of close listening to and understanding subjective experience. Both believe that non-judgmental acceptance of the patient, alongside a warm and humane relationship, are essential components of the therapeutic relationship. Despite the many differences (Rogers gave more weight to the patient's subjectivity, was less interested in the patient's past, stressed the here and now, rejected the notion of transference, and did not use interpretations), there is an unmistakable family resemblance. Kohut and Rogers seem to have more in common than Kohut and Melanie Klein, who also established a school of psychoanalytic thought.

Robert Stlorow, in one of his earliest publications, wrote:

> There appear to be striking parallels between the techniques, therapeutic processes, and ideal outcome formulated in the analytic treatment of narcissistic disorders . . . and the techniques, therapeutic processes, and ideal outcome of client-centered therapy as conceptualized by Rogers. The understanding and treatment of narcissistic disorders may thus provide an unexpected area of rapprochement between psychoanalytic and client-centered therapists.
> (Stolorow, 1976, as cited in Kahn and Rachman, 2000)

Like other psychoanalysts, Kohut had little respect for non-psychoanalytic techniques, which he thought were superficial, cosmetic, and incapable of bringing about structural change. Never mentioning Rogers by name, Kohut compared him to technicians who try to fix old clocks. Technicians, like Rogers, he believed, have no fundamental understanding of the clock's inner workings – the analyst's particular province – though they know how to clean and oil its parts, thereby creating the impression that the clock is fixed (Kohut, 1978a).

In a comprehensive study of the mutual influence between these two approaches, Kahn and Rachman (2000) argue that Kohut wished to be seen as having invented the notion of therapeutic empathy even though decades before Kohut Rogers used empathy as the cornerstone of his technique. Rachman argues that Kohut failed to acknowledge Ferenczi's impact, the first to have used the concept in the psychoanalytic literature (298).

Kohut and Other Anti-positivists

Self-psychology was not the first psychoanalytic theory to have departed from the positivist model. Psychoanalysis had never been monolithic, and there were always divisions and controversies on many issues. For instance, Sandor Ferenczi had already held somewhat non-positivist therapeutic views (emphasizing experience rather than objective external reality), even in Freud's lifetime – views that inspired the postmodern approaches of today. Heinrich Racker and Heinz Loewald, too, strayed from positivist therapeutic principles. Therefore, other anti-positivist voices had been heard before Kohut and were indeed known as he published his work. One of the most prominent among them was that of Donald Winnicott, who also greatly impacted postmodern theories in the United States, for instance, Jessica Benjamin's developmental theory. Winnicott wrote little on philosophical issues. However, the importance he attached to the subjective phase in the infant's life and illusion, imagination, and play formed a radically new perspective on the objective-subjective thread in development and technique.

Kohut and Winnicott combined theoretical innovation with philosophical conservatism, which Stephen Mitchell called "theory without meta-theory" (1993, 68). While both Kohut and Winnicott emphasize the patient's subjectivity within the therapy, this did not flow from a more general doubt concerning the objectivity and validity of analytic knowledge.

Mitchell was right: Kohut's commitment, in the end, was to a scientific-objective model. What Mitchell fails to take into account, it seems, is Kohut's intense preoccupation with epistemological questions. Throughout his writings, Kohut asks many philosophical questions. The answers he offers are exceedingly intricate. Due to the dominant place of ego psychology, with its idealization of science and its rejection of empathy as a therapeutic tool, Kohut had no choice but to delve into epistemological questions.

Characteristic of Kohut and what makes him distinct is his systematic attempt – both clinical and theoretical – to find new research tools for psychoanalysis. Such tools would be more valid than classical analysts' investigative methods because they believe in the separation between object and subject. His interest is not limited to development, therapy, and psychopathology but extends to epistemological questions – questions concerning truth, science, confirmation, and psychoanalysis's place among the sciences. Kohut (1984) is aware of the tension in the 20th century between the search for causal explanations and the search for subjective meaning. As opposed to the classical therapists before him and to the postmodern therapists after him, Kohut tries to make room for both. One could think of Kohut as situated in the middle of a bridge between modernism and postmodernism. On the one hand, unlike postmodernism, Kohut believes in the general applicability of scientific research and its ability to reach objective truth. On the other, he prioritizes interpretation and investigation of experience using empathy and introspection – i.e., subjective means.

Another difference between Kohut and other psychoanalysts who opposed the positivist framework is that Kohut – and his followers – established a school of thought in psychoanalysis that was as politically powerful as other, earlier major approaches like, for instance, ego psychology, Klein, or Anna Freud. As opposed to Winnicott – who, though highly influential, was not identified with a political organization – Kohut's self-psychology became very central and popular in the American psychoanalytical movement: Conferences were held, membership associations were run, and special training programs were conducted within the psychoanalytic institutes. Otto Kernberg (Bergmann, 2000) believed that the arrival of self-psychology spelled the end of Hartman's ego psychology. Kohut's influence, he argues, was powerful because he and his followers bravely stood up to their many opponents while staying in the mainstream, both in the US psychoanalytic movement and outside it, maintaining an ongoing dialogue. As a result, their fate was unlike that of other "deserters," and they made a significant contribution to the openness with which psychoanalysis treated various therapeutic approaches.

New Research Tools

In his paper, "Introspection, Empathy, and Psychoanalysis," published in 1959, Kohut argued that only through introspection and empathy can human experience be studied, and only these tools define the legitimate domain of psychological investigation. At the time, the concepts of empathy and introspection seem revolutionary.

When he designated empathy as a unique tool for studying the psyche, Kohut – perhaps unintentionally – introduced subjectivity through psychoanalysis' front door. This is Kohut's cardinal achievement.

Kohut argued that scientists investigate the physical world using the senses. They have developed research methods and sophisticated laboratories for this purpose. However, for psychological research, the senses do not suffice. Psychology's research data are thoughts, wishes, emotions, and fantasies. These abstract phenomena do not occupy space and are unavailable to study through the senses. For Kohut, we can only learn about the other's internal experience through vicarious introspection. Empathy and introspection are the tools we use to gather psychological data. Other types of observation belong to the physical domain.

Kohut was exceptional in calling to replace psychoanalysis' customary research tools in 1959, though he thought that his new model could fit into a positivist one. In the heyday of classical psychoanalysis and ego psychology, Kohut's emphasis on empathy was a dramatic departure.

Even though Kohut was already expressing radical ideas for his time, his paper "Introspection, Empathy and Psychoanalysis" still does not reflect his philosophical breakthrough. Here, Kohut's argument is more modest: If one wants to understand mental and emotional states, special instruments are required, other than the ones that have been in common use.

Charles Brenner (1968), a prominent classical psychoanalyst, criticized the paper. Brenner argued that Kohut introduced a radical, subjective, anti-scientific approach that made a false distinction between psychoanalysis and other sciences. Subjectivity, for Brenner, is synonymous with non-scientificity. He rejects Kohut's argument that psychoanalysis, being based on introspection, is unlike the natural sciences:

> There is a vitally important difference between the approach of a psychoanalyst to these data on the one hand, and of an introspective psychologist or philosopher on the other. The latter is concerned with his own thoughts and feelings, the former is concerned with the thoughts and feelings of another, who reports them to him.
>
> (688)

In response to Brenner, Kohut agrees that there is no essential difference between psychoanalysis and the natural sciences and stresses his commitment to a scientific model. In psychoanalysis, only the means of research differ. Biochemistry inspects tissues with biochemistry tools, and histology looks at the same tissues through a microscope (85). Every science, then, has its own means of investigation. To ensure he is not suspected of being insufficiently scientific, Kohut adds more arguments to signal his proximity to the classical positivist model: The main difference between an introspective approach and psychoanalysis is not inhere in data collection but in their processing. Every science has to formulate its assumptions at a certain distance from what the senses perceive. Psychoanalysis, including meta-psychology, is no exception to this rule: The data it collects using empathic observation constitutes the first stage. Scientific results are obtained when the data are processed through the theoretical conceptualization of the research object. In contrast with the psychoanalyst, who employs a scientific method, the philosopher's and the psychologist's thinking is grounded in introspection alone, either staying too close to the raw data or making a giant leap from this experiential input to abstract levels of generalization (philosophy):

> I was surprised by the implication of these statements that I had made erroneously conceived assertion that there is a basic distinction to be made between analysis and other natural sciences because analysis employs introspection and that, apparently, this error is due to a neglect of the difference between the approach of the analyst and the approach of the introspective psychologist or philosopher. There are differences, of course, and the methodology of a science defines to some extent the limits of the field that can be investigated and the nature of the data that are obtained. It is thus obvious that an examination of a tissue by biochemical means will lead to data that are basically different from those obtained with the aid of a microscope. If we wish to stress differences we may say that biochemistry is basically different from histology.
>
> (1968, 87–88)

Kohut's answer illustrates his commitment to a classical positivist model – so much so that it is hard to tell him apart from the group of ego psychologists presented in the previous chapter, who claimed that subjectivity was crucial in therapy only because it promotes the scientificity of psychoanalysis.

Judy Teicholz (1999) claims that Kohut's revolutionary effect on psychoanalysis was limited. Kohut, she writes, if he can be considered postmodern at all, should be seen as a moderate postmodernist who represents a conservative revolution – in contrast with current radical postmodernists and their radical revolution.

Empathy in the Service of Science

Here is how Kohut defines empathy:

> The capacity to think and feel oneself into the inner life of another person. It is our lifelong ability to experience what another person experiences, though usually, and appropriately, to an attenuated degree.

> (1984, 82)

Kohut tries to insert empathy, too, into a positivist frame of thinking. Empathy, by which one can understand the other, is a universally shared human experience and, therefore, can entail theoretical objectivity. In other words, empathy is not one person's subjective experience but the ability to "step into another person's shoes," see things from her perspective, and thereby gain true insight into her. It is not because of its subjective and emotional nature that empathy enables this understanding but because it can be applied, like any other research tool, in a wide array of cases – for instance, in all forms of human suffering and experience.

Kohut's conservatism is also reflected in the great weight he ascribes to processes of confirmation and verification. He believes the ability to achieve valid outcomes in psychology must be measured using two principles. The first relates to the observer's empathetic and emotional state. This state, from which data collection is done, requires stepping into the other's shoes but does not demand higher-level cognitive skills. The second principle touches on the cognitive aspect. The validity of the newly revealed outcomes must be founded on regular scientific logic. The observer must prove that various phenomena brought together under one new perspective yield previously unavailable meaning. When this is the case, psychoanalysts are entitled to state that their assumptions were proven correct and that they have attained a psychological truth.

Disengagement from Freud and Loyalty to the Psychoanalytic Establishment

In his book *The Restoration of the Self* (1977), Kohut first draws a line between himself and Freud, publicly announcing his diversion from classical theory. Freud's theory, he argues, has not done justice to a broad range of psychopathologies and psychological phenomena.

He argues that the main difference between himself and Freud concerns truth. Kohut observes that Freud expressed total commitment to truth both in his personal life and in the therapeutic objectives he set himself. Psychoanalysts followed

Freud, attributing truth the ultimate value. Kohut argues that the unquestioned preeminence associated with Freud's notion of truth should be reexamined (67). According to Kohut, Freud's notion of truth was influenced by the common perception of the Enlightenment that only when the object and subject of observation are distinct can ideal scientific objectivity be achieved. Whereas Freud's conceptualizations worked well for some mental phenomena, such as hysteria, which was very widespread during Freud's times, they fail to describe disorders of the self clinically. These latter, Kohut claims, call for a broader type of scientific objectivity than that of the 19th-century scientist, including introspective-empathic observation and the theoretical conceptualization of the experiencing self (68).

However, Kohut appears to be more conservative than how he presents himself, as a radical vis á vis Freud. His views reflect a certain hesitance. On the one hand, he criticizes Freud's concept of truth, the great importance Freud placed on it, as well as the strict separation Freud established between researchers and their subjects. On the other hand, he remains attached to notions of truth and objectivity and suggests new ways of realizing them. Kohut does not see himself as a relativist or postmodernist.

In contrast to what he writes, the significant difference between him and Freud is not in an essentially different approach to truth but in his use of different investigation tools. Kohut, like Freud, believes that objective knowledge about the world is possible. Like Freud, he looks to attain ideal scientific objectivity. He, however, believes this can be done by different means, for instance, through empathy. Moreover, Kohut thinks Freud's external investigation tools are still helpful for certain phenomena. It is only for some other clinical phenomena like narcissistic disorders that psychoanalysis requires another type of investigation.

Coming from the conservative psychoanalytic establishment, Kohut was facing complicated political problems. The Chicago Psychoanalytic Institute, to which Kohut belonged, suffered from severe political and management problems like other psychoanalytic institutes (Kirsner, 2000). Kohut's correspondence indicates (Cocks, 1994) that he meant to be working within the psychoanalytic movement, not to split off. He had relative intellectual leeway at the Chicago Institute (even though his colleagues refused to elect him for the psychoanalytical board of education in protest against his aberrations from Freudian orthodoxy). Kohut preferred, nevertheless, to stay in the institute. This intense wish to remain affiliated with the psychoanalytic establishment might have been one reason for his conservatism. The three requirements he formulates (1978b) for new psychoanalysis – i.e., self-psychology – testify to his strong wish to remain attached to the establishment: 1. The new self-psychology must be continuous with traditional psychoanalysis to protect its followers' sense of continuity. 2. The new theory must consider the relevance to classical psychoanalysis and, more particularly, ego psychology. 3. The new theory must be open to change and new developments.

Elsewhere, Kohut tries to reassure Dr Rudolf Heinz, who voiced objections against Kohut's deviation from the classical model. Three years before his death, in 1978, Kohut wrote to him that he had very much wished to stay part of the development of psychoanalysis and that it was for this reason that he decided to introduce theoretical changes only gradually. He decided to focus on the study of transference and to stick to self-psychology in the narrow sense only. Remaining faithful to the dynamic unconscious, he considers himself part of the mainstream approach to psychoanalysis:

> I am very eager not to encourage a break in the development of psychoanalysis and am therefore proceeding with theory change gradually. By basing myself on the investigation of transferences and by retaining a psychology of the self in the narrower sense, i.e., a psychology of a self within a mental apparatus (see *The Restoration of the Self*), I am retaining the concept of dynamic unconscious . . . and remain therefore in the mainstream of analysis, i.e., I do not encourage the development of a dissident school.
>
> (From: Cocks, G., (ed.) 1994)

In a 1978 letter to his friend and student Arnold Goldberg, he attempts to curb the latter's defiant enthusiasm, telling him that he thinks self-psychology is part of psychoanalysis, not outside it (367).

Another letter, dated 1981, to Robert Stolorow shows us a more argumentative Kohut, less fearful of his critics, expressing himself uninhibitedly. Here, he argues that all psychopathologies, including the Oedipal neuroses, are the outcome of disorders of the self. If we recognize, he argues, that we will never focus on the conflict itself, but always on the selfobject's (the selfobject is a significant object of the child who performs psychological functions that they cannot perform on their behalf) conflict and failures, then we will be able once and for all to set aside the old model (423).

A More Radical Approach toward the End of Life

In the 1980s, in his paper "Introspection, Empathy, and the Semi-Circle of Mental Health" (1982) and in his book *How Does Analysis Cure?* (1984), Kohut takes another step in near-revolution, which he sets into motion. Toward the end of his life, he drops some of the principles of positivism, though he holds on to others. More and more contradictions turn up in his epistemological premises. While he understands that positivism does not suit psychoanalysis as a theoretical model, he finds it hard to drop its basic tenets.

In these years, two questions especially preoccupy Kohut: The observer's influence on the object and the importance of empathy as a universal human value rather than merely a scientific tool.

Kohut is ready to admit that humans are not closed systems that can be known objectively from within (using empathy). People are constantly exposed to external influences, and these form their personalities. However, even during these years, Kohut maintained a conservative outlook and did not entirely concede to the objective perspective. It appears that he considers the observer's influence on the object of study as a form of interference that must be removed. That the therapist's personality impacts her or his perception of the patient does not contradict the existence of objective reality and objective science:

> Do these considerations imply that there is no objectivity, that what we want to call objective science is always some sort of moral pressure or propaganda veiled in the cloak of scientific respectability?
>
> Again, I do not think so. If we initially have the courage to acknowledge the fact that scientific objectivity in the sciences of man must always include the objective assessment of the observer . . . then we can clarify our methodology. Through such clarifications we, we acquire the ability to separate the wheat from the chaff.
>
> (40)

Thus, although they were important, Kohut's epistemological contributions remained modest. In his late writings, he admits that it is impossible to attain objective truth and is willing to acknowledge that the observer affects the object of observation. However, he cannot give up on the traditional argument whereby the psychoanalyst's ability to reach the truth is a desirable ideal. Moreover, Kohut also regards subjectivity as an impediment to the search for truth in his late writings. In brief, **Kohut never moved away from his original position concerning the existence of objective truth, whose revelation is the psychoanalyst's praised ideal.** The fact that he consistently compares psychoanalysis and physics illustrates how he did not abandon the rhetoric of the classical approach.

Moreover, it seems that Kohut was bent on clarifying that he had nothing to do with non-positivist approaches and expressing his reservations about them. A note in one of his last papers, "Selected Problems in the Theory of Self-Psychology" (1980b), shows his affinity for philosophical ideas as well as his worry about being identified with the more innovative philosophers like Wittgenstein or even with someone like Popper who in his way also departed from the conservative positivist model of scientific thinking. In this note, Kohut mentions that we should not confuse his argument that reality as we know it can never be free of the observer's point of view with, for instance, Wittgenstein's or Popper's claim that it is scientists' theory that determines both what they are looking for and, to a considerable extent, also what they find. Kohut argues that scientists' physical and psychological presence is part of their research field, affecting their findings. Kohut's philosophical argument, in other words, is weaker than that of Wittgenstein or Popper, who did not only talk about the observer's "influence" on the findings but also about how scientists "create" theory-reality.

Innovation and Conservatism in Development Theory

Kohut's developmental theory asks one central question: How does the infant develop a sense of self through relations with significant others, which affords an optimal expression of the infant's personality?

A key concept in Kohut's developmental theory is the *selfobject*. The selfobject is a significant object in the child's life that carries out psychological functions. Infants experience this object regarding their specific functions rather than their personality traits. In the early stages of development, the infant does not perceive the parents as separate persons in their own right, with their own feelings and needs. The parents, so long as they perform their functions, are perceived as parts of the infant's self. The infant discerns them as separate and distinct only when parents do not fulfill their role.

Kohut describes two structures vital to early development performed by the selfobject: the *idealized parental imago* and the *grandiose self*. These two unconscious structures develop simultaneously; each includes a collection of unconscious needs, wishes, feelings, fantasies, and memories. Together, they make up the infant's attempt to revert to a former state of perfection, when all needs were gratified and there was no frustration. Because they emerge as the result of an early unconscious effort to maintain original perfection, Kohut calls these *archaic narcissistic configurations*. The first structure, that of the idealized parental imago, includes the perfect fantasy with which the infant wants to become one. Unification with this omnipotent object is gratifying and gives a sense of power and wholeness. The illusion of unification yields a sense of perfection, whereas breaking the illusion may result in fragmentation and intolerable anxiety. During normal development, the idealized parental imago transforms into the various ideals a person pursues.

The second structure that emerges in early development is the grandiose self: it grows out of the fantasy of a perfect self. Here, perfection is attributed to the self and imperfection to the outside world. The grandiose self is marked by omnipotence, grandiosity, and exhibitionistic narcissism. The child feels the "master of the world," unsurpassed and with unlimited power. In adult life, the grandiose self forms the basis of our ambitions.

The normative child develops two defense structures, the idealized object and the grandiose self, to protect herself from imperfection – both her own and the world's. This is their primary mechanism: "I am perfect" = the grandiose self; "You are perfect, but I am part of you" = the idealized object. According to Kohut, the intensity of these structures diminishes over time through a process he calls *passage through the object* (1971). Aggrandizement gradually lessens as the child experiences the parent's actual limitations. This process enables the child to internalize the specific qualities of parental positions, reactions, and feelings. Another process in which the two defense structures gradually lose power is called *transmuting internalization* (1977, 30–32) and resembles mourning, as Freud described it in "Mourning and Melancholia" (1917). Withdrawing from her investment in parental aggrandizement, the child reinvests the energy in herself, building new structures that replace the psychological functions so far performed by the selfobject. The main engine of development is frustration, which urges the child to do what, hitherto, the parent has done. In the case of optimal frustrations – i.e., age-appropriate frustrations the child can tolerate, the child internalizes the functions the selfobject fulfilled until then.

We can draw two main conclusions from Kohut's developmental theory: First, **subjectivity is the main significant factor in development**. Developmental disorders are not the outcome of difficulties in the shift from the pleasure principle to the reality principle, but they originate from a non-empathic attitude to the child's subjective needs.

The second conclusion is that **Kohut, in his developmental theory, much like in his epistemological assumptions, is situated on the line between modernism and postmodernism**. One can discern many conservative elements in his theory, especially in his earlier writings. Much evidence suggests he believed in an objective reality – though he knew it was challenging to unveil it. He thus argued that the child's self was an isolated internal structure, including an inborn potential nucleus that would flourish in an optimal empathic environment. In this, he stays faithful to the Freudian model, in which the psyche is a fixed and stable structure that does not change from one interaction to another.

Kohut's developmental theory focuses on the self – the individual's experience in the world. This focus deviates significantly from the question that preoccupied Freud and classical psychoanalysis, namely, how the infant attains proper, unfalsified, and mature knowledge of objective reality, in other words, how he sheds subjectivity to observe reality as it is. Kohut is more interested in investigating the healthy, consolidated, stable, protected, and secure sense of self, allowing the child to believe in himself, develop ideals and ambitions, and belong to other human beings.

In Freud's theory, infants are miniature scientists. They learn about reality and its constraints in a way that resembles a scientific experiment. Under the domination of the pleasure principle, infants try to satisfy their urges. Initially relying on subjectivity (in this period, the baby is subject to the pleasure principle), this soon turns out not to help realize the infant's wishes. Gradually, through repeated frustration (a type of trial and error), they come to apprehend reality as it is, which leads to better-adjusted ways of attaining gratification.

The developmental direction Kohut described is the opposite: It is precisely the parents' boosting of the infant's subjective aspects and their responsiveness to her unrealistic, irrational wishes in the early stages of development that are necessary for development and growth. In his developmental theory, Kohut vacillates between his wish to maintain the existence of objective reality and the significant place he wishes to make for subjective factors. **However, Kohut argues that building up the child's reality-distorting subjective sides in early development is essential.**

The infant has unrealistic illusions and perceptions of herself. Healthy development takes the form of the parents bolstering self-illusions and perceptions (while protecting the toddler's life). In the initial period of the infant's life, it is the parent's task to reinforce the distortions of subjective perception while not allowing the infant near reality. Though he never says so explicitly, Kohut considers parents' role in these early stages of development to act like supporters of distortions and purveyors of illusions, protecting the child from a painful and frustrating reality.

Growth and development can happen when parents respond positively to their infant's subjectivity rather than curb it. This early phase of being subject to the pleasure principle is not merely regarded as a necessary evil that the baby should simply pass or a time devoid of real achievements; it is perceived as the most crucial phase in forming the child's personality. When subjectivity is denied at a too early stage – or, as Kohut calls it, where there is insufficient empathic response to the child's needs at this point, this might be one of the significant sources of psychopathology.

For example, responding to a scrawl by her little daughter, the mother says, "That is the most beautiful thing I ever saw!" Is she lying? Objectively speaking, yes, she is. She has obviously seen more beautiful drawings. However, regarding her experience, the mother is telling the truth about herself and her daughter. This is a time in the toddler's life when she must know she is "the best in the world" no matter what she does. Such a need clearly does not support the reality principle. But at this early stage, the parents' task is to support and underwrite their daughter's grandiosity. Remarkably, the parents genuinely believe what they say. The mother admires the child's drawing, not because she thinks this is what she is expected to say. She truly admires her child's achievement. The emphasis, thus, shifts from validation concerning an objective, distinct reality to an experiential, subjective truth. Though it may be incorrect regarding reality, it is accurate from a subjective perspective.

Kohut believes the self cannot be left in its own care in early development. The self requires an object that will fulfill a psychological function that she or he cannot. In his writings, he mentions four selfobject needs which come to build and strengthen the self (1971, 1977, 1984): a) the need for soothing, containment, and emotional regulation (using omnipotent merging); b) twinship experiences, which enable the infant to experience similarity between herself and significant others; c) the need for confirmation and mirroring of all dimensions of experience, both physiological and psychological; d) the need to aggrandize a parental figure.

It is illuminating to pause at what is missing from this list: taking proper cognizance of reality, reducing subjectivity, and learning to achieve goals appropriately and in a well-adjusted manner – none appear as essential basic developmental functions. Kohut considered the reality principle to have an essential function in the infant's development. As said, through transmuting internalization, the child learns to "take over" these functions, thereby reducing the importance of the selfobject. For Kohut, these structures develop naturally if the object has supplied the child's needs in the earlier stages. That is to say, the child's consciousness of reality (awareness of her own and her parents' limitations, the gradual lessening of self or object aggrandizement) comes naturally. However, the infant cannot become independent without the first subjective phase. To get rid of illusion, one must first have an illusion, and there is no way for the child to become familiar with reality without initial distortions of reality and without these distortions being supported and reinforced by the parents.

Without parental (selfobject) recognition of the child's exhibitionism and omnipotence, the grandiose self will keep its archaic form disconnected from the ego; it will be left untouched by the external world and will not be part of the personality texture. This description is also valid for the idealized parental imago (Kohut, 1971, 28).

Kohut believes that raising children according to the rational-positivist model is bound to unsettle the stability and cohesion of the self. One of his clinical illustrations (1977, 146) touches on how psychoanalysts raise their children. Kohut treated children who had grown up with parents who were classical psychoanalysts. What was the problem with the parent's attitude to their children? Kohut observed that the psychoanalyst parents shared, in great detail and from an early age, their insights about what their children were thinking, wanting, and feeling. No matter how accurate this communication was, it was based on the parents' assumption that they knew more about their children's internal and emotional experiences than the children themselves. However, this impeded the consolidation of the children's self. The children became secretive and reticent to defend themselves against their parents' intrusiveness.

The psychoanalysts Kohut describes believed that by passing their children the knowledge they had about the children's thoughts, feelings, and wishes, they contributed to their education (see the case of Gillian Silverman, recalled in the preface). They were trying to raise their children on a rationalist-positivist model that considers self-knowledge, freedom from subjectivity, and correct knowledge about reality as the focus of development.

And Yet: The Supremacy of the Reality Principle

The conservative elements in Kohut's developmental theory are straightforward to identify. First, Kohut believes that optimal frustrations are what allows the child, in the course of development, to progress from the subjective to the objective stage. Here, Kohut remains faithful to Freud: Starting with certain illusions concerning themselves and their parents, through a process of frustration, children slowly adjust to reality. Admittedly, it is the role of the selfobject to support defensive and reality-distorting structures – i.e., to shore up subjectivity through the early stages of development. However, Kohut, too, considers the subjective stage as somehow lower in the developmental order: a stage children must overcome on their way to a more objective grasp of reality.

Second, the description of this process in his first book, *The Analysis of the Self* (1971), illustrates Kohut's early writing well. The book, in its entirety, renders Kohut's effort – abandoned later on – to combine innovative ideas with Freud's meta-psychological rhetoric and Hartman's ego psychology (3). This effort, undertaken with particular enthusiasm, to include classical psychoanalysis epistemological assumptions was one factor preventing Kohut from making an epistemological path-breaking contribution. In explaining his notion of transmuting internalization, for example, Kohut attempts to embed the concept in ego psychology. This structure, he believes, develops in close association with the early development of the mental mechanism's maturation processes, as Hartman described them (49–50). Thus, for instance, Kohut attempts to combine failure of maternal empathy (which, when tolerable to the infant, will trigger development and growth) with Freudian meta-psychology – something which, from a present perspective, seems utterly misguided. Consequently, wherever the mother fails to be empathic, misunderstands, or inadequately cares for the infant, the infant takes back some of the energy invested in the archaic representation of the mother. The released energy is then re-invested in the internal psychological structure that replaces the role of the mother in maintaining a narcissistic equilibrium (64).

Here, we see a self-psychology that refuses to separate from Freud's meta-psychology, putting notions like energy or libidinal investment together with, for instance, selfobject and empathy.

In this passage's fascinating, almost surreal note, Kohut wants to affirm his adherence to classical theory further. He cites an empirical finding to the effect that people suffering from narcissistic disorder have difficulty sensing their body temperature and maintaining it. They rely on others to provide them not only with emotional but also with physical warmth. The blood supply to their skin is insufficient, making them susceptible to cold temperatures. Even regular people who do not habitually suffer from a narcissistic disorder tend to feel cold when they sustain narcissistic injuries (64). This strange note, which is not supported by any reference and seems to have perhaps based on a patient's reports, indicates how much value Kohut attached to being able to suggest self-psychology's "biological-medical nature" and the lengths he was prepared to go to achieve this.

Developments in the Concept of the Selfobject

On October 29, 1978, at the home of his friend Ernest Wolf, Kohut celebrated a momentous occasion: From now on, he had decided, in any future publication, to cancel the hyphen between *self* and *object* (Siegel, 1996). No longer self-object but selfobject. This change expresses, maybe more than anything, how the concept of the selfobject had evolved in Kohut's thinking. There was no longer a hyphen to separate between self and object, between inside and outside, between subjective and objective. Its removal meant another step back from the classical psychoanalytic frame of reference.

Teicholz (1999) argues that his concept of the selfobject turns Kohut's theory into a postmodern one. "Breaking" the boundaries of the self and between self and other, the selfobject anticipates the current psychoanalytic discourse regarding subjectivity, objectivity, and intersubjectivity (83).

It seems that what Teicholz has in mind are later developments of Kohut's concept: The selfobject in 1971 is not the same as in 1977, and neither one of them is the same as the selfobject in 1984.

In 1971, Kohut maintained the distinction between the subjective and the objective. He differentiates between: 1. the archaic selfobject; 2. psychological structures develop following the withdrawal from the investment in the selfobject and carry out psychological functions that were hitherto carried out by external forces; 3. actual objects – loved or hated – have been invested with libidinal energies. The relation to these objects develops once the person has separated from the selfobject, developed autonomous structures, and acknowledged the separateness and the various needs of the other (50–51).

In this early version of the selfobject, we observe the traditional dichotomy – between fantasy and reality, objectivity and subjectivity, true and distorted. The experienced object is subjective and archaic. It is a distortion of the real object. The selfobject is external. The selfobject initially performs psychological functions for the infant. However, once the infant grows, she can turn the "external" into the "internal" and carry out these functions herself. At this stage, a significant difference exists between the actual object and the selfobject, which is nothing but the infant's projection. When a person can distinguish a real object, this is a sign that a high level of maturity has been reached.

This is not much more than a slightly subtler version of the classical model, which holds that development consists of an apparent movement from a subjective state – identified with dependency, immaturity, and reality distortion – to a state of maturity and a better separation between inside and out.

Kohut changed his concept of the selfobject again in 1977. He no longer considers it a primitive and archaic product of the infant's subjective phase. Instead, Kohut argues that selfobject experiences occur throughout life in different modes. He writes in a note that the normal adult's narcissistic resources are insufficient. The normal adult needs mirror responses of the self provided by another person.

So, Kohut's therapeutic theory includes specific elements that are classical and conservative and others that are postmodern and contemporary. Like his notion of truth and developmental theory, his therapeutic theory evolved and became more detached from the classical approach.

The Metaphor of the Archeologist

Kohut emphatically disengages himself from the image of the psychoanalyst as an archeologist. He thereby renounces one of the most critical therapeutic objectives of classical theory, which considers itself a science: to unveil childhood facts, whether they happened in reality or fantasy.

Here, too, Kohut's thought developed over the years. In *The Analysis of the Self* (1971), his first book, he is ambivalent about the therapeutic contribution of the patient's recollecting the initial traumatic event (6). Regressions in the therapy, he believes, are the result of empathic failure. Understanding them during the treatment is extremely important for the patient. The point of the therapy, however, is not to focus on the patient's current regression. Interpretations should mainly address the traumatic event before the regression (137).

In his last book – *How Does Analysis Cure?* (1984) – Kohut expresses an opposite view, whereby it is not right to direct the patients to focus on their primary trauma (6). Elsewhere in the book (43), Kohut rejects the technique of looking for early trauma, also for neurotic patients who suffer from structural disorders entailed by failure in the Oedipal stage. Now, he believes that, even if retrieving the traumatic memory was possible, it would not benefit the patient.

Both Kohut and Freud think that there is no way to raise the earliest traumatic memory in the therapeutic session. While Freud gives up on retrieving these memories on pragmatic grounds and considers the transference as a tool for retrieving the actual event, Kohut no longer finds it therapeutically meaningful to try and bring it to conscious memory. Though he does not deny the existence of such a truth, he does not think that bringing to consciousness the memory of the traumatic event is a desirable ideal. The evolved self, he believes, withdraws from the frustrating traumatic events and constructs compensatory structures that allow coping with the narcissistic injury. In the transference relations, the therapist encounters the compensatory structures, not the primary self structures that initially coped with the trauma.

Kohut also renounces the metaphor of the surgeon (1984, 112). Freud, he argues, used terms that were appropriate to the state of medical science and research of his time, but they did not meet the demands of modern science. He believes that Freud's metaphors are alien to the domain of psychology, whose main research tools are empathy and introspection. Freud, he argues, treated the unconscious as "abscess that had to be drained" (112). The patient's sick tissue must be removed by the surgeon, who is able to neutralize her or his feelings, including feelings of sympathy and affection. Kohut claims that this approach led therapists to deal excessively with mechanisms and to focus on the patient's instinctual wishes, defenses against these wishes, and resistances (113–114). These concepts, he thinks, being influenced by the frame of reference of the pleasure principle as opposed to the reality principle, have limited explanatory power.

The Parent Metaphor versus the Scientist Metaphor

One innovative element in Kohut's theory, compared with classical psychoanalytic theory, is a total avoidance of the scientist metaphor in the context of therapeutic relations. Instead, Kohut used a parent-child metaphor. The early injuries of the self are enacted in the patient-therapist ties, and the therapist, as it were, conducts a process of reparation for parental deprivation. In the therapy, the patient's developmental fixation re-emerges, and this allows the therapist to offer a kind of reparation of the damaged self.

Classical theory, too, saw the patient as a child, arguing that patients' conflicts in their early relations with their parents rise to the surface in therapy. However, classical psychoanalysts did not think therapists should assume the role of parent; they believed they should stay in the role of the scientist. From its very inception, these two metaphors – of the psychoanalyst as a scientist or as a parent – have haunted psychoanalysis (Freud and Ferenczi, Klein and Winnicott, Kohut, and Hartmann), and one can find expressions of each in almost each of these theories.

Kohut adopts the controversial term "corrective emotional experience" (78), which was coined by Franz Alexander (though he does not use it the way Alexander did). He considers it a concept suitable to describe his approach. Empathy is the therapist's primary tool and the most essential developmental factor.

Kohut's notion of the role of the therapist parallels his notion of the role of the parent. Both parent and therapist must not confront the child with reality or criticize the child's selfobject needs. The child's perceptions derive from her subjectivity, so they distort reality. However, like the parent, the therapist must support the patient's subjectivity and avoid confronting her with the reality principle. In his early writings, this idea is clear to Kohut when he argues that therapists' difficulty with allowing their patients to idealize them is mainly the therapist's emotional difficulty (Kohut, 1971, 262–263).

In his final book, Kohut articulates this much more explicitly:

the self psychologist does not confront the patient with an 'objective' reality that is supposedly more 'real' than his inner reality but rather confirms the validity and legitimacy of the patient's own perception of reality, however contrary it might be to the accepted view of reality held by most adults and by society at large.

(1984, 173)

Empathy, as Opposed to Interpretation

Kohut's attitude to interpretation grew more and more ambivalent toward the end of his life. He remained faithful, to the end, to the notion that interpretation is the primary tool of therapy. In his final writings, however, he no longer considers interpretation a unique instrument. One of the conservative elements in his writings is that he refers to true and false interpretations, correct interpretations, and ones that are deceptive and misguided. In his first book, *The Analysis of the Self* (1971), he argues that, at times, empathic understanding is preferred to interpretation. The empathic therapist, he believes, recognizes that sometimes, not even the most accurate interpretation suits the patient who is looking for understanding (121). Bringing unconscious contents into consciousness is only one aspect of the therapeutic process (Kohut, 1977, 30–31).

However, even in *How Does Analysis Cure?*, Kohut continues to ascribe a vital role to interpretation. He emphasizes that empathy is only a tool for data collection concerning the patient's inner life. Moreover, he repeatedly states that empathy is a scientific instrument that expands the therapist's knowledge. He underlines the difference between understanding, which is "close to experiencing," and an explanation that is "remote from experience." These two processes, occurring alternatingly and with a degree of mutual adjustment, achieve "structural change."

Kohut is inconsistent regarding the principles of psychotherapy. He presents two arguments on empathy, a weak and a strong one, which do not cohere. The weak argument is that empathy is merely an instrument for data collection. Once they are collected using empathy, this data must be understood in terms of self-psychology. The strong argument is that the therapist's empathic intervention positively affects the patient regardless of the therapist's theoretical views.

Empathy serves as an interpretation in the first argument, which sees empathy as a means for collecting data. Therapy uses two principal methods that contribute to the generation of structures. The first of these is an intervention aimed at understanding. Here, the psychoanalyst collects information about the patient's inner life using empathy for her experience. The therapist shares her insights at the appropriate points in time. Empathy, in its weak version, is not a therapeutic method per se; the patient's experience that she has empathically understood is essential to her psychological life. Empathy, thus, has secondary therapeutic benefits. The second principle is intervention, which explains that the psychoanalyst "connects" an understanding of the patient's early life with the attempt to understand a situation in the patient's current life. While the explanations are very sensitive, they are nevertheless somewhat detached from the patient's immediate experience. This relative distance enables the patient to reflect on the event in the context of her life and contributes to the establishment and consolidation of self-structures. Thus, it can be seen, in contrast with received ideas, that Kohut's empathy does not come to replace classical psychotherapy's central tool – interpretation.

At Kohut's explanation stage, the psychoanalyst supports the patient because the latter constitutes a selfobject for her. The psychoanalyst enables the patient to be more objective toward herself and her problems. Initially, the psychoanalyst simply shared her insights regarding the patient's experiences, but as the process continues, she may move to express more objective perceptions. The movement toward objectivity is proof of progress in the therapy (185).

However, Kohut also holds an opposite view, which considers empathy exclusive. In his later works, Kohut's indecision concerning subjectivity and objectivity is so salient that it leads him to serious contradictions. So, for instance, in a fascinating and surprising passage in the book (1984, 91), Kohut argues – in contrast with what he said about the importance of interpretation – that empathic understanding can be helpful even when the underlying theory is invalid! How can this be read against the background of his statement, only a few pages earlier, that empathy is a mere data-collecting instrument in the service of interpretation?

Kohut's illustration in this context shows how close he was to giving up on positivism altogether. While he raises questions that reflect his doubt about the assumptions of positivism and almost draws the obvious conclusions, he grinds to a halt at the very last moment to revert to a conservative way of thinking.

Kohut recounts a case presented by a South American therapist, a Kleinian, during a psychoanalytic conference. The therapist gave her patient a Kleinian interpretation, which Kohut disagreed with:

> To my surprise this, to me, farfetched interpretation of the patient's mental state elicited a very favorable response from the patient. She began to talk more freely, reported that she was now aware of the fact that her jaw muscles had

been very tight since the last session, was able to verbalize a number of "biting' fantasies . . . and ended the session again on good terms with the analyst. . . ."

Although I happen to have chosen an illustration pertaining to the theories of a specific, recognizable school of thought in analysis – the Kleinian school . . .- I did not intend to serve as a vehicle of criticism directed against this specific school. Had the analyst, in other words, responded to the patient by saying that she had withdrawn because she had experienced the analyst's cancellation in terms of being abandoned by the mother who was locking the bedroom door in order to engage in sexual intercourse with the father, the point at issue was just as valid.

The point I wish to make rests not only on the claim that in all these instances, the patient might feel genuinely understood, but on the strongest claim that *in all these instances, the patient's feeling of being understood would, in essence, have been in harmony with the facts.*

(93[1])

Kohut did not want to come up with a "weak" argument, namely, the patient, feeling understood, responded positively. He wished to present a "strong" argument – i.e., that the therapist's understanding had been correct. Simultaneously, however, he believed the Kleinian therapist's theory was misguided!

It would seem that Kohut's argument clearly clashes with the conservative view of truth: Different interpretations, when they cause the patient to feel understood, are equally valid. What makes the interpretation right is the patient's subjective feeling that she is understood. Kohut, however, finds it hard to leave it at this: he is eager to make amends:

No reader who is familiar with my outlook will now, on the basis of my pre-ceding statement, suspect me of utter nihilism vis-a'-vis the tenets of psycho-analytic theory, experience near or experience distant. And indeed I am not a nihilist. Specifically, I am convinced that only one of the three preferred inter-pretations is closest to the mark. . . . The fact is that all these proposed inter-pretations are irrelevant. Indeed, they exemplify "wild analysis" because they are not based on the analyst's prolonged empathic immersion in the patient's associations.

(93)

As he refuses to relinquish the truth of interpretation and in his effort to base this truth on a subjective element, Kohut exposes himself to irresolvable contradictions.

Kohut's argument, first, is problematic due to its circularity: Interpretation that meets the criterion of verbal agreement (the patient responds positively) is the true interpretation. If it were not, the patient would not respond positively. This is the circularity Freud wanted to avoid when he argued that the patient's response does not testify to the interpretation's correctness. Whereas traditional psychoanalysis expresses its skepticism regarding the patient's responses, Kohut argues:

> If there is one lesson that I have learned during my life as an analyst, it is the lesson that what my patients tell me is likely to be true – that many times when I believed that I was right and my patients were wrong, it turned out, though often only after a prolonged search, that my rightness was superficial whereas their rightness was profound.
>
> (1984, 94)

This position diminishes the importance of the patient's unconscious and inner complexity. While classical psychoanalysis perceived the patient as an elusive, tricky, and complex creature whose words and feelings (conscious and unconscious) do not always harmonize, Kohut's attitude toward the patient is more straightforward, and he tends to rely on the latter's emotional responses. In contrast with Szasz, who compared psychoanalysis to a game of chess – a complex human behavior involving two clever rivals and endless possibilities and truths – Kohut gives up on this complexity and attaches less weight to the concept of the unconscious, stressing the interpersonal relations between therapist and patient.

The question of empathy and interpretation takes us back to the most urgent issue regarding this book's main thesis: Is his contribution to therapeutic theory significant because it replaced Freud's theory of drives with a model referring to the self – i.e. because he replaced one theory with another – or are we talking about an essential change on the epistemological level?

Kohut seems to tackle this question, but he fails to come up with a clear answer. Even though, in his final book, he tends to draw attention to the differences between self-psychology and classical psychoanalysis, he does not have an alternative perspective to offer, one on which he wishes or can lean. In the end, Kohut criticizes modernism but does not suggest an alternative:

> The contrast between traditional psychoanalysis and psychoanalytic self psychology vis-a'-vis defenses and resistances resides in contrast between the formers' commitment to a scientific objectivity that typifies the nineteenth century and the latter's commitment to a scientific objectivity that incorporates the breakthroughs of our century.
>
> (111)

The Two Analyses of Mr. Z.

In Kohut's famous case study, "The Two Analyses of Mr. Z." (1979), he describes two analyses he conducted with the same patient, taking two different perspectives. In the first analysis, Kohut treated Z. when he still adhered to the Freudian drive-defense theory. When Z. returned to therapy five years later, the analysis was done with a self-psychological orientation. These two periods – each taking four and a half years of five weekly sessions – allowed Kohut to compare the two theo-retical points of view: the Freudian and the self-psychological.

Mr. Z. was in his mid-twenties when he first came for psychoanalysis. He com-plained about a sense of social isolation, difficulties in making contact with women, and masochistic sexual fantasies. Though his academic achievements were exem-plary, he felt he did not fully realize his abilities. He expressed some moderate physical complaints: A tendency to sweat and alternating spells of diarrhea and constipation. The patient's father fell ill when the boy was three and had to be hospitalized. In the hospital, his father fell in love with a nurse, and when he was released, he left home to live with her.

At the outset of the first stint of therapy, the patient demanded much attention and consideration from the therapist. Kohut understood and interpreted this demand in Oedipal terms. Unconsciously, the patient wanted to reproduce the experience of enmeshment with a mother who gave abundant warmth, love, and attention in the father's absence. The patient angrily rejected this interpretation. Throughout this first year, Z. expressed much anger toward Kohut. He felt Kohut refused to admire him. After one year, this rage passed, and the patient no longer thought his expectations were reasonable. Kohut explained this change by the patient having succeeded in processing his narcissistic delusions. Rejecting this interpretation, the patient argued that change has to do with something Kohut had said: "I had, he said, introduced *one* of my interpretations concerning his insatiable narcissis-tic demands with the phrase 'Of course, it hurts when one is not given what one assumes to be one's due'" (6). Kohut argues that he did not understand the signifi-cance of these words at the time. Kohut continued to believe the patient had taken control of his rage as a result of processing his narcissistic demands. During the first analysis, Kohut believed that the patient's conviction of his own uniqueness and of having no equals must be related to the long period of his father's absence in his childhood when he remained alone with his mother. Kohut understood the patient's narcissism, expressed in his sense of being special, as a denial of the fact that his father returned home to take sexual possession of his wife, the patient's mother. The patient's sense of being unique, that is, came to protect him from the competitive existence of his father and castration anxiety. During the first therapy, Kohut refused to comply with the patient's wishes:

> I consistently, and with increasing firmness, rejected the reactivation of his nar-cissistic attitudes, expectations, and demands during the last years of analysis by telling the patient that they were resistances against the confrontation of deeper and more intense fears connected with masculine assertiveness and competition with men.
>
> (8)

Eventually, the patient's narcissistic demands subsided and grew more realistic. In his work, the patient became more assertive. Kohut, at the time, believed that the therapy had succeeded thanks to his theoretical approach, which, thus, stood confirmed. From his perspective as a traditional psychoanalyst, he assumed that the positive changes in the transference relations and the patient's life resulted from a structural change in the patient's personality, made possible by becoming conscious of unconscious conflicts.

Five years after termination, the patient contacted Kohut again, complaining he felt stuck. He lived alone; he described his relations with women as unsatisfactory and superficial. While successful at work, he did not feel satisfied there either. His masochistic fantasies had continued and grown more intense, making up for a considerable part of his sex life. In this second round of psychoanalysis, the patient's feelings improved rapidly from the first meeting. Kohut began to notice the patient's idealizing transference relations toward himself. This time, Kohut allowed for the aggrandizement. The patient became increasingly demanding, expecting perfect empathy, exactly as he had done at the beginning of his first analysis. This time, too, he responded with rage at the slightest disappointment from Kohut. However, Kohut now coped differently with these feelings. He no longer thought of narcissism as a defense mechanism. Now, he saw it as a situation from a traumatic childhood that re-emerged in the analysis.

This new approach, he thought, prevented the rage that had marked the first round of psychoanalysis. This time, Kohut interpreted the patient's demanding behavior as a reflection of his relations with his mother. She had been willing to fulfill the patient's wish as long as he met her expectations.

Kohut lists the differences between the first and second analyses. In the first analysis, he considered the patient an independent, responsible subject. Therefore, he expected that psychoanalytic insights would help him see his life in a clearer light, give up his narcissistic demands, and enhance his growth. In the second analysis, he was less intent on the aim of growth, which would take care of itself as long as he could offer himself as the patient's selfobject. Rather than emphasizing values of mental health and maturity, he concentrated on the early stages of the patient's experience, especially his pathological enmeshment with the mother (145).

The second analysis was terminated successfully, with a real rather than a pseudo success. Kohut believes that the key achievement of the second analysis is in undoing Z.'s symbiotic relationship with his mother. As a result of analyzing the transference relations with Kohut, the patient was able to reconnect with his father's masculinity. This led to developing the emotional core of the self's enfolded aspirations, ideals, and competencies. Now, the patient experienced these needs as part of himself, as something he owned, and he went on to realize his life objectives through the activities of an independent, autonomous self rather than as a form of masochistic obedience – as he felt it after his first psychoanalysis. Years later, Kohut was told that the patient got married and had a daughter, which was another sign that the therapy was successful.

I have quoted Kohut's paper at length to illustrate, once more, how hard it was for him to replace classical theory's positivist epistemology with an alternative epistemology. The paper's terminology, to start with, is essentially classical and positivist. It is an effort to present things as a kind of scientific experiment: Two analyses with the same patient, the first, using a discredited theory, failed in its results. The second, which employed a well-grounded theory, was a success. What we have here, then, is a simple linear model whereby mental healing depends on the rightness of the theory. This way of presenting things, as though we were talking about established data, is evidence of positivist thinking. From a meta-theoretical perspective, it is unclear what was behind the difference between the first and the second rounds of analysis. Was it caused by changing from an erroneous theory to a correct one? Was it due to empathy, a factor in the second analysis but absent in the first?

All this takes a surprising and fascinating turn – postmodern in how it shatters expectations – when it transpires that Mr. Z. may well have been Kohut himself. In his introduction to the book, Cocks (1994) writes that those who were close to Kohut – relatives and friends alike – were convinced that the case study was based on Kohut's biography. The first analysis, Cocks believes, was the one Kohut underwent with Ruth Eissler in the 1940s. The second was a self-analysis Kohut conducted in the 1960s. Cocks does not go into Kohut's reasons for doing this strange thing: writing his most detailed and serious case study about himself. Kohut's biographer, Strozier (2001, 308–316), presents many points of similarity between Kohut and Mr. Z. However, suppose Mr. Z. is no one but Kohut himself; one has to wonder: Is this a case of forgery, or is it merely another instance of the legitimate camouflaging of identity that is habitual in the writing of case studies? Gedo (2002) mentions Kohut's way of fooling people and concealing certain details about his life and he considers Mr. Z.'s case study morally unacceptable. However, the choice between forgery or camouflage may also involve Kohut's doubts about staying faithful to the classical approach and his wish to be revolutionary and groundbreaking. Kohut needed an unambiguous case to adjust himself to the classical rhetoric. Had he fully identified with the positivist-scientific epistemology of the classical approach, he may not have resorted to forgery-camouflage; he may have worked on a real case study (his writings are larded with plenty of actual case descriptions), to "scientifically" prove the principles of therapy on the lines of self-psychology. That Kohut thought that a self-analysis could serve as "proof" could have been a sign of a "postmodernism" direction in his thinking, as the assumption that a subject can testify to a subject much like an object can testify to a subject is a postmodern one. However, he obviously did not – or else he would have explicitly brought the case as his own. This also seems to keep him well out of the rubric of postmodernism: This type of reflexivity is a self-conscious, explicit "trademark" of postmodernism.

Again, we encounter Kohut's two hats: He tries to act according to classical psychoanalysis while not wholly identifying with its research instrument. Kohut's forgery/camouflage of the Mr. Z. case may reflect all of his ambivalence regarding the classical approach: Kohut's two analyses – the one he did with Eissler and his self-analysis – represent his subjectivity, which led him to develop a new theory, self-psychology. Unlike classical psychoanalysis, but similar to Freud, Kohut accepts his subjectivity as a sufficient theoretical justification for developing a new theory. He knows, however, that this is not enough. He must prove the theory, not in the same manner as he discovered it, but objectively, following the criteria of classical psychoanalysis.

The problem, though, is even more nettly. Doesn't self-analysis stand in square contradiction with all of self-psychology's most fundamental assumptions? If the most significant aspect of therapy and parenting is a corrective experience based on a relation with a selfobject then self-analysis does not seem to possess a curative potential.

Suppose one can be, as it were, one's own selfobject. Doesn't this entirely do away with the argument that both pathology and healing wholly depend on concrete relations with external objects (mother-analyst)? In contrast, self-analysis can be a possibility for an approach emphasizing a modern positivist epistemology, which regards truth and knowledge as therapeutically important.

Conclusion

Kohut's theory reflects ambivalence in its view of science: On the one hand, a commitment to the scientific model and objectivity and, on the other hand, a focus on subjective elements in development and therapy.

One possible explanation might be that **the main change in his theory, unlike Freud and ego psychology, relates not to its view of science but to its view of the human mind**. Freud and ego psychology think differently about mental structure than Kohut. Freud and the ego psychologists consider the individual in terms of energies, defenses, and drives; that is, in mechanistic terms. If the processes in the mind resemble those in other living creatures and if they obey similar physical and neurological rules, then there is no sense in investigating humans using subjective approaches and empathic understanding. The mechanistic approach shared by Freud and the ego psychologists requires investigative tools that refer to an external understanding of the patient.

Kohut holds a radically different view of the mind's structure. He believes that the fundamental problem in life is existential: The centrality of significant others is crucial for the healthy self development. The child's self – his or her subjective experience – is more critical than energies and drives. **The confusing ambivalence in Kohut's work arises from the fact that, while his view of the human subject undergoes a significant change, his epistemological stance remains unchanged.** While one can find expressions of doubt in Kohut's oeuvre about the appropriateness of psychoanalysis to a positivist approach, there is no transition to an alternative worldview that may support this radical change in his perception of the human subject. The instruments of investigation – empathy and introspection – become more subjective and existential, but they are used for the same purpose: to attain, by scientific means, valid knowledge about the world. Thus, the problem is that, throughout his life, Kohut tried to maintain that the figure of the new human individual – the tragic person torn by existential doubts, whose subjectivity is essential – can be studied and understood objectively and scientifically.

In the years after Kohut's death, psychoanalysis underwent another transformation when it incorporated a new postmodern philosophy – intersubjectivity. The intersubjective approach began as an essential philosophical perspective to self-psychology. However, as it evolved, it has departed from self-psychology, which was perceived as too conservative both clinically and philosophically.

Note

1 Italics are mine.

References

Bergmann, M.S. (Ed.) (2000). *The Hartmann Era*. New York: The Other Press.

Bohart, A.C. (1991). Empathy in Client-Centered Therapy: A Contrast with Psychoanalysis and Self Psychology. *Journal of Humanistic Psychology*, 31, 34–48.

Brenner, C. (1968). Psychoanalysis and Science. *Journal of the American Psychoanalytic Association*, 16(4), 675–696.

Cocks, G. (Ed). (1994). *The Curve of Life: Correspondence of Heintz Kohut 1923–1981*. Chicago: University of Chicago Press.

Cushman, P. (1995). *Constructing the Self, Constructing America – A Cultural History of Psychotherapy*. Boston: Adison-Wasley Publishing Company.

Freud, S. (1917). Mourning and Melancholia. *Standard Edition*, 14, 237–258.

Gadamer, H.G. (1960/1994). *Truth and Method*. 2nd revised edn, trans. W. Glen-Doepel, rev. J. Weinsheimer and D.G. Marshall. New York: Continuum.

Gedo, J.E. (2002). Heinz Kohut: The Making of a Psychoanalyst. Charles B. Strozier. *American Imago*, 59, 91–102.

Habermas, J. (1968). *Knowledge and Human Interest*. Boston: Beacon Press.

Kahn, E. (1985). Heinz Kohut and Carl Rogers: A Timely Comparison. *American Psychologist*, 40, 893–904.

Kahn, E. (1989). Carl Rogers and Heinz Kohut: Toward a Constructive Collaboration. *Psychotherapy*, 26, 555–563.

Kahn, E. and Rachman, A.W. (2000). Carl Rogers and Heinz Kohut – A Historical Perspective. *Psychoanalytic Psychology*, 17(2), 294–312.

Kirsner, D. (2000). *Unfree Associations: Inside Psychoanalytic Institutions*. London: Process Press.

Kohut, H. (1959/1978). Introspection, Empathy and Psychoanalysis: An Examination of the Relationship Between Mode of Observation and Theory. In P. Ornstein (Ed.) *The Search for the Self*. Vol. 1. New York: International University Press, 259–261.

Kohut, H. (1968). The Psychoanalytic Treatment of Narcissistic Personality Disorders – Outline of a Systematic Approach. *Psychoanalytic Study of the Child*, 23, 86–113.

Kohut, H. (1971). *The Analysis of the Self*. New York: International Universities Press.

Kohut, H. (1977). *The Restoration of the Self*. New York: International University Press.

Kohut, H. (1978a). Conclusion: The Search for the Analyst's Self. In P.H. Ornstein (Ed.) *The Search for the Self*. Vol. 1. New York, NY: International Universities Press, 931–939.

Kohut, H. (1978b). Psychoanalysis in a Troubled World. In P.H. Ornstein (Ed.) *The Search for the Self*. Vol. 1. New York: International Universities Press, 205–232.

Kohut, H. (1979). The Two Analyses of Mr. Z. *International Journal of Psychoanalysis*, 60, 3–28.

Kohut, H. (1980a). Reflections. In A. Goldberg (Ed.) *Advances in Self Psychology*. Madison, CT: International University Press, 473–554.

Kohut, H. (1980b). Selected Problems in Self Psychological Theory. In P.H. Ornstein (Ed.).

Kohut, H. (1982). Introspection, Empathy, and the Semi-Circle of Mental Health. *International Journal of Psychoanalysis*, 63, 395–407.

Kohut, H. (1984). *How Does Analysis Cure?* ed. A. Goldberg and P. Stepansky. Chicago: University of Chicago Press.

Kuhn, T.S. (1962). *The Structure of Scientific Revolutions*. Chicago: University of Chicago Press.

Laudan, L. (1977). *Progress and Its Problems – Towards a Theory of Scientific Change*, Berkeley: University of California Press.

Mitchell, S. (1993). *Hope and Dread in Psychoanalysisx*. New York: Basic Books.

Ricoeur, P. (1970). *Freud and Philosophy: An Essay on Interpretation*, trans. D. Savage. New Haven: Yale University Press.

Siegel, A.M. (1996). *Heinz Kohut and the Psychology of the Self*. London: Routledge.

Strozier, C.B. (2001). *Heinz Kohut – The Making of a Psychoanalyst*. New York: Ferrar, Straus, and Giroux.

Teicholz, J.G. (1999). *Kohut, Loewald, & the Postmoderns – A Comparative Study of Self and Relationship*. Hillsdale, NJ: The Analytic Press.

Tobin, S.A. (1990). Self Psychology as a Bridge Between Existential-Humanistic Psychology and Psychoanalysis. *Journal of Humanistic Psychology*, 30, 14–63.

Postmodernism and Intersubjectivity

Before describing postmodern psychoanalytic approaches, I will first briefly discuss the concepts of postmodernism and intersubjectivity. This brief introduction does not aim to review all the postmodern directions in the professional literature. Instead, it intends to guide the reader towards several lines of thought that have inspired contemporary psychoanalysis.

The term "postmodern" has various meanings. There are many postmodern theories, and their tenets often clash. This inconsistency coheres with postmodernism's questioning of originality or uniqueness and its aspiration not to be identified with one position. "Postmodernism" sparks off various associations, stretching from extremely sophisticated sensibilities to a simplistic, nihilist, and cynical way of thinking that marks contemporary culture (Dochetry, 1993). Indeed, this lack of definition takes up a considerable portion of the postmodern discourse.

Ihab Hassan (1987), referring to this problem, argues that the word has a strange quality because it includes what it comes to oppose – i.e., modernism. Unlike other movements, such as classicism, the baroque, or rococo, postmodernism contains its rival adversary.

> The word postmodernism sounds not only awkward and uncouth; it evokes what it wishes to surpass, modernism itself. The term thus contains its enemy within, as the terms romanticism and classicism, baroque, and rococo do not. Moreover, it denotes temporal linearity and connotes belatedness, even decadence, to which no postmodernist would admit. But what better name have we to give this curious age? The Atomic, or Space, or Television Age? These technological tags lack theoretical definitions. . . . Or better still, shall we simply live and let others live to call us what they may?
>
> (86)

In Richard Rorty's postmodernism (1989), there is no one valid way of representing the world. Rorty's radical argument is that changes in scientific perceptions are neither findings nor observations but language. According to him, Europe did not decide to adopt the terminology of Roman poetics, socialism or Galilean

DOI: 10.4324/9781003498162-6

physics because of certain findings or because some new facts about the world were revealed. Europe adopted these terminologies not by choice and not because they were presented with persuasive arguments but because it lost the habit of talking in certain words and acquired new habits, including new words. It was neither due to telescope observations that the Europeans decided the Earth did not occupy the center of the universe nor that all scientific activity needs to aim for observation and verification. Following a century of doubt and uncertainty, the Europeans spoke about these interconnected theses as though it was a matter of course. Cultural changes of this order are not decided on the strength of some criterion, much like a person's decision to be an atheist or religious or to change partner or friends is not a matter of criteria (6).

Another branch of postmodernism is associated with Jacques Derrida's post-structuralism. Poststructuralism emerged in response to institutionalized structures such as authoritarianism in general. Derrida's deconstructive critique aims to shatter the illusion that texts have stable meanings. Because of this, philosophy and criticism cannot claim authority in textual interpretation. Interpretation, for Derrida, is a free activity that resembles a playful activity rather than a rule-governed analysis. Derrida attacks the authoritarianism he observes in Western thought, especially in its essentialist aspect. The most prominent illustration of this is Derrida coins *logocentrism*, the belief that words are representations of meanings that pre-exist in the speaker's mind. Derrida rejects the notion of meaning as a stable entity awaiting representation using a word – whether spoken or written. Instead of stable meanings and the authority of critical thinking, Derrida proposes the undecidability of meaning and language games (Llewelyn, 1986). Deconstruction broadly means accepting the contradiction instead of trying to eradicate it. All ideas are contradictory for Derrida. If sentences in language are vague and therefore contradictory, then the idea of the sentence is contradictory because the sentence must both carry meaning and cannot carry meaning. The sentence cannot be inaccessible as a meaning component from its context, so it does not occur in a stable self-identical way, as the same sentence may have different meanings in different contexts. The sentence must both be what it is and not what it is. The same applies to all aspects of meaning (Stocker, 2006, 68).

For Jean-François Lyotard (1993a), postmodern artists or authors resemble the philosopher. The text they write or their composed art does not evolve from predetermined rules and cannot be judged through the accepted categories of judgment (78). Lyotard rejects broad explanatory and inclusive theories. These, he calls "grand narratives" or "meta-narratives." In his book *The Postmodern Condition* (1993b), Lyotard uses the term narrative to denote a series of events. The narrative simply exists, and herein lies its justification. It does not need any meta-narrative to operate or exist. The narrative is perceived as liberating personally, while the meta-narrative is seen as authoritarian and totalitarian.

Like Derrida, Lyotard believes that value judgments should be overcome or sidestepped. He thinks all types of discourse are equal, with none having a special claim to priority. Whatever discourse we can think of is nothing but a narrative:

a series of ideas that might or might not be reasonable to the public, pleasant or unpleasant, but always a series that cannot claim or prove transcendental authority. Lyotard wishes to release the defensive individual from the shackles of the meta-narrative – i.e., from earlier explanatory systems.

In this book, I refer to postmodernism in its general, broad sense, as characterized by the following three criteria: 1. the view that supposed truths are no less subjective values than any other beliefs or opinions (Vattimo, 1985) and the rejection of general truths and rules in favor of contextual, relative, unique, and personal "truths"; 2. claiming the plurality of meanings of texts and events; 3. declaring the "death" of the subject, the self, or the individual; and 4. rejection of the subject's true ontological status (e.g., Chaikilin, 1992; Polkinghorne, 1992).

Intersubjectivity exists between subjects, is shared by all, is open and public, and involves relations with others. Through intersubjectivity, we can know how the other feels, what he or she believes and wants, and who and what they are (Malpas, 2000). The main question concerning intersubjectivity in modern philosophy is our ability to know the subjectivity of others.

The notion of intersubjectivity has several philosophical implications. Husserl (Ricouer, 1967) tried to understand how we manage to understand one another without access to each other's mind. In his opinion, we can only know our own subjectivity and mind. This is why our understanding and perception of others can only be based on the imaginary projection of our own experiences to the other. The process is achieved in the following manner: The other has a body identical to ours, and the other moves in a manner identical to how we move. Since both our movements and body are experiential and conscious, we assume that the other possesses vitality and consciousness. There is much room for confirmation or refutation in understanding the other. A person will think of the other as a conscious object and will transfer feelings she or he imagines the other has (based on what the person knows about her or himself), as long as the other acts in ways that are intelligible for the person – from a conscious perspective. The pair is a key concept for Husserl. When we perceive things, no matter what types of things, as being similar, we tend to believe they have similar attributes and act toward them in similar ways. We act toward them as though they were a pair. In fact, this is our self, which we link with the perceived object that we perceive, turning them into a pair. Awareness of the self always includes awareness of the other. These are relational terms: Neither one of them has meaning without the other. No self-awareness or self-knowledge, therefore, is possible in the absence of awareness of the other. Husserl rejects the existence of the isolated monadic soul because the soul cannot know itself without the other (Ricouer, 1967).

Husserl claims that we experience others as subjects who experience and know the world and who experience and know us as part of the world. We thus experience ourselves as being experienced by others.

In the writings of Hegel, Buber, Levinas, Heidegger, and Arendt, the intersubjective takes on further meanings (for an exhaustive summary of this notion in philosophical discourse, see Crossley, 1996).

The Finish social psychologists Gillespie and Cornish (2010) listed at least seven definitions of intersubjectivity (and other disciplines have additional definitions): people's agreement on the shared definition of a concept; people's mutual awareness of agreement or disagreement, or understanding or misunderstanding each other; people's attribution of intentionality, feelings, and beliefs to each other; people's implicit or automatic behavioral orientations towards other people; people's interactive performance within a situation; people's shared and taken-for-granted background assumptions, whether consensual or contested; and the variety of possible relations between people's perspectives.

Why does it make sense to consider the intersubjective or relational approaches to psychoanalysis as postmodern approaches? First, some authors define themselves as such (Aron, 1996; Benjamin, 1995; Spezzano, 1993). Second, the term "postmodern" coheres with the relational research objective, namely, to situate the developments in psychoanalysis in a broad cultural context. There is hardly any intellectual domain that has not been affected by postmodernism. Postmodernism has left its mark on academic disciplines and cultural practices, such as architecture, zoology, biology, geography, history, law, and politics (Dochetry, 1993).

In the present study, the term postmodern reflects the view that the main questions preoccupying psychoanalysts run parallel to those postmodern philosophers deal with. Knowledge, in the postmodern age, is no longer securely based epistemologically speaking, and it has become almost impossible to justify a preference for certain types of knowledge over certain other types of knowledge. In the postmodern era, there is no epistemological justification for one type of knowledge. In the face of this, the authority vested in certain social forces, like scientists and diverse kinds of advisers and consultants, who, in past times, claimed to possess valid knowledge, has waned.

Current psychoanalysis struggles with similar problems. Using the rhetoric of modernism, psychoanalysis believed itself on firm epistemological grounds. The classic psychoanalyst struggled to replace emotion with reason to reveal the patient's inner truth. In his attempt to attain objectivity and neutrality, he wished to insulate the clinic to eliminate the burden of subjectivity and be able, together with the patient, to draw valid therapeutic conclusions. But, postmodern analysts argue that the classic psychoanalyst himself was "tainted" by his own subjective ideology, which held that theoretical models could match the state of affairs in reality and that reality could be probed through logical, causal argumentation as it was done with the laws of nature. The psychoanalyst himself, they argue, turned into a burden distorting our grasp of the world with his own values and culturally biased ideas.

What Characterizes Postmodern Authors?

Regarding their worldviews, postmodern psychoanalytic theories declare irreducible complexity as their key feature. They do not try to resolve contradictions or paradoxes. In general, one may say that they do not adopt an empiricist-positivist model of knowledge and tend to be suspicious of any theory that presents itself as true, valid, scientific, or universal. The therapeutic reality, they would have it, is constructed rather than revealed, and they tend to put a prime value on the subjective aspect of development and therapy. While they attempt to keep themselves apart from relativist or solipsistic approaches, they do not provide clear criteria for validating theories as the classic theoreticians did.

According to Teicholz (2009):

For postmodern analysts, there is an emphasis on process over structure in conceptualizing the mind, and on nonlinearity over linearity in conceptualizing development. There is a perception of multiplicity, complexity, or chaos of experience rather than unity or organization. Postmodern theorists also tend to conceptualize apparent opposites in terms of dialectics and paradox, and they prefer theoretical pluralism over the claims of any single explanation. They reject the interrelated concepts of foundational knowledge; essences and universals; cause-and effect relationships; grand or meta-narratives; and the notion of scientific progress.

(74)

Also, the concept of a singular self gives way to a stance of multiple-selves-in-relation-to-multiple-others. The terms "subjectivity" and "intersubjectivity" suggest greater flexibility in the experience of self and selfobject. The analyst's subjectivity is recognized and seen as crucial to the treatment process, with analytic neutrality no longer an ideal.

While the classical theory was influenced by positivism and committed to an orthodox scientific model, postmodern authors have been affected by philosophers supporting an anti-positivist approach, like Hans-Georg Gadamer, Ludwig Wittgenstein, Richard Rorty, and Richard Bernstein.

Postmodern authors object to the modernist tendency of psychoanalysis and its aim to understand the patient using totalizing theories. Emanuel Berman aptly writes:

Intersubjective and relational approaches to psychoanalysis also reflect changes in the zeitgeist. The time of monolithic and total, grand theories seems to be over. The wish for objectivity clears the field for an interest in and respect for the subjective. Postmodern schools of thought encourage the critical dissection or deconstruction of received truths – many of which stand revealed as simplistic mythologies.

(Berman, 1997, 181)

A significant property of postmodern psychoanalysis is that, rather than proposing a new theory, it defines its ideas as a "sensibility" or a "different type of understanding." Postmodern analysts like Louis Aron, Stephen Mitchell, and Robert Stolorow refer back copiously to earlier psychoanalytic theories and do not offer an alternative. They express few positive arguments about "psychic facts" and focus mainly on therapeutic questions. However, as I intend to show, they believe that sensibility is not just a poor replacement for a robust theory (see Chapter 6). It has enormous implications for the clinical encounter.

Several questions touching on postmodern psychoanalysis are also relevant to the cultural role of postmodernism. Has the postmodern approach in psychoanalysis produced a method of its own, or is its only contribution to pointing out the limitations of classical psychoanalysis? Does postmodern psychoanalysis have a new theory to offer in the fields of development and psychopathology? In short, do postmodern theories stand in their own right, or are they parasitical on classical psychoanalysis, feeding on its rejection? Are they, indeed, theories at all?

Postmodernism is even more problematic in its role in psychoanalysis than in other cultural domains. For over and beyond being a theory, psychoanalysis is an actual praxis, offering counsel to people in distress. It is a therapeutic method that defines the ways, methods, and objectives relevant to helping people cope with their mental afflictions. Researchers who belong to the US postmodern school of thinking are psychoanalysts themselves. Patients regard them as a professional authority and turn to them for help. Are their postmodern assumptions transparent to their patients? Can a person present herself as a professional authority and consider herself a postmodernist simultaneously? How do these psychoanalysts deal with this contradiction?

There is little doubt that psychoanalysis was transformed in the last decade with the appearance of the relational movement. Its questions and insights, its new understanding of therapeutic relations, truth, and subjectivity, set an agenda for psychoanalysis that has influenced the entire psychoanalytic thought. Whatever their shortcomings, superficial criticism of these texts is always to be rejected. Their questions are responsive to new concerns that did not emerge during the modern era of psychoanalytic schools.

As Roger Frie (2009) writes:

Postmodernism in psychoanalysis, like philosophy, takes many forms. Indeed, there is no overarching "postmodern" theory of psychoanalysis, just as there is no single way of practicing analytic technique. In the broadest sense, the emergence of a postmodern position in psychoanalysis has played a constructive role in calling attention to many of Cartesian rationalism's oversights. Within the North American context, postmodernism is most frequently linked to the emergence of the relational school of psychoanalysis. In Europe and South America, by contrast, postmodernism is associated chiey with Lacanian and post-Lacanian versions of psychoanalysis.

(11)

In the following two chapters, I will present the postmodern turn in psychoanalysis through its two main theories: the relational and intersubjective approaches. These two theories are wide-ranging and include a host of great thinkers and clinicians.

I do not attempt to review the entire literature but to show how they incorporated questions about truth, knowledge and authority.

I chose to center around two contemporary analysts whose philosophical and clinical critique of their predecessors changed how they perceive therapeutic relations: Robert Stolorow and Irwin Hoffman.

Stoloro and Hoffmann were significant players in the 1990s and 2000s when psychoanalysis had an important conceptual crossroads. During this period, innovative ideas that had always accompanied psychoanalytic thinking grew into a mature and sophisticated philosophy that gathered an entire growing community.

References

Aron, L. (1996). *A Meeting of Minds – Mutuality in Psychoanalysis*. Hillsdale, NJ: The Analytic Press.

Benjamin, J. (1995). *Like Subjects, Love Objects: Essays on Recognition and Sexual Differences*. New Haven & London: Yale University Press.

Berman, A. (1997). Mutuality and Intersubjectivity in Therapeutic Encounter: The Historical Background of Relational Psychoanalysis. *Sihot – Israel Journal of Psychotherapy*, 11(3), 172–182.

Chaikilin, S. (1992). From Theory to Practice and Back Again: What Does Postmodern Philosophy Contribute to Psychological Science? In S. Kvale (Ed.) *Psychology and Postmodernism*. Newbury Park, CA: Sage, 194–208.

Crossley, N. (1996). *Intersubjectivity: The Fabric of Social Becoming*. London: SAGE Publications.

Dochetry, T. (Ed.) (1993). *Postmodernism A Reader*. New York: Harvester Wheatsheaf.

Frie, R. (2009). Introduction: Coherence or Fragmentation? Modernism, Postmodernism, and the Search for Continuity. In R. Frie and D. Orange (Eds.) *Beyond Postmodernism: New Dimensions in Clinical Theory and Practice*. London: Routledge/Taylor & Francis Group/, 1–23.

Gillespie, A. and Cornish, F. (2010). Intersubjectivity: Towards a Dialogical Analysis (PDF). *Journal for the Theory of Social Behaviour*, 40(1), 9–46. https://doi.org/10.1111/j.1468-5914.2009.00419.

Hassan, I. (1987). *The Postmodern Turn*. Colombus: Ohio State University Press, 84–96.

Llewelyn, J. (1986). *Derrida on the Threshold of Sense*. London: Macmillan.

Lyotard, J.F. (1993a). Answering the Question: What is Postmodernism? In T. Dochetry (Ed.) *Postmodernism A Reader*. New York: Harvester Wheatsheaf.

Lyotard, J.F. (1993b). *The Postmodern Condition: A Report on Knowledge*. Manchester: Manchester University Press.

Malpas, J. (2000). Between Ourselves: Philosophical Conceptions of Intersubjectivity. *International Journal of Psychoanalysis*, 81, 587–592.

Polkinghorne, D.E. (1992). Postmodern Epistemology in Practice. In S. Kvale (Ed.) *Psychology and Postmodernism*. Newbury Park, CA: Sage, 146–165.

Ricœur, P. (1967). *Husserl: An Analysis of His Phenomenology*. Evanston: Northwestern University Press.

Rorty, R. (1989). *Contingency, Irony and Solidarity*. Cambridge: Cambridge University Press.

Spezzano, C. (1993). A Relational Model of Inquiry and Truth: The Place of Psychoanalysis in the Human Conversation. *Psychoanalytic Dialogues*, 3(2), 177–208.

Stocker, B. (2006). *Routledge Philosophy Guide to Derrida on Deconstruction*. London: Routledge.

Vattimo, J. (1985). *The End of Modernity*, trans. J.R. Snyder. Baltimore, MD: Johns Hopkins University Press.

Chapter 4

The Intersubjective Approach

The "rules of the game" change when the aspiration for scientific objectivity is completely abandoned and replaced by a deep understanding of patients' needs, a desire to respond to them, and ethical responsibility for their well-being. However, the most significant change is the attitude toward strict rules. Like social revolutions that disgustingly reject the old social order, many analysts during the 90s enjoyed a new sense of freedom and could now violate strict principles that have prevailed for decades:

> It happens with some patients that they feel not sure whether their therapist remembers them between meetings: they experience considerable difficulty around separating from the therapist. When, in extreme cases, a patient is not reassured that he has a place in the other's heart, he may experience panic and terror. Such patients, who are often labelled as suffering from borderline personality disorder, are in need of therapists who are capable, at times, to depart from psychoanalytical rules. One therapist told me that he had a patient who asked him to phone him every day at a certain time. Some months later, the daily phone call became redundant when the patient had become able to experience the continuity of his existence both in the therapist's mind and in his own experience. Another patient gave her therapist a book on loan when the latter went on vacation: in this way she ensured that he would remember her when they were not meeting. Yet another patient once gave me a fridge magnet which was also a Christmas decoration. When she asked in February, I replied I had removed it from the fridge after Christmas and that I was keeping it in another place. The patient became low and sad. Having suffered severe harassment in childhood, her self experience was fragmentary and discontinuous. What she needed was for me to remember her every single day in order to feel she was part of humanity.
>
> (Orange, 1995, 153)

DOI: 10.4324/9781003498162-7

Against the Isolated Mind: Intersubjectivity and Self-Psychology

The so-called "intersubjective" school consists of a group of American psychoanalysts: Robert Stolorow, George Atwood, Donna Orange, Bernard Brandchaft, and others. From now on, they will be referred to as The Intersubjective Group. The group started with a collaboration between Robert Stolorow and George Atwood, two analysts who are still collaborating to the present day. The two had studied the personal lives and theories of Freud, Jung, Reich, and Rank. The result was a psychobiographical study of the personal, subjective origins of the theoretical systems that formed the basis of their first book, *Faces in a Cloud²: Subjectivity in Personality Theory* (Stolorow and Atwood, 1979). From these studies, Stolorow and Atwood concluded that psychoanalysis needs a theory of subjectivity– a unifying framework capable of explaining the psychological phenomena that other theories deal with and the theories themselves (Stolorow, 2004). According to Stlorow (2004, 546), although intersubjectivity was not introduced in the first edition of *Faces*, it was implied in their description of how the personal and subjective world influences theoretical writing. The first explicit use of intersubjective in their work appeared in the paper *"The Representational World in Psychoanalytic Therapy"* (Stolorow et al., 1978). They conceptualized the interplay of transference and countertransference in psychoanalytic therapy as an intersubjective process reflecting the interaction of the different organized subjective worlds of the patient and the analyst (249). Continuing much work, they examined the impact on the therapeutic process of unfamiliar communication and gaps – intersubjective combinations and disconnections – between the patient's and analyst's world of experience.

Stolorow's and Atwood's first ideas were formulated precisely when Kohut began publishing his papers. Stolorow's first encounter with Kohut occurred in 1977 when he was asked to review the latter's first book. From that point on, Stolorow's connection to Kohut's ideas was quick and natural. Stolorow (2004) writes:

"I was immediately attracted to the revolutionary nature of his theoretical proposals, in which he was throwing off the shackles of classical metapsychology and recasting psychoanalysis as a "developmental phenomenology of the self," . . . This new theoretical paradigm, emphasizing the motivational centrality of self-experience, seemed to fit like a glove with the suggestions for a psychoanalytic phenomenology that Atwood and I had set forth in *Faces*. Kohut was attempting, as we were, to reframe psychoanalysis as pure psychology.

(547)

To begin with, the intersubjective group strove to continue Kohut's self-psychology without the burden of classical psychoanalysis's presuppositions. However, the intersubjective group later set themselves apart from self-psychology and emphasized their differences. They aimed to form an independent psychoanalytic approach, and they see their relationship with self-psychology as a family resemblance (Orange, 1999). No longer committed to sustaining a positivist rhetoric, these researchers adopt a radical, subjective, postmodern epistemology while simultaneously taking on a considerable part of Kohut's ideas concerning development and therapy. Beginning in 2000, Stolorow started a systematic study of Heidegger's existential philosophy. He (2016) found a theoretical framework for his psychoanalytic contextualism and many of his former ideas in Heidegger.

> When I read the passages in *Being and Time* devoted to Heidegger's existential analysis of *Angst*, I nearly fell off my chair! Both his phenomenological description and onto-logical account of *Angst* bore a remarkable resemblance to what I had concluded about the phenomenology and meaning of emotional trauma some two years earlier. In short, Heidegger's analysis of *Angst*, world-collapse, uncanniness, and thrownness into Being-toward-death provided me extraordinary philosophical tools for grasping the existential significance of emotional trauma. . . . My dual aim in this work has been to show both how Heidegger's existential philosophy enriches post-Cartesian psychoanalysis and how post-Cartesian psychoanalysis enriches Heidegger's existential philosophy.
>
> (Stolorow and Maduro, 2022, 444–445)

Heidegger's direct influence on Stolorow is another example of how philosophy shapes psychoanalysis.

The intersubjective group believes that psychological phenomena can be understood only in their intersubjective context. They define psychoanalysis as the science of intersubjectivity, which looks at the reciprocities between the separately organized domains of the observer and the observed (Orange et al., 1997).

The subject position, they argue, always emerges in the intersubjective space, not outside it. This confirms the central role of empathy and introspection as the exclusive research methods.

Here, I will not deal with Heidegger's influence on Stolorow. Heidegger's influence on Stolorow stemmed mainly from Stolorow's painful personal journey after his wife's death and his sense that Heidegger's ideas in *Being and Time* could help him cope better with personal trauma (Stolorow and Maduro, 2022, 443). But, the intersubjective group in the 1990s and the first decade of this century was immersed in psychoanalytic theory and heavily influenced by Kohut's ideas.

My main interest is in that crucial shift in the 90s, during which significant changes in the epistemology of psychoanalysis took place. The intersubjective group contributed significantly to psychoanalysis's radical change during these years.

The intersubjective group considers themselves a critic of the traditional view of psychoanalysis, which posits a mind isolated from the interpersonal contexts affecting it from the outside. Kohut conceives of an isolated mind when he sees the self as an autonomous existential entity enclosing an innate core that turns to an empathic environment to realize its potential (Stolorow et al., 2002).

The interpersonal method, by contrast, is a breakthrough to a new epistemology. They argue that there is an ongoing mutuality between the inner experiential domain and the external world. Thus, intersubjectivity abandons the old dichotomy of the classical approach, which separates the internal and the interpersonal (Stolorow and Atwood, 1992). Here, there is an issue, among other things, with the notion of a "two-person psychology" replacing traditional analytical "one-person psychology" (i.e., that of the patient). Classical psychoanalysis conceives of the individual as a closed biological system. Assuming the individual as the fundamental unit of research, the instinctual and defensive sources of anything interpersonal or subjective must be considered part of the subject's inner world (Aron, 1996). The intersubjective approach, by contrast, zooms in on the dyadic system that marks therapy and any other relationship between people. Psychoanalysis is the science of inter-subjectivity – i.e. the reciprocal interplay between diverse subjective domains – between the subject and the object of observation. What is singular for the intersubjective groups compared to other scientific disciplines is that the observer is also the object of observation here. The only existing reality is subjective: " 'Reality', as we use the term, refers to something subjective, something felt or sensed, rather than to an external realm of being existing independently of the human subject" (Stolorow and Atwood, 1992, 26–27).

This implies an acknowledgment that there are other aspects of reality that the intersubjective group does not deem relevant to this discussion. What we see here is an expression of the early, radical – but also naïve – intersubjective approach, which rejects realism and argues that reality as such does not exist. Realism claims that physical objects have an independent existence, regardless of the experience or the consciousness of those who think about them. The intersubjective group relates to those who adhere to realism in a manner reminiscent of Freud's attitude toward religious believers in "Future of an Illusion" (1927). According to the former, it is not merely that the only reality relevant to a psychoanalytic investigation – empathy and introspection – is the subjective reality of the patient, the psychoanalyst and the field between them, but that any notion of "objective reality" is a "concretization" – a symbolic conversion of subjective experience into events that are perceived as objective (Stolorow and Atwood, 1992, 333).

This is an extreme and highly paradoxical argument. On top of there being no objective reality, those who believe in its existence are deemed distorters of reality! In the 1980s and the early 1990s, adherents of intersubjectivity used the terms "subjectivity" and "intersubjectivity" as the approach's more or less exclusive epistemological basis.

As Eagle (2009) writes:

Just as the postmodernist does not accord physical reality a status independent of social constructions of it, similarly the "new view" analyst does not accord mental reality (i.e. the patient's mind) a status independent of interpretive construction and social interaction.

(32)

In its earliest days, the intersubjective approach adopted a naïve philosophical position and defined itself as relativist (Stolorow, 1988, 335). Rejecting the existence of a universal truth, relativism argues that knowledge always depends on theoretical, social, or cultural context. Adherents of the intersubjective approach argued that diverse outcomes of case descriptions are all entailed by the fact that psychoanalysis does not refer to external criteria, defining itself using intersubjective boundaries (Stolorow and Atwood, 1992, 193).

The main danger of Stolorow and Atwood's arguments is the same as relativism: If all perspectives are equally valid and certain, how are we to differentiate between them? How to choose? Why would anyone prefer psychoanalysis to any other therapeutic approach, religion, or mystical belief?

By defining in a somewhat naïve manner the criteria for a valid psychoanalytic theory, Stolorow tried to address this question (1988).

> However, this avowedly subjectivist and relativist position should not be taken to mean that we believe that any psychoanalytic interpretation or explanatory construct is as good as the next.
>
> (1988, 336)

However, his solutions are easy bait for analytical philosophers. Here are some of Stolorow's proposed questions that may help in ascertaining the validity of a psychoanalytic theory:

- Does the psychoanalytic theory allow for greater generalization than previous theories?
- Does it allow the generalization of a broader range of experience than competing theories?
- Does it include a self-reflective and self-corrective element?
- Does it give access to rich and complex subjective domains?

Obviously, Stolorow and Atwood believe that intersubjective theory meets all these criteria. But their problematic nature is glaring. First, their search for unified validation criteria is itself a modern rather than a postmodern project. Second, intersubjective theory has only one type of well-grounded psychoanalytic knowledge: a person's knowledge while interacting with another person at a certain time. This is a severe constraint, not just for psychoanalysis but for the entire intersubjective approach. The intersubjective group, in this earlier phase, it would seem, risks cutting off the branch they are sitting on: If the only type of valid knowledge occurs in an intersubjective situation, unrelated to any external objective reality, how are they to convince others of the correctness of their arguments? Richard Moore (1999) claims that the intersubjective group's assumptions make it impossible to present it as one psychoanalytic theory that competes with others. He argues that the group wishes simultaneously to preserve a subjective, relativist frame of reference while constituting a theory that tries to present persuasive truths.

The Late 1990s: A Sophisticated Philosophical Position

Over time, the intersubjective groups engaged with these shortcomings by introducing additional philosophical concepts, like contextualism and perspectivism (Orange, 1995; Orange et al., 1997). The authors shifted away from a radical postmodern position rejecting the existence of any external reality to a more moderate, realistic one that rejects and negates relativism.

What caused this mitigation in the intersubjective position on the status of reality?

The understanding was that psychoanalytic theory could not support postmodernism in its most extreme form. Postmodern radicalism is bound to remove the ground from underneath the therapist's authority. If the relevant epistemology underlying psychoanalysis is relativism, how can the therapist say anything significant about what is happening in the therapy?

The problem also attaches to the concept of knowledge and the knower's confidence in intersubjective theory itself. Suppose knowledge is achieved empathically while relying on intersubjective shared reality; how can intersubjective theory make claims that it knows or apprehends reality any better than the other theories it criticizes?

It must be noted that all postmodern psychoanalytic theories, including the intersubjective approach, have been trying to defend themselves against accusations of relativism. Much like classical theoreticians tried to counter the claim that they were nonscientific, the postmodernists argue fervently that they are moderate and haven't conceded their realism; their debate with relativism is no less harsh than their debate with positivism.

When we consider the philosophical assumptions of the intersubjective approach more in depth, the following question arises: Does the newer version of intersubjective theory manage to steer clear from relativism?

In their book, *Working Intersubjectively: Contextualism in Psychoanalytic Practice* (1997), Orange, Stolorow, and Atwood try to avoid radical relativism. Donna Orange, a clinical psychologist and philosopher who contributed much towards developing the sophisticated epistemological aspect of the intersubjective approach, attempted to explain why Husserl's phenomenology cannot serve as an epistemological basis for psychoanalysis. The ahistorical nature of Husserlian phenomenology, she believes, clashes with the influence of experience on the individual's subjectivity. For the intersubjective approach to be considered psychoanalytic, it must encapsulate the past's impact on the present. It must, therefore, be less radical than Husserl's theory. The fact that intersubjectivity focuses on the subjective organization of experience does not imply it embraces radical solipsism (56).

Orange's book *Emotional Understanding: Studies in Psychoanalytic Epistemology* (1995) attempts to find a new philosophical frame for psychoanalysis. The new approach it suggests, replacing positivism in psychoanalysis that Orange called *perspectival realism*, is associated with the work of philosopher Richard Bernstein. Bernstein's (1983) epistemology suits Orange's purpose because the former rejects positivism and objectivism while shunning relativism and avoiding yielding realism. Bernstein considers reality a social product that must be understood as a social process: Each participant in the investigation brings their own perspective, which affords them an aspect of reality. Individual understanding is always partial because people can only see things from their angle. Communication with the other enables one to approach a more comprehensive truth. Theories and cultures, similarly, are viewed as perspectives on the truth.

However, psychoanalysis loses many qualities if one takes on this view. The traditional approach holds that the declared truth, the perspective the person consciously expresses and which Orange looks for, is only one out of many. Another part of the individual, the unconscious, is inaccessible to the patient but no less vital than the conscious perspective. One of classical psychoanalysis' basic assumptions concerns the elusiveness of the unconscious. In the traditional approaches, the unconscious is considered a kind of "otherness" inherent in every person. Classic examples of this thinking abound in traditional psychoanalytic case descriptions: The prudish woman who consciously fears any contact with a man is unconsciously defending herself against repressed sexual desires. The worried and obsessive mother who consciously fears the catastrophes that will befall her children unconsciously would like them to die; the husband who expresses unfounded conscious jealousy toward his wife is suffering from unconscious homosexual fears; and so on.

According to classical psychoanalysis, rather than mere "bits of truth" or perspectives, the contents the patient brings to the clinic are forms of clever camouflage for other contents that are conflictual and consciously inaccessible. It is not as though the therapist incorporates the patient's "bit of truth" with that of the patient to create a more complete mosaic. Instead, the psychoanalyst's role is to identify this "otherness" of which the patient is unconscious and put it to use. In Orange's model, by contrast, the patient and therapist share their knowledge about the patient and the world, expanding the range of truth of both patient and therapist. The status of the unconscious, which is more than anything the hallmark of psychoanalysis, is subverted and emptied of meaning.

An Alternative to Theory or Metatheoretical Sensibility?

In their *Working Intersubjectively: Contextualism and Psychoanalytic Practice* (1997), Orange, Atwood, and Stlorow declare that they do not consider intersubjective theory a clinical theory that competes with existing theories or as a theory from which therapeutic implications can be derived. Their theory, they argue, displays commonalities with all the various psychoanalytical schools. They prefer to think of intersubjectivity as a "sensibility" rather than a theory (ix). Rather than a clinical theory, the intersubjective perspective offers a metatheory, a set of questions posed to theories (88).

Clearly, this is one of the critical questions for any postmodern theory: Does it constitute a new theory that replaces its predecessors, or does it preoccupy itself with clarifications, sensibilities, and new wordplay? Does it suggest a new set of facts and insights?

Here, we see a change in the theory's epistemological direction: Its initial objective, in the 1980s and the early 1990s, to constitute an alternative to earlier psychoanalytic theories relying on pure subjectivity was replaced by a more modest aim. Now it aspires to be a "sensibility," a "metatheory," or a "set of questions" addressed to other theories.

The following illustration bears out the problematic nature of this approach. Let us assume that a psychoanalytic institute decides to become intersubjective and teach the intersubjective approach. What will the candidates study? Since even its own originators do not define intersubjectivity as a theory, it is hard to believe that they will be studying it as a sole theory. Will they set aside classical theory and the drive's model? They cannot explain the "sensibility" they developed if they do. The curriculum will likely emphasize Kohut's self-psychology, but as the previous chapter has shown, that theory adopts large parts of the positivist epistemology of classical psychoanalysis. Thus, candidates at this institute will first have to learn traditional theories of development and therapy – whose assumptions have been repeatedly criticized by the intersubjective approach. Here again, we conclude that postmodernism does not stand alone on its own feet but always relies on the modern realm that preceded it.

The Intersubjective Infant

In analyzing the developmental theory of the intersubjective approach, the following questions, among others, must be raised: How did the intersubjective portray development if they rejected all investigative tools other than introspection and empathy? How does the infant develop a perception of reality if reality is perceived as subjective? Do they offer new facts about development beyond those Kohut has already introduced? What is the place of the unconscious – the private and personal component that is not accessible to the subject herself in a theory that negates the existence of the isolated mind?

Psychological Development

Given that the intersubjective approach rejects a positivist approach, it is remarkable how often it cites from and relies on empirical case studies. Adherents of the intersubjective approach refer to influential researchers with a psychoanalytic orientation, some of them supporters of self-psychology, who conducted laboratory observations of parent-infant interactions. These researchers wanted, among other things, to find out how the child's sense of self emerges due to interrelations with the parents (Beebe and Lachmann, 1988; Lichtenberg, 1983, 1989; Stern, 1985, 1989, and others). This type of empirical research that centers on the caregiver-infant dyad is prevalent now, yielding a body of knowledge in its own right. Here is another paradox in psychoanalytic history: In Freud's and self-psychology's "scientific era," few empirical studies supporting developmental theory were carried out. Freud, Hartman, Eissler, and others did not consider themselves empirical researchers doing controlled observations in laboratory conditions. In fact, some of the originators of the most central schools of psychoanalytic thought – Freud and Kohut – who conceived highly complex and rich developmental theories hardly saw a child in their clinic. Their developmental theories are entirely grounded in their work with adults, their observation of their own children, and their access to their childhood memories (Govrin, 2016). Postmodern psychoanalytic theories, by contrast, which oppose a scientific-positivist approach, feel obliged to scientifically prove their developmental theory and shore it up with empirical evidence.

Teicholz (2009) writes that "the convergence between postmodern psychoanalysis and these diverse fields of research is strange because, from a postmodern viewpoint, there is no scientific truth "out there" beyond what can be mutually agreed upon through intersubjective negotiation" (71).

It is nothing other than an attempt to achieve a modern narrative relying on empirical studies and to prove the validity of their clinical descriptions.

Thus, based on these studies, the intersubjective group concludes that the child's experiential organization is the product of a mutual regulatory system between the child and caregiver (Stolorow and Atwood, 1992, 23). They refer to Louis Sander's (1985, 1987) research in which he argued that the infant-mother system regulates and organizes the infant's inner world. Self-regulation can only unfold based on the mutual relations between parent and child. The individual's sense of singularity and separateness emerge from a developmental system that features synchronization and "specific adjustment" between the child's changing states of being and the parent's ability to identify them (Sander, 1985). They also cite Beatrice Beebe and Frank Lachmann (1988), who argue that the infant's earliest representations reflect relations with the mother. These representations are structures of interaction that cannot be represented only by one of the parties (23).

The intersubjective group cites this research to prove that various principles that unconsciously organize the child's experience result from recurrent patterns of interpersonal attachment between mother and infant. They call these principles the "pre-reflective unconscious" (see as follows). According to the authors, these principles are the building blocks of personality development.

But are these unconscious organizing principles, which the individual carries wherever she goes, not simply another version of the "isolated mind" so forcefully rejected by the intersubjective approach? The contradiction, the authors argue, is only an apparent one. Though the unconscious organizing principles were established in early childhood, the choice of which principle a person will employ at any given moment is made in the intersubjective context (24).

Despite this explanation, it seems difficult, if not impossible, for a theory to call itself "psychoanalytic" and not to include some version of the isolated mind. The authors, too, concede that each individual brings something of her or himself to the intersubjective encounter, which does not depend on the intersubjectivity of the encounter but was formed early in life.

The Child's Sense of Reality

How does the infant come into a sense of reality in a world wholly made up of intersubjective experiences? If we want to answer this question, it is crucial, to begin with understanding what the adherents of the intersubjective approach consider reality. The intersubjective group argues that reality is subjective and that it is experienced or felt. They argue that reality is not an external thing isolated from the human subject. In their view, Freudian theory, which perceives reality as external to the individual, considers psychological development as a gradual process in which the infant encounters the limitations of external reality.

These things were written when the intersubjective approach supported the radical version of postmodernism and rejected realism. Its developmental theory remained faithful to this early version of radical postmodernism and did not adjust to the more moderate and subtle epistemological assumptions of the 1990s when Donna Orange joined the group. As a result, even though the intersubjective approach no longer rejects the existence of an external reality as of the late 1990s (Orange, 1995), it lacks a new developmental theory that highlights the child's perception of a reality that exists independently of herself.

The intersubjective theory of development takes a stand against one central assumption shared by all psychoanalytic theories: that frustration affords growth and development. Frustration presumably makes the child move from a primitive state of non-differentiation, illusion, and omnipotence to a developed state of more adult realistic perception and a better ability to identify her or his limitations. The intersubjective group holds that the child's developmental achievement is not the result of her increasing ability to acknowledge reality for what it is. After all, reality as such does not exist. The child develops a sense of what she or he **experiences as true** due to the parent's sensitive confirmation. Resonating the child's subjective experience on a broad spectrum of powerful emotional experiences – positive and negative – the parents provide the sense of reality. Reality becomes apparent in the face of an emotional encounter sensitive to subjectivity (Orange, 1995, 27). This reality-confirming function is what the authors call the "self-delineating selfobject function" (Stolorow and Atwood, 1992).

Along with its perception of trauma (see as follows), this seems one of the innovative elements in intersubjective development theory. Reality is not validated as the result of a linear, sharp transition from one phase to another: From a subjective era that includes reality distortions and illusions to an objective one when freed from subjectivity, the child comes into a realistic and objective vision. Rather than learning about true reality, **the child develops a sense of reality**, which she manages by means of subjective confirmation (Stolorow and Atwood, 1992). The child does not learn about the world like a scientist, through trial and error or gratification and frustration. The intersubjective relations with the child's parents validate her emotional experiences, which is how the child learns what is true.

This development theory makes two new contributions, one postmodern and the other modern. **The postmodern innovation is that the dichotomy between** objective and subjective is canceled for the first time in developmental theories. **Unlike other theories that consider the objective to be located outside the child, in external reality, and the subjective inside, in the child's internal world, the intersubjective approach claims that subjectivity always mediates reality perception. In normal development, the child is not released from subjectivity at some stage. Parents support, validate, and reinforce The child's subjectivity. Though Winnicott also presents a version of this view, it is revolutionary in American psychoanalysis.**

The second modern contribution is a positive factor in the developmental description of reality perception. It is a fact about development, not merely a theoretical sensitivity. Here, the intersubjective approach determines that this and not otherwise is how the child develops. Doing so points to a new fact in the development process. **Whereas Kohut believed empathy to be crucial to the self's development, intersubjective thinkers assume the empathic response to be crucial to reality perception.** The intersubjective theory of development, including these two innovations, seems to aspire to be more than just a "sensibility" or meta-theory, offering as it does a particular alternative to existing developmental theories.

Trauma

More than anything else, trauma presents the intersubjective approach with some complex clinical and epistemological dilemmas. If the most important thing is the perceived reality as it emerges and stands confirmed in the intersubjective context, what is the place of actual, traumatic events in the child's life? Do parental responses always mediate them?

Stolorow and Atwood (1992) could not be more outspoken in their affirmative answer to this question. They begin with a critique of Freud's model of trauma as a deterministic theory that overemphasizes the individual's inner world. They see it as a representative instance of the isolated mind.

Following Freud, ego psychology, according to the intersubjective group, conceived of trauma in economic terms when it defined psychological trauma as a psychologically intolerably intense stimulus.

Classical therapists, they believe, tend to cast doubt on whether the trauma occurred – a doubt that re-traumatizes the patient. Instead, they consider trauma as part of the child's fantasy world that results from the failure to regulate her or his impulses. The intersubjective approach holds that the child who has been subject to harassment and is desperately in need of his parents cannot turn to parents who fail to respond emphatically and doubt his experience. Similarly, if there is pressure coming from the therapist, a patient who suffered harassment might either repress his painful feelings or blame himself for them. Such a therapeutic approach blames the victim and results in the recurrence of the initial trauma symptoms (Stolorow and Atwood, 1992, 56). Kohut's concept of trauma, too, comes under criticism. He argues that traumatic frustration occurs when the child's disappointment with the object takes "intolerable proportions" (52). He thus emphasizes the "quantity" of frustration and the "intensity" of depressive feelings, assuming they are the main components in determining whether disappointment is pathological or enables growth.

Stolorow and Atwood (1992) argue that the environment's response is the crucial factor in the occurrence of trauma – its response to the child's depression and other reactions. They substitute self-psychology's focus on the child's optimal frustration with parents' sensitive attention to the infant's feelings or affect attunement.

Like Freud, they believe that essentially trauma is about intolerable feelings. However, the intensity of the feelings does not entail the inability to discharge excessive energy. **The difficulty is not in the traumatic event itself but in the parent's failure to regulate the child's feelings**. Early childhood trauma originates in a formative intersubjective context, whose main component is a failure of affective attunement. Failure of parental regulation might result in an emotionally catastrophic situation for the child. The painful or frightening emotion transforms into something traumatic only when the responsiveness is not forthcoming. The child needs an empathic response to overcome the painful emotions and regulate and contain them. Again and again, the authors underline that it is not the event itself that is traumatic but rather, the failure of the surroundings to react appropriately. In the wake of such failure, the child is bound to doubt the reality of what happened to him.

How about the traumatic severe events to which children are exposed in concrete reality? Stolorow and Atwood (1992) come up with a radical answer: They believe that serious injury sustained in childhood, like, for instance, the loss of a parent, is not in itself traumatic or pathological as long as it happens in an empathic environment. Pain is not pathology. It is only the absence of empathy and sufficient attention to the child's pain that causes the development of trauma. They believe this is true for all the descriptions of mental anguish in childhood that appear in the psychoanalytic literature: extreme injuries, milder ones that involve holding (Winnicott), hyper-stimulation (Grinker), and narcissistic injuries (Kohut).

Referring to Alice Miller, Orange (1995) mentions an additional need for a selfobject: that of the selfobject in the role of the eyewitness. She believes that people who underwent severe trauma in their childhood require a witness who will share their pain, validate it, and make it real. Without such a witness, the child cannot experience the injury as externally or actually. Instead, she experiences the event and its internal implications as torture that must be endured.

Their approach to trauma shows that Stolorow Atwood hold their epistemological position, even when their assumptions lack strong internal validity. Can an empathic response from a parent transform an experience of sexual abuse into something non-traumatic or merely painful and temporary? Though it is clear that parental response to a traumatic event is critical and may well help the child's coping with it, is it not too far-reaching to call it the central trauma? As a result of its ambiguous relations with reality, the intersubjective approach seems to put excessive emphasis on parental response and, at the same time, to underplay the importance of the actual trauma.

The Unconscious in the Intersubjective Approach

The unconscious presents a problem for the intersubjective approach because it is a private component inaccessible to self and others. The unconscious does not express itself directly in the social domain or the intersubjective encounter. The unconscious is the product of a "one-person psychology," a private component of the individual.

As said, the unconscious is the central shared concept of all psychoanalytic theories. Surprisingly, it is also central for Stolorow and Atwood (1992), despite the contradictions this poses for the fundamental tenets of their approach. This central position results from criticism of classical psychoanalysis leveled at self-psychology's minimal emphasis on the unconscious (Kernberg, 1982). However that may be, its emphasis on the unconscious testifies to how the intersubjective approach includes elements of the isolated mind. Eventually, the group had to admit that the individual consists of a private, inaccessible part beyond intersubjective contexts.

How, then, do intersubjective thinkers conceive of the unconscious? Stolorow and Atwood (1992) distinguish between three types of unconscious:

1. **The pre-reflective unconscious:** The organizing principles that unconsciously constitute a person's experience are included here. These principles might raise specific experiences to consciousness and prevent others from so doing. Pre-reflective structures of experience develop due to the interactions between infants and parents.
2. **The dynamic unconscious:** Experiences that threatened and endangered the self's needs and did not rise to consciousness come under this category. Intersubjective therapists avoid using the term "repression" in order not to describe the unconscious in metapsychological terms. Even in describing the unconscious, they prefer to stick to experiential terms. They believe conflicts occur when the child's primary affective states cannot be integrated because they fail to evoke an attuned response.
3. **The unvalidated unconscious:** includes experiences that could not be perceived and understood because they received no attunement and no confirming response. The child's experience becomes gradually conscious due to attunement responses from outside. If these are not provided, some features of the child's experience may remain unconscious. These experiences are not necessarily painful, but they cannot be intelligible to the child, and they stay in the unconscious in the form of raw and unprocessed content.

Stolorow and Atwood (1992) liken these three types of unconscious to a storeyed building with a cellar. Consciousness can be compared to the above-ground parts of the building. The highest floors represent the developed and integrated parts. The dynamic unconscious is the cellar, located below ground and hidden. Here is where the parts left out of the conscious reside, which are tied to intolerable

conflict and subjective danger. The pre-reflective unconscious is the plan according to which the architect constructed the building. It is a structure of organizing
principles that define the types of relations between the different parts of the building. Pre-reflective structures are not the same as contents: They are principles that
organize the experiential contents into typical patterns. The unvalidated unconscious can be compared to the bricks, the planks, and all the other materials that
were not used and never became part of the building, though they could have been.
These details represent experiences that were never understood and were left unintegrated by the conscious mind.

The Intersubjective Therapist

The intersubjective group (Stolorow and Atwood, 1992; Stolorow et al., 1987)
extensively covers the differences between their therapeutic method and ego psychology and object relations. Object relations is a theory developed in the UK that
stresses the role of the significant other – whether in actuality or in our internal
world. Prominent representatives in the UK were Melanie Klein, Ronald Fairbairn,
Donald Winnicott, Margaret Mahler, and Otto Kernberg in the US). Traditional
psychoanalysis, they believe, relies on the dichotomy by which the patient distorts
the transference relations while the therapist perceives them objectively as they are
(Stolorow et al., 1987; Stolorow and Atwood, 1992). The criticism also refers to the
traditional psychoanalytic notion of therapeutic authority. To illustrate what happens when a therapist is convinced of the truth of his experiences and the distorted
perception of the patient, they cite a case description by Otto Kernberg. Kernberg's
therapeutic approach was a combination of Kleinian ideas and ego psychology.

Kernberg presents the case of a female patient who complains that he, Kernberg,
is trying to seduce her. He mentions that he examined his own feelings and failed
to find any erotic attraction toward the patient. This leads him to conclude that the
patient is relating her own repressed erotic feelings to him – an indication that the
mechanism of projection is at work. At a later stage of the therapy, Kernberg does
come to have sexual feelings toward the patient. But these, too, he understands
as a complementary Oedipal paternal position, triggered by the sexual fantasies
the patient projects onto him. The intersubjective group argues that Kernberg uses
his experience raw data as facts. These "facts," based on subjective experience,
persuaded him that the patient was distorting the transference relations. Kernberg,
they believed, failed to probe why the patient felt he was seducing her. The therapist's subjectivity is elevated to objectivity and the patient now must accept the
therapist's experience for a fact, part of the therapeutic alliance: "[For Kernberg]
one reality, the analyst's, is apparently real; the other, the patient's is false! The
therapeutic task is to account for the 'distortion'" (Stolorow et al., 1987, 100).

The authors clearly point out a frequent phenomenon in psychoanalytic treatments. Psychoanalytic journals abound with cases in which therapists turn to their
feelings, "examine" them, and then use this examination as an objective meas-
ure of the therapeutic reality. The patient's feelings are another matter: They are

perceived as falsified, distorted, or projected. Therapy aims to help the patient see things more realistically in the way the therapist does. The outcome frequently is a condescending therapist who takes her subjective assumptions as self-evident.

The intersubjective approach proposes a radically different way of understanding transference relations (Stolorow et al., 1987). The one relevant reality accessible to psychoanalytic investigation is subjective: that of the patient, the therapist, and the emergent psychological field between them. They think therapists have tended to be defensive about their feelings regarding the patient. The notion that there is an objective reality that is vulnerable to distortion has led psychoanalysts to locate pathology exclusively on the side of the patient without reference to the intersubjective context. This has led therapists to avoid examining their influence on the patient. This influence is constant and inevitable – part of the nature of therapeutic relations. For them, the idea that therapeutic success is based on identification with the therapist is tantamount to demanding obedience and conformity from the patient. Often, the patient, wanting to maintain independence and singularity, will express resistance. This resistance will draw a circular response: When the patient rejects the therapist's interpretations, this only proves the therapist is right.

Stolorow and Atwood (1992) have different ideas about the therapeutic alliance. This alliance, they believe, is the outcome of the therapist's genuine commitment to understanding the meaning of the patient's emotional states. Understanding arises from the patient's subjectivity – it does not originate somewhere outside it. This position, they call "sustained empathic inquiry" (1992, 93). Taking such a position requires a considerable investment on the therapist's part. The therapist's attempt to see reality through the patient's eyes rather than through his subjectivity puts his own sense of self and reality at risk. A focus on subjectivity helps diminish persistent resistance and enrich the psychoanalytic dialogue by re-centering the frustrations, disappointments, and mismatches in the transference relations. Such mismatches are not simply the patient's errors or distortions; they express the therapist's impact on the patient's subjective world.

They argue that treating transference as distortion may sometimes be destructive to the patient's self. Many patients suffer from a compromised basic sense of their internal experience. The confirmation of their subjective world is crucial to them. The ability to believe in the subjective reality of their experience was damaged because it was a threat to their parents: It became easily subverted and pushed outside the margins of consciousness. When a person cannot trust her perceptual reality, this may sometimes lead to psychotic states (1992).

One can see why the authors would want to encourage a more empathic stance of therapists by putting them in the patient's place. However, their stipulation that therapists equate their subjectivity and that of the patients not only is not realistic, it also leads, paradoxically, to an objectivization of psychoanalytic therapy and a return via the backdoor of therapeutic neutrality! Suppose the patient's and the therapist's subjective perceptions are equally subjective. In that case, the therapist must equate her assumptions regarding the therapeutic relationship with the patient. If the therapist is simply one subject meeting another, her assumptions are no more valid than the patient's. This is an impasse. **The intersubjective group paradoxically reverts to a scientific-objective position that calls to overcome therapists' subjectivity.** In doing so, they negate the therapist's subjectivity as subjectivity. Subjectivity, in essence, regards itself as valid and prefers itself over the other's subjectivity.

Critique of the Neutral Therapist: A Straw Man or Common Organizing Principle?

More than anything, the intersubjective approach is perhaps identified with its criticism of the therapist's presumed neutral position. This critique is not new in the psychoanalytic literature. Even in Freud's lifetime, some objected to his advice that therapists should work with surgical emotional chill (Hoffman, 1983). In the 1980s and early 1990s, voices of opposition against the therapist's neutral, objective, and anonymous position counted as radical and path-breaking. In some instances, the idea that therapists might reveal something of their private lives was simply outrageous. The common belief was that patients distort reality in the transference and that therapists have the authority to understand reality properly. Of course, even in the time they wrote their books, hardly any psychoanalysts supported the therapist's neutral and objective position.

However, the Intersubjective Group, aware of the popularity of the critique of the neutral therapist, believes their critique to be relevant. The notion of the neutral therapist, they believe, is so deeply enshrined in the psychoanalytic tradition that it continues to function as a fundamental organizing principle, powerfully marking the therapeutic encounter. As a result, therapists tend to ignore the intersubjective dimension. The Intersubjective Group believes that neutrality is wielded especially heavily whenever therapists' sense of self comes under threat in the therapy (Orange et al., 1997, 35–36).

The intersubjective approach regards the neutral therapist as authoritarian. The authors puncture the "myths" associated with the notion of the neutral therapist. Such myths assumed the possibility of interpretation without suggestibility, "clean" transference relations, the objective therapist, and the isolated mind.

Moreover, they point out contradictions in Kohut's concept of neutrality: Though Kohut objected to a lack of emotional responsiveness in psychoanalysts, he held on to the idea of neutrality, which he considered a positive aspect of therapeutic work. However, the authors believe it is impossible to maintain a simultaneously empathic and neutral position. Their alternative is empathic and introspective investigation – another Kohutian concept.

The most significant recent contribution of the intersubjective approach is that the psychological organization of the therapist's experience must also be considered. Therapists must consider their own personality and use it rather than hide or ignore it. The critical factor in the therapeutic activity is the analysis of the intersubjective dimension of the patient-therapist dialogue. This view clashes with an earlier position of the intersubjective approach, whereby the therapist should see

things exclusively from the patient's perspective – something that calls for therapists to resign their subjectivity.

However, the authors mention some constraints in their new position. The therapist's subjectivity does not rule out the structural inequality of the psychoanalytic
situation. It is not supposed to evoke indiscriminate emotional responses on the
therapist's part; it does not replace interpretation (!), nor is it meant to encourage
the therapist to initiate self-disclosure.

Again, we confront the chief problem with postmodern psychoanalytic theories:
How can we be postmodern – i.e., questioning some essential tenets of psychoanalysis – and yet maintain the essence of psychoanalysis?

Conclusion

The analysis of its notion of truth, development, and therapy leads us to question
the contribution of the intersubjective approach. Does it amount to a specific theoretical sensibility, or has it generated a new theory? Does it exist apart from the
classical psychoanalysis which it criticizes?

Its foremost achievement seems to be in making analysts more sensitive to a
different type of human motivation in infant development and therapeutic relations.
Classical psychoanalysis operated on Kant's famous definition of enlightenment.
Here, the individual relinquishes various forces that dominate her pre-adult life
to obey the universal laws of reason exclusively. This is a fundamental principle
of the theory of development and the therapeutic technique of classical psychoanalysis. For Freud, the patient, to get rid of unconscious conflicts and to discover
the unconscious otherness within him, hires the services of a psychoanalyst, who
functions as an authority figure. This transforms the patient into a more rational
creature. As I noted in the previous chapter, self-psychology also remained loyal
to this worldview in some ways. The intersubjective approach tried to free psychoanalysis from its modern liberatory ideal. Instead, the objective is to understand the patient's subjectivity using the psychoanalyst's ability to put herself in
the patient's place and understand her subjectivity. The empathic stance can only
happen if the analyst is aware of her subjectivity, not pretending to be an objective observer. A safe, supportive, empathic, and non-judgmental environment thus
arises in which the patient's subjectivity can be studied and understood.

Orange writes, in her eloquent style (2001),

> To understand a person, I cannot enter that person's mind, catalog its mental
> furniture (ideas, affects and fantasies), and write a case report. Rather, in the
> only conception of "empathic immersion" that makes sense in post-Cartesian
> thinking, the participants in the conversation immerse themselves in the inter-
> play of personal worlds of experience. Instead of asking myself (as a clinician)
> "what is wrong with this person?" or "what misrepresentations reside in this
> person's mind?" I may ask, "what could be the aspects of a person's experiential
> world that would lead her to believe or feel that she is a murderer?" "What is

the personal lifeworld like of someone who sits or lies on my couch and says he is not really in the room?" "What can a person who feels in this way expect or hope for?" Such questioning attitudes, possible within most psychoanalytic communities, assume that what the other says is reasonable and that the task is understanding, not evaluation, classification, or judgment.

(17)

The intersubjective approach was not the first to stress subjective dimensions like empathy. Kohut, as mentioned, had discovered empathy earlier. But, to an extent unrivaled before, it put intersubjectivity at its very focus. This is, indeed, an epistemological change that challenges the perceptions and conventions of classical psychoanalysis.

However, even though those who articulated the approach define their connection with Kohut's self-psychology as a mere family resemblance, it is hard to conceive them as two separate theories. Intersubjective theory qua theory does not exist independently, uncovering new facts about development and therapy. Most of its developmental and therapeutic assumptions lean on self-psychology. The intersubjective approach, instead, states new things about "reality." Its adherents conceive of their patients' needs and pathologies in terms that are almost identical to those of self-psychology, and in their therapeutic work, they respond in very similar ways. To this, they add the sensibility of the intersubjective dimension between patient and therapist.

Following the cited writing of Stolorow, Atwood, and Orange, the intersubjective therapist is more sensitive to certain aspects that were not sufficiently prominent to therapists before them. She is more modest, less self-confident, less reserved, and inclined to attach more importance to the patient's truth. However, her understanding of the patient and her interventions does not stray far from those of self-psychology. The main difference between self-psychology and the intersubjective approach is their underlying philosophy. **The intersubjective approach has given self-psychology what it lacked: a philosophy in harmony with its perception of humans and its views of therapeutic objectives.** In the next chapter, I describe the most influential representative of the postmodern turn in psychoanalysis: the relational approach. Though the intersubjective approach of Stolorow and his colleagues share many philosophical assumptions with the relational approach, the relational approach is much more diverse. It consists of a cluster of writers with various fields of interest. They all share the assumption that the analyst's subjectivity is an essential part of the analytic situation.

References

Aron, L. (1996). *A Meeting of Minds – Mutuality in Psychoanalysis*. Hillsdale, NJ: The Analytic Press.
Beebe, B. and Lachmann, F.M. (1988). The Contribution of Mother-Infant Mutual Influence to the Origins of Self Object Representations. *Psychoanalytic Psychology*, 5, 305–337.

Bernstein, R.J. (1983). *Beyond Objectivism and Relativism*. Philadelphia: University of Pennsylvania Press.

Eagle, M. (2009). Chapter 1: Postmodern Influences on Contemporary Psychoanalysis. In R. Frie and D. Orange (Eds.) *Beyond Postmodernism New Dimensions in Clinical Theory and Practice*. London: Routledge, 27–51.

Freud, S. (1927). The Future of an Illusion. *Standard Edition*, 21, 1–56.

Govrin, A. (2006). The Dilemma of Contemporary Psychoanalysis: Toward a "Knowing" Post-Postmodernism. *Journal of the American Psychoanalytic Association*, 54, 507–535.

Hoffman, I.Z. (1983). The Patient as Interpreter of the Analyst's Experience. *Contemporary Psychoanalysis*, 19(3), 389–422.

Kernberg, O. (1982). Review of Advances in Self Psychology. *American Journal of Psychiatry*, 139, 374–375.

Lichtenberg, J.D. (1983). *Psychoanalysis and Infant Research*. Hillsdale, NJ: The Analytic Press.

Lichtenberg, J.D. (1989). *Psychoanalysis and Motivation*. Hillsdale, NJ: The Analytic Press.

Moore, R. (1999). *The Creation of Reality in Psychoanalysis – A View of the Contributions of Donald Spence, Roy Schafer, Robert Stolorow, Irwin Z. Hoffman and Beyond*. Hillsdale, NJ: The Analytic Press.

Orange, D.M. (1995). *Emotional Understanding: Studies in Psychoanalytic Epistemology*. New York and London: The Guilford Press.

Orange, D.M. (1999). Reply to Curtis. *Psychoanalytic Psychology*, 16(2), 309–311.

Orange, D.M. (2001). From Cartesian Minds to Experiential Worlds in Psychoanalysis. *Psychoanalytic Psychology*, 18, 287–302.

Orange, D.M., Atwood, G.E. and Stolorow, R.D. (1997). *Working Intersubjectively: Contextualism in Psychoanalytic Practice*. Hillsdale, NJ: The Analytic Press.

Sander, L. (1985). Toward a Logic of Organization in Psychobiological Development. In H. Klar and L. Siever (Eds.) *Biologic Response Styles*. Washington, DC: American Psychiatric Association, 20–36.

Sander, L. (1987). Awareness of Inner Experience. *Child Abuse & Neglect*, 11, 339–346.

Stern, D.N. (1985). *The Interpersonal World of the Infant*. New York: Basic Books.

Stern, D.N. (1989). The Representation of Relational Patterns: Developmental Considerations. In A.J. Samernoff and R.N. Emde (Eds.) *Relationship Disturbances in Early Childhood*. New York: Basic Books, 52–69.

Stolorow, R.D. (1988). Intersubjectivity, Psychoanalytic Knowing, and Reality. *Contemporary Psychoanalysis*, 24(4), 331–338.

Stolorow, R.D. (2004). Autobiographical Reflections on the Intersubjective History of an Intersubjective Perspective in Psychoanalysis. *Psychoanalytic Inquiry*, 24, 542–557.

Stolorow, R.D. (2016). Using Heidegger. *Journal of the American Psychoanalytic Association*, 64, NP12–NP15.

Stolorow, R.D. and Atwood, G.E. (1979). *Faces in the Cloud*. New York: Jason Aronson.

Stolorow, R.D. and Atwood, G.E. (1992). *Contexts of Being: The Intersubjective Foundations of Psychological Life*. Hillsdale, NJ: The Analytic Press.

Stolorow, R.D., Atwood, G.E. and Orange, D.M. (2002). *Worlds of Experience: Interweaving Philosophical and Clinical Dimensions in Psychoanalysis*. New York: Basic Books.

Stolorow, R. D., Atwood, G. E. and Ross, J. M. (1978). The Representational World in Psychoanalytic Therapy. *International Review of Psychoanalysis*, 5, 247–256.

Stolorow, R.D., Brandchaft, B. and Atwood, G.E. (1987). *Psychoanalytic Treatment: An Intersubjective Approach*. Hillsdale, NJ: Analytic Press.

Stolorow, R.D. and Maduro, P.N. (2022). Trauma and Illusion: A Conversation between Robert D. Stolorow and Peter N. Maduro. *Psychoanalytic Inquiry*, 42(6), 436–448. https://doi.org/10.1080/07351690.2022.2094687.

Teicholz, G.T. (2009). A Strange Convergence Postmodern Theory, Infant Research, and Psychoanalysis. In R. Frie and D. Orange (Eds.) *Beyond Postmodernism: New Dimensions in Clinical Theory and Practice*. London: Routledge/Taylor & Francis Group, 69–91.

Chapter 5

The Relational Approach

A Clinical Vignette

A patient called me to see if I could get her for treatment. She wasn't sure I was the right therapist for her: "I just wanted to know what method you follow. I don't want a classical analyst who is often silent and passive. I am looking for someone who adopts a more relational approach."

Since I did not know what she meant by the term "relational," I told her I combined different therapeutic approaches, adapting my method to meet the patient's needs.

"If that is so," said the patient, "I presume that you are sometimes unyielding and silent and at other times open and warm, depending on the type of patient you are treating."

I suggested we should meet. Into my office walked a young woman in her thirties who, I learned, had only recently given birth to a daughter. She told me that her uncle – her father's brother – had sexually abused her when she was a child. She asked that I treat her according to the "Jody Davis method."[1] She wanted me to be sexually open with her, including the disclosure of any erotic feelings I may have toward her. She had never read Jody Davies's work. She had only heard what Davies had said to a patient, which greatly appealed to her. In her view, such a two-person relational approach was the only way she would be able to recreate the trauma she had experienced and live in peace with what had happened to her. She wanted us to begin at once.

What the patient said surprised and confused me. I took my time to think about how to react. My silence, in turn, led the patient to respond by saying that, contrary to my earlier promise, it turned out that I was a therapist of the old school and that my approach was obsolete.

The patient apparently expected me to take the sort of risks taken by Davies and bring my own sexual desires into the therapy so that, together, we would be able to repeat the trauma she had experienced in favorable, secure conditions and, as a result, ease her suffering. She wanted me to be enticed by her, emphasizing that she meant this to be in a playful way only. I believed her. Such an approach, she said, would enable her to unashamedly feel aspects of her sexual desire and have

DOI: 10.4324/9781003498162-8

her desire acknowledged by me. The patient was fascinated by the new method she imagined Davies had developed and berated her previous analyst for his conservatism and interpretations. These, according to her were dry, passive, and dull without a shred of vitality. She tagged him "the Potz."

This example shows that the relational approach changed how therapists think about their patients. But it also changed – and will almost certainly continue to alter – the patients' expectations of what it means to be in therapy. The patient of bygone years underwent therapy, hoping and believing that the analyst would "uncover what there is in my subconscious." More recently, patients go into therapy expecting an authentic experience in therapeutic relations beyond interpretation and silence. The wish now is for something like "let us play" "let us see what can happen between you and I."

The relational group was first formed in the 1990s, at New York University's postdoctoral program in psychoanalysis. Its name derives from the fact that relationships and human connectedness, rather than the concept of the drives, are perceived as central to the individual's being and motivation. It attaches much importance to the relations between people, regarding them a decisive factor in how their inner world and behavior evolves. They see the mind as "striving for connection and communication, rather than discharge and gratification of endogamous instinctual pressures" (Dunn, 1995, 724). Relational analysts "see the clinician and the patient co-constructing the clinical data from the interaction of both members' particular psychic qualities and subjective realities" (Dunn, 1995, 723–724).

Members of this group include psychoanalysts like Stephen Mitchell, Lewis Aron, Jessica Benjamin, James Fosshage, Philip Bromberg, Emanuel Ghent, Donnel Stern, Anthony Bass, Steven Kuchuck, Karen Meroda, Galit Atlas, and Neil Altman. In 1991, they founded *Psychoanalytic Dialogues – The International Journal of Relational Perspectives*, which was first published under the editorship of the late Stephen Mitchell.

Charles Spezzano (1995) calls this group "the middle group" (in parallel with the British middle group who refused to choose between Melanie Klein and Anna Freud) in order to indicate its location between two approaches at New York University: ego psychology and intersubjective psychology. Unlike Stolorow's group, which tends to write papers together and express a unified view, the relational group represents a plurality of opinions, positions, and world views. A further difference between the two groups is in the sources that influenced them. While Heinz Kohut's self-psychology informed the intersubjective group, relational analysts are inspired by various sources.

Sources of Inspiration

Postmodern relational authors have looked into two directions for their sources. The first is a postmodern reading of major psychoanalytic figures such as Freud, Klein, and Bion (Benjamin, 2021; Stern, 2013). The second are authors from the past whose revolutionary ideas were not hitherto recognized: Now, they were discovered by the postmodernists and used to bolster their ideas. This method suits postmodernism very well: It does not claim novelty and interprets the old through its own readings.

The work of Sandor Ferenczi, the Hungarian psychoanalyst who was one of Freud's close associates but later departed from him because of theoretical differences, presents early signs of relational thought in psychoanalysis (Aron and Harris, 1993). Ferenczi's clinical experiments with mutual analysis and his theoretical proposals regarding trauma are among the most controversial novelties in the history of psychoanalysis (Aron, 1998). His therapeutic explorations led to theoretical, clinical, and technical discoveries concerning trauma, dissociation, the use of countertransference, and enactment within the transference-countertransference matrix. These ideas echo much of the relational thought (see Aron and Harris, 1993).

Ostracized for many years by the European psychoanalytic community, Ferenczi was seen by US psychoanalysts as a sensitive relational psychoanalyst willing to bravely question some of the most hallowed truths of the discipline. Ferenczi was the first to recognize that there was a dimension of mutuality in the therapeutic dyad; that is to say that the patient's influence on the therapist is no less than, vice versa, that of the therapist on the patient. He developed a "mutual therapy" technique in which the patient and therapist take turns on the couch. This method clashed with conventional approaches and led Ernest Jones to call Ferenzci "crazy." Ferenczi's technique was so extravagant that even today's postmodernists express their reservations and use it in an attenuated form. Lewis Aron argues that Ferenczi's experiments went too far. He claims Ferenczi mistook equality for reciprocity, which caused him to fail to safeguard the necessary analytic space between therapist and patient (Aron, 1996, 174–175).

Another psychoanalyst often cited by relational practitioners is Heinz Loewald, a prolific American psychoanalyst who was unconventional. Relational analysts believe him to be a prophet of innovative, bold, epistemological, and clinical ideas (Mitchell, 2000; Teicholz, 1999). Bergmann (2000, 61) has argued that Loewald's classic paper "On the Therapeutic Action of Psychoanalysis" (1960) inaugurated the end of the Hartmann era in psychoanalysis. Loewald was influenced by the philosopher Martin Heidegger (Mitchell, 2000). They studied philosophy together at Freiburg University – before Loewald turned to the study of medicine. It is especially in his attitude to language that Mitchell identifies Loewald's contribution.

Loewald, who lived and worked in the heydays of ego psychology, used a language taken from Freud and the psychoanalysis commonly practiced in Loewald's times.

As Orange (2014) writes:

Basic concepts in psychoanalytic theory lose their strangeness in Loewald's hands. "Cathexis" becomes organizing activity, bonding, and sometimes even love. "Primary process" becomes the richness of our ongoing access to our earliest and embodied mother-infant experience, constantly alternating with the differentiated, more organized linguistic life. "Secondary" in his view gains the connotation of secondary as coming later in the process of psychological organization and integration of experience. "Primary process" completely loses its shamefulness and becomes the rich resource of imaginative, cultural, and even, perhaps, transcendent life. A close reader of Freud who never left the American Psychoanalytic and never founded a school of thought, Loewald recognized the baby-watchers and Winnicott as his kindred spirits.

(561)

His writings include many unusual ideas, though initially not recognized as radical. Loewald, for instance, offered interventions that were far more expansive than official psychoanalysis would allow (McLaughlin, 1996). He conceived of the psyche in terms of human interaction, much more than drives and impulses. He tended to consider oppositional pairs – like primary and secondary processes, inside and outside, object and self – in a more integrative and less dichotomous way than his contemporaries. The meaning of human experience, he believed, arose from a dialectic, mutual tension between reality and fantasy, with each requiring its opposite to emerge. Loewald's interpretation, a response to the dialectics between the objective and the subjective in Freud's work, did not settle well with the official interpretations of his period.

Harry Sullivan's writings, too, made a substantial impact on the relational school. Some of its members are followers of Sullivan's interpersonal approach. This approach flourished in the late 1930s, offering the first significant US alternative to classical psychoanalysis. Sullivan is one of relational psychoanalysis' most highly respected authors. His writings have had a powerful impact on contemporary psychoanalysis. As Greenberg and Mitchell (1983) write

Sullivan has been one of the most influential, most ambitiously radical, and most frequently misread figures in the history of psychoanalytic ideas. His role has been elusive and paradoxical. His work, although rarely studied comprehensively and in the original, has had enormous influence on modern American psychiatry and contemporary psychoanalytic thinking. It has been suggested that Sullivan "secretly dominates" much of modern clinical psychiatry in the United States. Sullivan's concerns and formulations, derided by classical authors during his lifetime, or ignored, have resurfaced, at times in strikingly unaltered form, within the most important and popular Freudian authors of the past decade. Yet he is rarely credited with originating these approaches and ideas.

(80–81)

After having elaborated on Freud's way of treating psychotic patients, Sullivan proposed a psychotherapeutic technique based on the "interpersonal field" as the core unit of analysis. He also described how cultural and social aspects shape our personal identity (Conci, 2013).

Influenced by the pragmatism of Herbert Mead, Charles Cooley, Robert Park, Jane Adams, Thomas, and Edward Sapir, Sullivan was a rare voice against objectivity and neutrality in the work with patients, especially with schizophrenic patients. He was ambivalent toward Freudian psychoanalysis: On the one hand, he employed many terms that derive from classical drives theory (albeit in his own idiosyncratic way). Sullivan was one of the first analysts to stress the extent to which sexual impulses rendered primary yearnings for meaningful relations with the other. He had his qualms against Freud's dogmatism and thought the latter's therapeutic technique unsuitable for the US lower classes. Sullivan (1964, 220) was perhaps the first psychoanalyst to express his antagonism to the concept of the isolated mind.

Ronald Fairbairn, a psychoanalyst from Edinburgh, also was a source of inspiration for postmodern psychoanalysis. For Mitchell (Greenberg and Mitchell, 1983; Mitchell, 2000), Fairbairn and Sullivan developed the purest and most precise expression of the transition from the drives theory to a relational model.

Fairbairn's main contribution, which was to become the theoretical foundation of the British Independent Group's Object Relations Theory, was his concept that the primary motivation of human experience, thought, and behavior is the search for the object (i.e., relationship) and not the search for pleasure (Tubert-Oklander, 2018). This he posed in the following terms, "libido is primarily object-seeking (rather than pleasure-seeking, as in the classic theory), and that it is to disturbances in the object-relationships of the developing ego that we must look for the ultimate origin of all psychopathological conditions" (Fairbairn, 1944, 82).

Fairbairn also had a background in philosophy. He was among the first to reject the assumption that human experience is based on drives to reduce tension. Instead, he argued that human behavior aims to find and cultivate connections with the other. Psychopathology, for him, is not the outcome of conflict around forbidden and unsatisfied drives. Instead, it reflects disorders in relations with others.

Merton Gill is mentioned (especially by Hoffman, 1998) as another early source of postmodern psychoanalysis. Gill was considered to have crossed the lines when, from being a classical psychoanalyst, he became a relational psychoanalyst. Questioning the positivist assumptions of psychoanalysis, he also gave much space to the therapist's personal involvement in the therapeutic process (Gill, 1982).

Then, there are Heinrich Racker's (1968) ideas about transference relations, which are also considered advanced. The following well known paragraph by Racker inspired Irwin Hoffman, a significant figure among relational psychoanalysts:

The first distortion of truth in 'the myth of the analytic situation' is that analysis is an interaction between a sick person and a healthy one. The truth is that it is an interaction between two personalities, in both of which the ego is under pressure from the id, the superego, and the external world; each personality has its internal and external dependencies, anxieties, and pathological defenses; each is also a child with its internal parents; and each of these whole personalities – that of the analysand and that of the analyst- responds to every event in the analytic situation.

(Racker, as cited in Hoffman, 1998)

Thomas Ogden, who expanded and conceptualized the theories of Klein, Bion, and Winnicott, was another psychoanalyst who left his mark on relational psychoanalysis. Though Ogden used classic therapeutic techniques in the past, emphasizing silence, discretion, and reservation on the therapist's part, his therapeutic approach is intersubjective. Ogden believes that the therapist's and patient's minds can be penetrated by mutual influence, which then creates a "third" subjectivity (Ogden, 2004) – an intersubjectivity that is distinct from the subjectivity brought into the therapy by the therapist and patient each (Mitchell and Aron, 1999, 459–461).

How a New Worldview Changed the Understanding of Therapeutic Relations

Historically, changes in how analysts perceived patient-therapist relations were based on pragmatic reasoning. The changes were part of an attempt to refine the technique. Despite their clinically innovative features, the changes still followed a conservative epistemology. But the relational approach wanted to do much more than perfect the technique. It railed against the conventional worldview that the analyst holds the key to the patient is unconscious, that is, to his truth, and that the therapist holds a monopoly on this truth. The change, then, originates outside psychoanalysis in the worldviews of analysts. What, then, has changed?

One of the answers has to do with images of knowledge (Elkana, 1981). Elkana (1981) argues that images of knowledge are socially constructed perspectives on knowledge itself, distinct from views on nature or society. These images encompass beliefs about the role of science (such as understanding and prediction), the nature of truth (whether it is certain, probable, or attainable), and the sources of knowledge (whether it is acquired through reasoning or sensory experimentation). Together, these elements form time- and culture-dependent images of science, which in turn influence what is deemed important, interesting, worthwhile, absurd, or risky. The relational approach's radical conceptualizations were greatly encouraged by a new image of knowledge nurtured by philosophical changes in Western culture. These epistemological changes included the erosion of positivism's dominance and the rise of new epistemologies, such as modern hermeneutics, postmodernism, post-structuralism, and feminist theories. As Jon Mills (2012) notes:

> Relational psychoanalysis has largely embraced the hermeneutic postmodern tradition by closely examining the dialogic interactions and meaning constructions that emerge within the consulting room. They questioned the validity of absolute truth claims to knowledge, objective certainty, and positivist science. Meaning, insight, and conventions of interpretation are primarily seen as materializing from within the unique contexts and contingencies of interpersonal participation

in social events, dialogical discourse, dialectical interaction, mutual negotiation, dyadic creativity, and reciprocally generated co-constructions anchored in
an intersubjective process. This redirection from uncritically accepting metaphysical realism and independent, objective truth claims to reclaim the centrality of subjectivity within the parameters of relational exchange has allowed for
a reconceptualization of psychoanalytic doctrine and the therapeutic encounter.
(3)

At first, these cultural changes permeated into psychoanalysis through modern hermeneutics (Paul Richer, George Klein, Donald Spence, and Roy Schafer). Later
on, the discipline was even more radically affected by postmodernism and the relational approach. Racker and Ferenczi's theories were only acknowledged after a
profound change had occurred in psychoanalysis's images of knowledge. Influential ideas in Western cultural thought suggested that truth should be perceived as
essentially unstable, open to interpretation, and dependent on a social, political,
and historical context. Only then did many analysts abandon the classic conceptualization of therapeutic relations and opt for the relational approach. This neces-
sitated the adoption of the view expressed by Aron (1996), according to which
meanings that are seen as a product of universal laws lose their value when doubt
is cast on the very ideas of objectivity, reality, and truth.

But how was the new image of knowledge accepted and internalized? Did thousands of therapists begin to take an interest in philosophy and delve deeply into
the ideas of postmodern thinkers and their perceptions of the truth to form a new
psychoanalytic approach? Of course not. Images of knowledge are not acquired
consciously and intentionally; they are the outcome of an indirectly internalized
cultural, educational, and social environment. There is no need to have any knowledge of philosophy to change an image of knowledge. Analysts simply began
to feel uneasy about the psychoanalytic models they had worked with for years,
which they perceived as closed, rigid, limited, and monolithic. That was a sufficient
reason for a new and more youthful approach to emerge, bringing a wind of change
offering pluralism and democracy and attracting a mass following.

The process looks like this: In the wake of profound philosophical changes,
there are radical changes in philosophy's concepts of truth and their perception of
knowledge. A small group of analysts, open to new ideas and familiar with them, is
quick to assimilate the change and develop innovative psychoanalytic conceptualizations (within the relational approach, this small group included Stephen Mitchell, Lew Aron, Irwin Hoffman, Jessica Benjamin, Emmanuel Ghent, and Philip
Bromberg). The group quickly understood that postmodernism could potentially
enhance a real revolution in therapeutic relations and would have massive implications. The masses of therapists who follow in their footsteps do not know much
about the philosophical sources of these ideas. However, they quickly agree with
the new implications more compatible with the spirit of the times. The roots of the
latest image of knowledge were philosophical and cultural. However, the outcome
was far more critical than its origins.

The pragmatic clinical implications were far more important than philosophical abstract ideas. These profound implications signaled an end to the era of the knowing, authoritative therapists who portrayed themselves as holding the key to the patient's unconscious, an end to a period in which therapists struggled to hide their personalities and blur their subjectivity to ensure that the patient's emotional projections were "clean," and not subject to the effects of therapists' countertransference. A new era had begun. Jon Mills (2012) describes it best:

No longer do we get an image of the sober, cerebral, emotionally sealed-off analyst who greets the analysand with a curt social acknowledgment, then walks back to his chair saying nothing, standing in thick uncomfortable silence with an expressionless face waiting for the patient to lie on the couch or sit down. Rather we imagine the analytic encounter aspiring toward an interpersonal ideal of relational fulfillment and mutual recognition that serves a nurturing and validating function for both the patient and the therapist, similar to the consummate holding environment envisioned by Winnicott or a milieu of optimal empathic attunement identified by Kohut, with the supplementary exception that the analyst is also recognized, or at least acknowledged, as being a human subject with a distinct personality and needs.

(98)

The change is not only in abstract philosophy about the nature of analytic knowledge; it is much broader. Psychoanalysis has become less "heavy-handed," takes itself less seriously, seems less satisfied and self-content, and is freed from being honorable and old-fashioned. Analysts have "thrown away their books" (Hoffman, 1998), which is to say they have become less devoted to teachers and belief systems. They maintain a tension between ritual and spontaneity (Hoffman, 1998). They now talk to their patients and do so as equals, creating a more genuine relationship with them instead of working in line with a system of fixed and rigid principles of interpretation. The relational approach also encouraged independent thought, experimentation, innovation, spontaneity, creativity, genuine self-expression, humor, and playfulness. It allowed therapists to choose the most appropriate intervention given every patient's unique needs and characteristics (Mills, 2012).

An additional contribution to the success of the relational approach was its openness to political, social, and gender-related topics – subjects that had been excluded from psychoanalysis in the past. Relational analysts influenced by the interpersonal approach conceptualize the inner world as being affected not only by early experiences and family dynamics but also by social factors such as sex, race, and social standing (see Altman, 1993). All of these factors contribute to conscious and unconscious mental states. Some say that even the relationship with nature influences the human mind and that the changing relationships between people and ecosystems affect the intra-psychic (see Bodnar, 2008).

As strange as it may sound, relational analysts are successors of Freud in one significant way: Like him, they are the product of their era. In much the same way as he had done, they also brought their time's cultural, philosophical, and social world into psychoanalytic theory. Like the discipline's founding father, they, too, were willing to absorb and be influenced by the ambiance of their culture and their epoch. Finally, the relational analysts followed Freud, taking a keen interest in a vast range of non-psychoanalytical areas of study. It began with their inquiry into infant studies and progressed to include postmodern philosophy and hermeneutics, the philosophy of science, feminist theories, theories of gender and race, and eco-logical theories. Like Freud, whose curiosity was insatiable, relational analysts also tried to find their way through the maze of varied sources and bodies of knowledge. Though they discovered no new "facts" about infant development or the differing types of psychopathology (facts, we have seen, require the adoption of realism and the correspondence theory of truth, both of which were rejected by relational analysts), they most definitely recognized psychoanalysis's cultural climate and reconceptualized the therapeutic relationship.

The relational approach awarded psychoanalysis with two precious gifts: being eclectic and contemporary. In line with the spirit of the times, it freed analysts from committing to a single, consolidated, uniform worldview. It offered them a vast range of perspectives they could identify without requiring them to commit to any particular one. It has also provided a sense of belonging to various communities of therapists around the world who felt they had no place they could call professional home. These therapists held pluralistic views or wanted to conduct a dialogue with other schools of thought while remaining loyal to a specific therapeutic approach. In addition, the relational analysts succeeded in updating psychoanalysis, which had stagnated and had become obsolete, thus enabling a fresh touch and a lively revival. Its interest in social and political development in all areas rejuvenated psy-choanalysis and made it relevant to the contemporary world. It replaced an isolated discipline, preoccupied with its purity, with a discipline that was vibrant, lively, and capable of self-deprecating humor, involved in the issues of the here and now, such as gender, culture, and politics, and employing images from the world of jazz, literature, and the cinema. The relational approach has many strengths. It also possesses a remarkable capacity for self-reflexive humor and the acceptance of criticism both from within and beyond. The approach encourages dialogue and criticism and is not afraid of either one.

However, I think the revolutionary phase ended when the relational approach became established and successful. We now face a quite different and entirely new stage. At the end of the 1990s and the beginning of the 2000s, the relational approach was preoccupied with criticizing the conventionally accepted worldview. From an epistemological point of view, Mitchell rejected the contention that the therapist was a neutral, objective onlooker armed with the correct psychoanalytical theory. He dismissed the idea that the therapist had "a singular scientific knowledge and authority *vis-a vis* the patient's mind" (16).

In Mitchell's (1997) view, therapists cannot discover or expose what lies hidden in the patient's mind. The only expertise a therapist possesses, claims Mitchell, is the creation of meaning, self-reflection and the shaping and reorganization of the patient's experience. He rejects "traditional claims . . . that the central dynamics relevant to the analytic process are preorganized in the patient's mind" (18).

Further, the creation of meaning should not be forced rigidly but to be co-constructed and negotiated through dialogue.

This is an excellent example of how a revolution begins. In my view, this is not how therapists, including relational therapists, work. Nor is it desirable for them to follow such an approach. Is there really a therapist who isn't curious to discover what is in his patient's mind? Think about that initial, intuitive curiosity that grips you when the patient first walks into the room: Who is he? In what sort of mood has he come? What's happened to him? What thoughts are going through his mind? And the most important question: How can I understand him in a way that will enable me to help him more effectively? Not one of these simple, intuitive queries can be considered an intersubjective question. They all arise from what Stolorow terms the "isolated mind."

Here are several criticisms of analysts who think Mitchell has gone too far. Meissner (1998) writes:

It seems odd . . . that one would think of the patient, as he enters the consulting room for the first time, as without a history entirely of his own, without a developmental background, without a psychology and personality that he has acquired and developed in the course of a lifetime, all accomplished before he had any contact with the analyst.

(422)

Eagle (2009) writes:

Characteristic of the postmodern turn in psychoanalysis is the transformation of legitimate criticism into radical and, in my view, untenable philosophical positions. Thus, as we have seen, legitimate questions regarding the therapeutic efficacy of insight and self-knowledge are transformed into claims that there are no truths about the mind to be learned or discovered.

(30)

Eagle continues:

A recognition of the untenability of the blank screen model and of certain conceptions of analytic neutrality has become transformed into the claim that the patient-analyst interaction constitutes and organizes the patient's mind, as if there were no stable organization prior to and independent of these interactions.

(31)

However, from Mitchell's perspective and that of a newly launched revolutionary movement, he was right to give voice to extreme claims, even if exaggerated.

Powerful and extreme claims are necessary to spark a revolution. Without such claims, there would, at most, be just a fresh voice in the community – but no revolution.

But when the revolutionary movement becomes institutionalized, it invariably parts from such claims and deals with pragmatically entrenching its technique. During the 1990s and the 2000s, there was a substantial preoccupation with epistemological questions – a line of thinking led by Mitchell. His primary target was analysts fascinated by the theories they espoused. Ostensibly, to argue against the confidence analysts had in their theory, Mitchell did not have to abandon and replace the whole of the previous epistemology. It was enough for him to warn analysts to be more cautious in reaching conclusions. However, it turned out that this was not the case. Prior to the appearance of the relational approach, the psychoanalytic world was, from an epistemological point of view, anachronistic and at a standstill. To shake up this world, it was not enough to call for a modest confidence in psychoanalytic knowledge.

However, we are already beyond that point. In the last decade, the preoccupation with epistemological issues has declined to a great extent. It's a pity because epistemology and theory are essential. Without it, we are once again losing a vital dimension in psychoanalysis.

Here, as in the intersubjective approach, I am interested in that transitional phase in which philosophy has played a decisive role in the discussions of the relational approach. With its consolidation, most relational analysts lost interest in philosophy. They did not seem to need it anymore. The best representative of this phase is Irwin Hoffmann, who set the tone by proposing a new, radical philosophy called "social constructivism." Sharply criticizing the positivist model of his time, the philosophical aspect he conceived greatly influenced the relational approach.

Irwin Hoffman's Therapeutic Approach

Irwin Hoffman, an outstanding proponent of the postmodern school of American psychoanalysis, has a singularly ironic, provocative, and radical voice. Having started as a Rogerian therapist and, in time, branching out to other psychoanalytic approaches, Hoffman was influenced by the ideas of Merton Gill and Heinrich Racker, who were among the first in the US to depart from positivist psychoanalysis.

Identifying with a postmodern-oriented existentialism, Hoffman offers many descriptions of the postmodern condition. He considers death to be the one certainty in human existence. In his *Ritual and Spontaneity in the Psychoanalytic Process – A Dialectical-Constructivist Approach* (1998), Hoffman dedicates two chapters to death. He endorses philosophers like Thomas Nagel and Ernest Becker, who were interested in the dialectic between subjective and objective positions as a way of allowing people to live with the brutal truths of life. The crux of reality perception for Hoffman is the dialectic between recognition of and the refusal to recognize reality. A full recognition of reality will not let the individual live. The individual's chief challenge lies in his or her ability to recognize the severe limitations of self-consciousness and human freedom and to find viable ways to live with the terrible and absurd reality of life:

> We, the Slaves-that is, humankind-will, take what we can from the Mistress-Master, that is, from Nature, even though we know that Nature, ultimately, brutally disregards our needs and wishes, ravages us with illness and old age, abuses us, forces on our bodies the most grotesque kinds of physical deterioration, kills us in unspeakably horrifying and unexpected ways. We are not all, to be sure, adult survivors of childhood sexual, physical, or psychological abuse; but we are all adult endurers of the ongoing abuse of the human condition.
>
> (1998, 14)

Hoffman presents his position regarding death as Kohut's and Freud's antithesis. For Kohut, there was a dichotomy between healthy adjustment, marked by the serene acceptance of death, and pathological stance, characterized by denial and nihilism. Freud, too, who claimed that the death drive is part of the human constitution, tried in this way to fend off the despair and helplessness associated with death. Hoffman believes neither Freud nor Kohut took note of the adult, mature developmental position: the ability to tolerate ambivalence about death. This ability involves simultaneous existential fear and inescapable mourning together with a position that recognizes the existence of the self:

> It may be that the ultimative wisdom lies not with a "cosmic narcissism' that transcends individual narcissism and results in a calm acceptance of mortality, but with an ability to maintain in awareness both sides of the paradox posed by the prospect of death, namely that death renders life meaningful and meaningless, precious and valueless at the same time.
>
> (56)

According to Hoffman, humans are fated to live with the certainty of their death and that of those they love. They do not have the choice to be born, to live, or to die in a world where terrible events occur. Still, most people feel they want to live – they are happy to be in the world and believe they can have wonderful experiences. This absurd state of affairs implies that full consciousness is an impossibility as it necessarily would take humans to the very brink of despair. Instead, the individual is in a constant state of tension between the following two extremes: meaning and death. This dialectic is between construction and annihilation, determination and doubt, hope and despair.

Hoffman points out a similar paradox in the psychoanalytic situation: The therapist cannot but accept and exploit the magical, irrational authority with which the patient attributes falsely. This, too, is an irresolvable complexity – much like living in the shadow of death. The main achievement of the psychoanalytic situation is that both sides make the most of the therapeutic encounter – despite its absurd aspects, reflected in the act of paying money for love.

Therefore, Hoffman's notion of authenticity does not ethically resemble the values of self-psychology or classical psychoanalysis. The general meaning of *value* is the attribution of priority and preference to one human principle over others. On these lines, classical psychoanalysis prioritized objectivity and the search for knowledge over warm and open relations with the patient. Self-psychology chose the value of understanding subjectivity – i.e., the ability to step into the other's shoes – over and beyond finding the truth in therapy. However, Hoffman presents us with something else. His foremost principle is postmodern: the ability to live with contradictions rather than solve them. His thinking does not show a preference for one value over another. Authenticity is not the same thing for Hoffman as it is for Carl Rogers; for the latter, it means the negation of the therapist's subjectivity for the sake of joining the patient. Hoffman's authenticity takes off from the non-existent, acknowledging absence, death, and complexity. Rather than negating contradiction and paradox, this authenticity contains and learns to live with them. Slavin (2001) is correct in observing that when Hoffman refers to "dialectics," he does not have in mind a movement toward a synthesis of opposites, as would be the case in Hegel and Marx. The poles of this dialectic stay in place, and no resolution is reached: They are in constant tension and contradiction. For Stein (2001), Hoffman's dialectical constructivism is not just an epistemological position but also – and chiefly – a moral and spiritual stance that holds that meanings are constructed to deny death.

Infantile development is not one of Hoffman's strong interests. He does, however, mention the subject in his postmodern theory:

> Parents, the "gods" of infancy and childhood, can give children a sense of being "chosen," that is, of being valued as creative centers of experience and choice in their own right.
>
> (1998, 11)

The child needs parents who can take a sufficiently authoritative role and represent "Gods" so she can find personal meaning in the world.

It is the transference relations that occupy the center of Hoffman's attention. Hoffman's term for his position is "social constructivist" (1991, 137). Constructivist – because the therapeutic situation constructs the therapeutic reality and does not uncover a pre-existing reality. In using this concept, Hoffman also stresses an element of choice: The therapist chooses one interpretation from among many possible others. While this choice is affected by theoretical considerations, it is no less marked by the therapist's personality, interests, needs, and personal history. Hoffman believes the therapist's response cannot be predicted and should not be predicted. It is equally impossible to know whether other interventions – those not chosen – would have been better or worse (Stein, 2001). In the evolving relations between two people, nothing can be predicted. The patient's life story is not merely an historical reconstruction; it is also under construction right now in the interrelations that make up the therapy. Constructivism is social as a result of the dimension of interpersonal relations and the therapist's personal involvement in the therapy.

Later, Hoffman (1998) changed this erstwhile term to "critical or dialectical constructivism." He felt that "social" was identified with a radical relativism, which he strongly rejected:

> I want to emphasize . . . that postmodernism itself is heterogeneous and that certain versions of it, particularly radical relativism, are no more in harmony with my own thinking than extreme forms of objectivism.
>
> (1998, xxiii)

Hoffman criticizes positivism, in which the therapist's role is to read the patient's unconscious or unveil what was there. Regarding his dialectical constructivism, the patient and therapist in the therapeutic situation jointly construct something that did not exist before, something surprising and new to both. For both, the burden of responsibility is incomparably more significant. The activity between patient and therapist constitutes a kind of joint creation, one of many that could have developed between them. What is important in therapy is creating new meaning rather than disclosing existing thoughts (Hoffman, 1998, 150). The therapist is not merely unable to discover the patient's truth; he isn't even able to know the truth behind his own actions and interventions in the therapy.

Hoffman does not give up on either realism or essentialism. He writes (2013):

> The fact that a certain perspective emerges in a certain culture at a certain time does not in itself limit the validity of that perspective to that particular cultural, historical context.
>
> (289)

He does not believe that reality – in its general sense as well as in therapy – depends on social consensus. He believes in the existence of universal truths. Death, for instance, has an objective universal status. According to Hoffman, reality, exists in an independent, pre-given world so that the quality of human experience, despite its cloudy nature, also has an element of certainty, and specific actions can be authentically derived from it. Hoffman distances himself from scholars like Kenneth Gergen and Richard Rorty, who consider reality exclusively consensual, thus opening the door to relativism (x).

The new paradigm's central assumption is that the therapist is personally involved in the therapeutic process. The therapist's involvement seriously impacts her understanding of the patient. In this model, the therapist's understanding always depends on her perspective at any given moment. This understanding is vulnerable and open to the influence of the therapist's resistance. At any moment in the therapy, it can be substituted by another position that might arise in its place. Hence, no conclusive knowledge can be achieved in therapeutic relations: Understanding is always the product of two participants and their interaction at a given moment. Hoffman regards this assumption as a radical alternative to positivism.

The resulting therapeutic reality, Hoffman believes, depends on several factors, the two most important of which are the personal lives of the therapist and the patient, respectively. Experience comprises three components: 1. well-developed, certain, and distinct features; 2. vague positions, affective states, and undeveloped symbols; 3. potential, wholly indistinct mental frameworks (22). He accepts the existence of facts unrelated to the mind that thinks of them. These facts include two individuals who meet in the therapist's clinic at a certain time, for a particular duration, for psychoanalytic treatment. However, the experiences during this treatment remain vague and indeterminate – and unlike facts, they are not certain. Vague, though they are, these experiences are not amorphous. They have specific qualities and potentials that might develop in language or other modes of expression. The question remains unanswered: Which of these potentials actually develop and in what manner? Referring to Donnel Stern (1997), Hoffman writes that the movement between the unformulated and the formulated includes the dialectic between the given and the emergent (Hoffman, 1998, 23).

This is an unprecedented epistemological attack, not just on classical psychoanalysis but also on contemporary psychoanalysts. Setting himself up against thousands of papers published in psychoanalytic journals that draw theoretical conclusions from clinical examples or attempt to prove their theory through clinical illustrations, Hoffman claims that what happens in the therapeutic process cannot function as reliable evidence for theory, which remains extraneous to therapeutic relations. Psychoanalytic theory explains only a small part of the therapeutic reality. Most of that reality is explained by subjective factors related to the therapist and the patient.

Hoffman argues that since the dialectic-constructivist paradigm is new to psychoanalysis, it has not yet come into its own. He differentiates this paradigm from others, such as the transition from the drive model to the relational model (Greenberg and Mitchell, 1983) or Kohut's (1977) shift from interpretation to empathy. He argues that even new paradigms that have left behind the model of the drive still hold on to a positivist model by which the patient distorts the transference relations. Most object relations theories, he believes, have not adopted a radical anti-objectivist approach. At the same time, some classical psychoanalysis includes dialectical-constructivist ideas (in Racker's work, for instance). In other words, conceptual innovation in psychoanalysis, expressing itself in departures from the drive model, has not usually been accompanied by epistemological innovation.

Deconstructing the Analyst's Authority

Hoffman presents one of the key questions for psychoanalysis in the postmodern age: If the psychoanalyst is no longer a source of knowledge and truth, and if it is no longer her task to reveal a pre-existent unconscious – what can the psychoanalyst offer?

He thinks that the two justifications, which in the past served to confirm the therapist's authority, do not suit the epistemological assumptions he proposes. For classical Freudian psychoanalysis, therapists promised to search for the psychical truth – access to the unconscious. Such access became available through the development of neurosis in the transference relation. The therapist's remote and neutral attitude would trigger a regression in the patient's condition, generating neurosis within the therapy. The patient's early relations with her or his parents are reproduced in the therapeutic situation. Hoffman thinks such an approach is problematic, as it assumes that the patient distorts the transference relations and projects her repressed feelings toward her parents onto the therapist. In contrast, the therapist remains objective – a source of knowledge and insight.

In Kohut's and Winnicott's terms, psychoanalysis' second answer is that what counts in the therapeutic relationship is the therapist's love and recognition of the patient's needs (3). In this approach, therapist-patient relations can constitute a kind of second parenting, repairing the damage done by earlier, non-empathic parenting. This answer, too, is problematic for Hoffman because it makes the therapist's love conditional on payment. The fact that the patient pays the therapist casts doubt on the authenticity of the love and recognition offered. If love is procured using money, Hoffman asks, what is the difference between the therapist and the prostitute? Moreover, a treatment of 50-minute five sessions a week seems a poor substitute for parenting.

Layton (2013) writes: "For Hoffman, the patient's idealization of the analyst facilitates change. However, he also describes the multiple temptations for abuse that the analytic frame sets up. His contributions highlight how therapists benefit from compliance with a normative culture of 'expertise'" (278).

Thus, Hoffman agrees that, in the postmodern age, the therapist's confidence in her authority is lost: She no longer possesses truth and knowledge. Believing that the therapist has more knowledge than the patient does not make sense anymore.

However, as opposed to the intersubjective approach, which calls to reduce the therapist's authority, Hoffman paradoxically tells psychoanalysts to hold on to their authority.
Hoffman (2013) writes:

In a hermeneutic/constructivist paradigm, the analyst is only an influence; whatever the patient does in response is his or her choice. Ironically, that frees the analyst/therapist to assume much *more* responsibility than would be assumed conventionally because what is conventional are the conflations of influence and coercion, on one hand, and autonomy and isolation, on the other.

(294)

An inevitable dialectical process, he believes, happens in the course of therapy. The patient perceives the therapist simultaneously in two clashing ways: as another human being just like herself and as an authority figure endowed with knowledge, wisdom, judgment, and power. For the patient, the therapist's authority is ironic and intimate. There is something inescapable about this attribution of authority to the therapist since the therapeutic situation resembles, in some of its features, the parent-child situation:

> I believe there is a tendency in the work of some relational theorists, as an overreaction to the scientistic authoritarianism to which classical technique was prone, to denigrate the irrational aspects of the authority of the analyst to a degree that denies what is implicitly built into the analytic arrangement. In my view, unless the fundamental asymmetry of the analytic situation were to be dismantled, the analyst is likely to retain a certain residue of special power that cannot be undone by analysis, by interpersonal negotiation, or even by personally revealing behavior if it is consistent with the maintenance of the analytic frame.
>
> (10)

The therapist's role here is consistently caring – his weaknesses are kept out of view, and his relative anonymity is maintained. This drives the patient to reproduce the conditions allowing her to receive and absorb love (12).

This ironic-intimate dialectic, though based on an illusion (after all, the therapist is not the patient's parent) needs no resolution! It must be openly discussed as part of the therapy and the effort to achieve authenticity in the transference relations. **Hoffman believes the therapist should use the magical powers the patient projects onto him rather than try defusing them.** Being a psychoanalyst means taking on the role once set aside for the gods; in other words, the omnipotent parent. This view could be seen as an inevitable return to Freud's notion of suggestion. It is well known that Freud used hypnotic suggestion and only later expressed his reservations regarding this technique.

Hoffman believes that, even if he makes an effort, the therapist cannot undo the remarkable power he has for the patient. The therapist's authority is neither a religious nor a sacred type of authority but one that identifies a "universal human need." Instead of trying to nullify his magical power, the therapist should use it for the good of the patient. Paradoxically, he thinks that those therapists who deny their magical influence revert to the rational ideal of modernism and the enlightenment – which is the ideal classical psychoanalysis advanced.

We can draw a parallel with the British psychoanalyst Donald Winnicott's phase of omnipotence, which plays such a crucial developmental role. At this stage, the infant-patient believes in her or his omnipotence and powerful ability to control the mother and create her time and again (Winnicott, 1965, 146). Where development is functional, the mother enables this stage, avoiding disillusioning the child. In contrast to Winnicott, who believes that illusion forms the first stage of development, which must be followed by a next, objective stage of disillusionment, Hoffman does not assume such a second, objective stage. In fact, he believes that a rational, objective stage of disillusionment is impossible. He suggests that for maximum therapeutic gain the therapist must join the illusion rather than fight it.

Hoffman encourages his readers to reconcile themselves to the authority patients bestow on them and accept that psychoanalysts sometimes function as mentors, advisers, and guides along their patients' complex roads. He believes that most therapists, while accepting their authority role, have always tried to reduce it. Most psychoanalysts shun having too much of a decisive influence on their patients and prefer an uninvolved position. Most psychoanalysts would like to assume that their role is limited to bringing to the surface what is there and helping patients be more aware of what is involved in their significant life choices. However, Hoffman argues that therapists have realized that they cannot be neutral and objective. From this realization, they have evolved a new position: that they should try to keep their subjective influence at bay, which Hoffman wholly rejects.

In one of the most beautiful passages in his book, he writes:

> I am anticipating that some might argue that perfect empathy and attunement, like perfect objectivity, are merely ideals to strive for, with the understanding that we are always falling short of them despite our best efforts. My reply is that I do not think it is good to set up intrinsically irrational ideals that do violence to human nature. Aspiring to walk on water and striving to be able to do that are bound to interfere with learning to swim. Such a standard of locomotion is no less wrongheaded if we humbly "admit" that, since nobody is "perfect", those attempting to walk will surely get wet.

(86)

Hoffman looks pretty preoccupied with the question of the therapist's tactics or strategy. His main argument – that one must make the best of an inevitable situation (i.e., the therapist is necessarily a magical influence) – is pragmatic. Hoffman seems to suggest to psychoanalysts that, often, one should prefer pragmatic considerations to theoretical ones. Favoring pragmatic considerations is especially the case in the postmodern era, with the position of the theory's correspondence with reality considerably corroded.

One might add to Hoffman's arguments that only those who are persuaded of the therapist's authority in the first place will turn to therapy. We may also say that if therapists actually succeed in convincing patients that they are not a source of authority, they thereby cut off the branch on which psychotherapy is sitting. That would, indeed, be embarrassing and ironic. If we take Hoffman's advice, we seem to reach the following conclusion: The postmodern therapist knows she does not know the truth and that her knowledge is no more valid than that of the patient – but if the patient would reveal this knowledge, there would be no more room for therapy. The patient has no use for a therapist who does not consider herself a source of authority.

In many ways, Hoffman's approach is, in fact, no different from Freud's and classical psychoanalysis. Freud did not claim either that psychoanalysis derives its healing power from the psychoanalyst's knowledge and truth alone. Freud agrees that no successful psychoanalysis is possible without transference, that is, without illusion. The therapist has an impact not only because of what she knows but also

thanks to the robust nature of the transference relations. The power of these relations derives from illusion and the distortion of the therapeutic reality. Traditional
approaches also use an elusive component and do not rely on knowledge alone.
Unlike Hoffman, though, they believe it is the therapist's job to reduce the power
of illusion, helping the patient achieve a more adult and objective perception of
himself and reality.

However, even if we accept Hoffman's pragmatic considerations, according to
which we must exploit the situation for the patient's best interest, the following
question stands: **What is the therapist's source of authority in her own eyes?**
Hoffman does not address this question. It would seem that he falls into his own
trap. For there is at least one thing that the postmodern therapist knows and his
patient does not: that the therapist knows no more than the patient, and her way of
seeing reality is no more valid than his!

Hoffman calls for therapists to continue their work – not based on some ability
they have (knowledge, insight, access to the unconscious), but due to their patients'
faith in them. What does this remind us of? Perhaps the healer whose patients
believe in his magical powers while he knows that he has no such powers. However,
he offers them his help, not disclosing that he is an ordinary human who is not different from them. So, while in classical psychoanalysis, both the patient and therapist
believed that the latter had special knowledge (witches did believe in their own
powers!), for Hoffman, it is only the patients who harbor this belief. After all (bon-
afide), therapists can claim to have studied something (so may witches, by the way).

One might also ask what Hoffman has in mind when he argues that therapists
must use wisely (p. 10) the authority their patients vest in them or when he says
elsewhere that interventions must be made based on only one consideration: "the
long-term interests" (p. 199). Though he often repeats this advice, and though it
seems that from his perspective, this criterion replaces classical psychoanalysis'
search for the truth, Hoffman offers no guidelines for gaining a better idea of his
notions of "wise" and "long-term interest." Traditional psychoanalysis, by contrast,
included clear rules for "wise" and "long-term interest" interventions, and each
psychoanalytic theory had its distinctive therapeutic objectives.

Ritual and Spontaneity in Psychoanalysis

It would be a mistake to assume that Hoffman does not attach great importance to
the rules and laws of classical psychoanalysis. On the contrary, Hoffman is committed to psychoanalytic rules. He believes in a dialectics between psychoanalytic
rules (end of the hour, termination of analysis, payment) and the therapist's objectivity, on the one hand, and the therapist's personal involvement and occasional
departure from the rules, on the other:

> Thus, the moment in which the analyst allows himself or herself to surface as a
> desiring subject is not experienced with the same sharp edge of deviation that
> characterized it before. Now, instead of **throwing away** the Book, we place it
> temporarily in the background while the analyst's distinctive self-expression

moves into the foreground. The opposite holds as well. When the analyst's more standard, formal, detached, reflective, and interpretive stance is in the foreground, the aspect of the relationship that reflects his or her more personal engagement can still be sensed.

(199)

A dialectic movement exists between ritual and spontaneity. Malcolm Slavin (2001) comments that this idea resembles Winnicott's description of object use. Winnicott argues that, to be able to use the object (the therapist), the patient must perceive her as real rather than only through her projections, destroying certain aspects of the object as previously internalized. The object must both allow this attack and survive it. The form-background process is a Hoffmanian's version of the annihilation and survival of the object – this time, in two-person psychology. The patient wants to come out triumphant from an Oedipal struggle, changing the rules and the theory to which the psychoanalyst adheres. When the therapist "breaks" the rules by expressing his subjectivity, the patient feels special and "above the law" because he broke the rules for his sake. At the same time, however, to feel safe and protected, the patient needs these rules. Hoffman is clearly concerned that an unbounded collusion may arise between the patient and therapist. Though he uses the provocative phrase "throwing away the books," he stresses no less how important it is not to do so. While the frame – the rules – is destroyed (and thus turns into the background) by the spontaneous departures occurring in the mutual attachment of the therapy, it also endures. In this manner, the patient can gradually use the therapist through ritual and spontaneity and develop a more genuine relationship with her.

Therefore, Hoffman assumes that psychoanalytic therapy involves two axes. The first is theoretical, objective, reflexive, and formal. Theory in the "regular" psychoanalytic sense belongs here. Hoffman does not suggest which theory is the right one or by which criteria the choice of theory should be made. The second axis in which Hoffman is more interested is the creative and authentic way of participation. It includes subjectivity, personal expression, self-exposure, and deviation from rules. This axis is a-theoretical, and the general suggestion is, as said, for the therapist to act wisely following the patient's long-term interests.

The second axis, Hoffman believes, allows the therapist greater latitude in expressing what is on his mind than the first axis. There is no criterion for objective truth, so there is more space for spontaneous expression (p. x). However, it remains unclear on what basis this axis rests, what kind of dialogue therapists can have about it, and how therapists can be trained to work with it.

Stein (2001) remarks on Hoffman's deep identification with the patient, who is unsure whether the therapist is objective, reliable, and ethical and whether the therapist will look after his interests with integrity. Interestingly, although he stresses that uncertainty is a central element of therapy, Hoffman argues that psychoanalysts do not necessarily have to be skeptics and unsure of what they say or do. **Psychoanalysts can go on being convinced of what they tell their patients**. While the certainty in psychoanalysis derived from objective knowledge diminishes, certainty built on subjectivity, responsibility, and ethics grows. In the transition, the importance of what was known through theory, research, and accumulated clinical experience lessens somewhat, to be replaced by the therapist's subjectivity and experience as informing what she says or does (p. xx).

It would seem that the certainty to which Hoffman refers is not empirical; it is not a certainty based on knowledge. Instead, he talks about the certainty of authenticity. This authenticity is open to psychoanalytic skepticism and critical thinking. The authentic therapist knows herself and stays faithful to her position, even when others disagree. The question Hoffman fails to answer is how professionals should conduct a dialogue or persuade each other. Though it was rigid, at least traditional psychoanalysis played by clear rules: The one who manages to prove that her theory offers a better description of reality is the persuasive one. The criteria whereby therapeutic theories, interpretations, and positions are scrutinized are, however, less clear when we refer to the criterion of authenticity.

The Abolition of Ideologies

Hoffman calls for abolishing the old psychoanalytic ideologies (1998, 86). He pinpoints two chief ones. The ideology of classical psychoanalysis was perfect objectivity. According to this ideal, the therapist must reduce his subjectivity to achieve valid knowledge about the patient. The second ideology, espoused by self-psychology, is perfect empathy, where the therapist must reduce his subjectivity to put himself into the patient's position.

For Hoffman, not only are these ideals unattainable – there is no need to accept or act by them. He considers them misleading, false, and irrational. Any attempt to attain them has always involved the negation of the therapist's personality, the concealment of his motivation and feelings, and the effort to reduce his personal influence. Hoffman also has an answer for those moderate psychoanalysts who understand that neither objectivity nor empathy can be perfect but that they should still be pursued:

> I am anticipating that some might argue that perfect empathy and attunement, like perfect objectivity, are merely ideals to strive for, with the understanding that we are always falling short of them despite our best efforts. My reply is that I do not think it is good to set up intrinsically irrational ideals that do violence to human nature. Aspiring to walk on water and striving to be able to do that are bound to interfere with **learning** to swim. Such a standard of locomotion is no less wrongheaded if we humbly "admit" that, since nobody is "perfect", those attempting to walk will surely get wet.
>
> (86)

Hoffman believes the ideals of accurate, empathic listening and perfect neutrality lead to the development of impossible objectives. The therapist defensively deludes himself into that he's made "achievements" and forgives his own "mistakes." More than anything, these ideals distract the therapist from what Hoffman considers the main issue: the therapist's personal involvement in the patient's life.

We should consider the abolition of therapeutic ideologies and values as one of Hoffman's most revolutionary and vital contributions. Going by his postmodern approach, there is nothing else to strive for; there is no guiding ideal, no faith – neither in absolute knowledge nor in the goodness of humanity, neither in truth nor in love.

Hoffman's writing, detached as it is from the existing psychoanalytic tradition and with its peculiarities, fits in well with the postmodern tendency not to make up one more link in the chain of theories and to constitute, instead, a different voice with an ironic and unblinkered view of the modernist chain. Hoffman's writing harbors a kind of alien element – an "otherness" that is hard to pinpoint and formulate. Though he frequently quotes Freud, Hoffman's thinking does not constitute another link in the chain that began with Freud and grew in various directions. Despite his attempts to present his ideas as the ideas of a psychoanalyst, one senses that mainstream psychoanalysis and Hoffman do not speak the same language. Their fundamental assumptions are very different – perhaps reminiscent of the differences between modernism and postmodernism. Hoffman writes fascinatingly – his texts are unusual and engaging; they challenge all that's known and familiar in psychoanalysis – to the point that one sometimes wonders whether they don't tear themselves entirely away from its body of knowledge.

Conclusion

If one could summarize Hoffman's approach in one sentence it might be: "The emperor has no clothes, he needs new ones!"; as Hoffmann points his finger at psychoanalysis. He argues that almost everything on which psychoanalysts were raised and educated is not as authentic and correct as the psychoanalytic community would like to believe. However, Hoffman believes that psychoanalysis can go on as it is even after abandoning its most intrinsic assumptions.

As Altman (2013) writes: "Hoffman eschewed the comfort of authority based on the presumption of the analyst's objective pursuit of knowledge in favor of a rigorous examination of how two human beings construct and unpack their analytic interaction" (269).

For Hoffman, the "comfort of authority" is also found in the tendency of some analysts to privilege evidence-based research. Hoffman thinks that

the privileged status that this movement accords systematic research and neuroscience as compared with in-depth case studies and strictly psychological accounts of the psychoanalytic process is unwarranted epistemologically and potentially damaging both to the development of our understanding of the analytic process itself and to the quality of our clinical work.

(2009, 1044)

More than anything else, Hoffman wants to discuss the therapeutic situation and the encounter between the patient and the therapist. He is not interested in psychoanalytic conceptualizations concerning infant development or the uncon-scious. Hoffman does not argue with Klein's theoretical statements or those of Kohut, Hartmann, or Freud. He is not interested in them at all. Hoffman's interest, in theory, is another pointer in the direction of postmodernism: While modernism presents general mechanisms underlying phenomena, postmodernism introduces the personal and the expressive, what escapes the rules, whatever is in theory's backyard.

Hoffman's significant contribution is forcing the psychoanalytic community to reconsider concepts and norms about which there was an almost absolute consensus. After Hoffman, it would seem, psychoanalysts will no longer be able to have it both ways: to criticize the classical therapist for being neutral and a tabula rasa, on the one hand, and yet on the other to hold on to certain other, typically positivist assumptions.

When one thinks about the social-constructivist paradigm that Hoffman pre-sented, one realizes how far it is from any attempt to understand the therapeutic relationship through empirical and quantitative means. For Hoffman, systematic empirical research on the psychoanalytic process is part of the "comfort of author-ity." Such studies pull the unique therapist-patient dyad out of their cultural and social context and look at a one-time relationship as statistical data. Indeed, Hoff-man (2016) called analysts not to privilege empirical studies over case studies: "I believe that the current zeal about the grounding of psychoanalysis as science is at best highly imbalanced in this regard and at worst profoundly mistaken philo-sophically" (1043).

Hoffman asks all science advocates not to give epistemic superiority to realism and the correspondence theory of truth over a hermeneutic approach. He believes in a non-positivist approach as the only appropriate approach to therapeutic work. However, despite Hoffman's recommendation, it is clear that the psychoanalytic world has never lost interest in the positivist approach and the belief that psycho-analytic theory should be evidence-based and validated.

The desire to connect psychoanalysis with science, to validate and expand psychoanalytic assumptions through non-analytical fields of knowledge, is today more significant than ever. In the next chapter, we will see that positivism is alive and kicking through a new, emerging discipline – neuropsychoanalysis, a rapidly developing field of research that is gaining popularity alongside harsh criticism.

Note

1 The patient refers to Jody Davies' article "Love in the Afternoon" (1994), where Davies tells her patient, who suffered sexual abuse as a child, about her sexual attrac-tion to him.

References

Altman, N. (1993). Psychoanalysis and the Urban Poor. *Psychoanalytic Dialogues*, 3, 29–49.
Altman, N. (2013). Introduction: A Dialectical Constructivist Understanding of Self-Interest and Social Responsibility. *Psychoanalytic Dialogues*, 23, 269–270.
Aron, L. (1996). *A Meeting of Minds – Mutuality in Psychoanalysis*, Madison, CT: The Analytic Press.

Aron, L. (1998). "Yours, Thirsty for Honesty, Ferenczi": Some Background to Sándor Ferenczi's Pursuit of Mutuality. *American Journal of Psychoanalysis*, 58, 5–20.

Aron, L. and Harris, A. (1993). Sandor Ferenczi: Discovery and Rediscovery. In *The Legacy of Sandor Ferenczi*. Hillsdale, NJ: The Analytic Press, 1–36.

Benjamin, J. (2021). Tilting Back Toward Development: Response to Steven Cooper's "Donald Winnicott and Stephen Mitchell's Developmental Tilt Hypothesis Reconsidered". *Psychoanalytic Dialogues*, 31, 371–380.

Bergmann, M.S. (Ed.) (2000). *The Hartmann Era*. New York: The Other Press.

Bodnar, S. (2008). Wasted and Bombed: Clinical Enactments of a Changing Relationship to the Earth. *Psychoanalytic Dialogues*, 18, 484–512.

Conci, M. (2013). Sullivan and the Intersubjective Perspective. *International Forum of Psychoanalysis*, 22, 10–16.

Davies, J.M. (1994). Love in the Afternoon: A Relational Reconsideration of Desire and Dread in the Countertransference. *Psychoanalytic Dialogues*, 4, 153–170.

Dunn, J. (1995). Intersubjectivity in Psychoanalysis: A Critical Review. *International Journal of Psychoanalysis*, 76, 723–738.

Eagle, M. (2009). Chapter 1: Postmodern Influences on Contemporary Psychoanalysis. In R. Frie and D. Orange (Eds.) *Beyond Postmodernism New Dimensions in Clinical Theory and Practice*. London: Routledge, 27–51.

Elkana, Y. (1981). A Programmatic Attempt at an Anthropology of Science. In E. Mendelshon and Y. Elkana (Eds.) *Sciences and Cultures*. Dordrecht: Reidel, 1–76.

Fairbairn, W.R.D. (1944). Endopsychic Structure Considered in Terms of Object-Relationships. *International Journal of Psychoanalysis*, 25, 70–92. [Reprinted in Fairbairn (1952), 82–136.]

Gill, M.M. (1982). *The Analysis of Transference. Vol. 1: Theory and Technique*. New York: International University Press.

Greenberg, J.R. and Mitchell, S. (1983). *Object Relations in Psychoanalytic Theory*. Cambridge: Harvard University Press.

Hoffman, I.Z. (1991). Discussion: Toward a Social-Constructivist View of the Psychoanalytic Situation. *Psychoanalytic Dialogues*, 1, 74–105.

Hoffman, I.Z. (1998). *Ritual and Spontaneity in the Psychoanalytic Process: A Dialectical-Constructivist View*. Hillsdale, NJ: The Analytic Press.

Hoffman, I.Z. (2009). Doublethinking Our Way to "Scientific" Legitimacy: The Desiccation of Human Experience. *Journal of the American Psychoanalytic Association*, 57, 1043–1069.

Hoffman, I.Z. (2013). Response to Layton: Considering the Sociopolitical Context of Dialectical Constructivism. *Psychoanalytic Dialogues*, 23, 287–295.

Hoffman, I.Z. (2016). The Risks of Therapist Passivity and the Potentials of Constructivist Influence. *Psychoanalytic Dialogues*, 26, 91–97.

Kohut, H. (1977). *The Restoration of the Self*. New York: International University Press.

Layton, L. (2013). Dialectical Constructivism in Historical Context: Expertise and the Subject of Late Modernity. *Psychoanalytic Dialogues*, 23, 271–286.

Loewald, H. (1960/1980). On the Therapeutic Action of Psychoanalysis. In *Papers on Psychoanalysis*. Vol. 00. New Haven, CT: Yale University Press, 21–31.

McLaughlin, J. (1996). Loewald and the Clinical Work of Psychoanalysis. *Journal of the American Psychoanalytic Association*, 44, 899–910.

Meissner, W.W.S.J. (1998). Neutrality, Abstinence, and the Therapeutic Alliance. *Journal of the American Psychoanalytic Association*, 46, 1089–1128.

Mills, J. (2012). *Conundrums: A Critique of Contemporary Psychoanalysis*. New York, NY: Routledge (New Books Network).

Mitchell, S. (1997). *Influence and Autonomy in Psychoanalysis*, New Jersey & London: The Analytic Press.

Mitchell, S. (2000). *Relationality From Attachment to Intersubjectivity*. London, NJ: The Analytic Press.

Mitchell, S.A. and Aron, L. (1999). *Relational Psychoanalysis: The Emergence of a Tradition*. Hillsdale, NJ: The Analytic Press.

Ogden, T.H. (2004). The Analytic Third: Implications for Psychoanalytic Theory and Technique. *Psychoanalytic Quarterly*, 73, 167–195.

Orange, D.M. (2014). What Kind of Ethics? Loewald on Responsibility and Atonement. *Psychoanalytic Psychology*, 31, 560–569.

Racker, H. (1968). *Transference and Countertransference*. New York: International University Press.

Slavin, M.O. (2001). Constructivism with a Human Face. *Psychoanalytic Dialogues*, 11, 405–429.

Spezzano, C. (1995). "Classical" versus "Contemporary" Theory. *Contemporary Psychoanalysis*, 31, 20–46.

Stein, R. (2001). Review Essay: The Ethical and the Epistemological. *Psychoanalytic Dialogues*, 11, 431–450.

Stern, D.B. (1997). *Unformulated Experience: From Dissociation to Imagination in Psychoanalysis*. Hillsdale, NJ: The Analytic Press.

Stern, D.B. (2013). Field Theory in Psychoanalysis, Part 2: Bionian Field Theory and Contemporary Interpersonal/Relational Psychoanalysis. *Psychoanalytic Dialogues*, 23, 630–645.

Sullivan, H.S. (1964). The Illusion of Personal Individuality. In H.S. Perry (Ed.) *The Fusion of Psychiatry and Social Science*. New York: Norton.

Teicholz, J.G. (1999). *Kohut, Loewald, & the Postmoderns – A Comparative Study of Self and Relationship*. London: The Analytic Press.

Tubert-Oklander, J. (2018). Is Fairbairn Still at Large? *Contemporary Psychoanalysis*, 54, 201–228.

Winnicott, D.W. (1965/1984). *The Maturational Processes and the Facilitating Environment*. London: Karnac.

Part 2

The Post-psychoanalytic
Schools Era

Chapter 6

Back to Positivism

The Case of Neuropsychoanalysis

If one thought, until now, that positivism was overwhelmed and defeated by post-modernism, one should think again. There has been a new player on the scene for over 20 years – neuropsychoanalysis – and it is the most informed representative of positivist thought. With truly remarkable scholarly activities, including a prestigious journal, an annual conference, regional groups in more than 20 countries, research projects, and thought-provoking publications, neuropsychoanalysis became one of psychoanalysis's most influential and exciting movements. Scholars of neuropsychoanalysis show in many ways how neuroscience research could lead to a new understanding of subjects at the heart of psychoanalytic theory, such as the unconscious (Kessler, 2013; Solms, 2013), memory (Yovell, 2000), trauma (Saporta, 2003), dreams (Solms, 1997), and transference relations (Axmacher and Heinemann, 2012). The neuropsychoanalysis move has also made an essential contribution to the work of psychodynamic therapists. Neuropsychoanalysis has led to discoveries in the fields of trauma, memory, affect, and motivation (Panksepp, 2013), as well as theories of the mind (Westen and Gabbard, 2002) that can shed new light on clinical work.

This chapter tries to solve two puzzlements. The first has to do with the central thesis of the book. If the dominant philosophy of our culture shapes psychoanalysis, and if positivism was replaced by postmodernism, how come it made a comeback in the form of neuropsychoanalysis?

Second, orthodox psychoanalysis and neurospsychoanalysis share the same images of knowledge. Both traditions believe psychoanalysis is a scientific endeavor, and both believe in the correspondence theory of truth (Govrin, 2016). How come representatives of orthodox psychoanalysis became the most vocal critiques of neuropsychoanalysis? I will explore the intricate relations between neuropsychoanalysis and mainstream psychoanalysis in much of the chapter. I will show that resistance to change is not unique to orthodox psychoanalysis but a regular and widespread phenomenon among scientific communities. I will also suggest ways that neuropsychoanalysis can be even more relevant to the daily practice of psychoanalysts.

DOI: 10.4324/9781003498162-10

Neuropsychoanalysis in the Postmodern World

Let us start with the first question: How did positivism come back in a postmodern world? The simple answer is that it did not make a comeback because it has never disappeared.

First, major worldviews such as positivism and the correspondence theory of truth do not simply vanish. Therefore, they express deep psychological needs and cannot be dispensed with. According to Yadlin-Gadot (2017), the activity of our consciousness is not detached from our emotions and needs; its forms answer our deep need for certainty, security, and direction. Yadlin Gadot presents six truth axes that organize the world in certain paradigmatic ways: correspondent (equivalent to the positivist worldview), coherent, subjective-existential, pragmatic, intersubjective, and ideal. Each image of reality captures a possible yet incomplete, aspect of the experience. Its organic truth serves as a point of certainty within it. In each reality resides a characteristic self-state guided, directed, and motivated by its truth. Yadlin-Gadot writes,

> At the root of the Correspondent axis is the need to be in touch with external reality so as to enhance the chances of survival, through explaining, responding to and anticipating events that influence the exchanges between man and the mind-independent world around him.
>
> (65)

Second, two sensibilities – infant research and neuropsychoanalysis – are related to scientific bodies of knowledge (on sensibilities, see Chapter 7). Both were created not as an alternative to psychoanalytic theory but as a lighthouse theory directing analysts to be sensitive to the findings of those fields. Both come from what their supporters identify as a fundamental flaw of psychoanalytic theory: its detachment from science and its reduction into a language primarily determined by the therapist's subjectivity and the theory he or she believes in. Faith has replaced genuine knowledge, and there is a lack of scientific evidence derived by reason and logic from sensory experience.

Neuropsychoanalysis, in particular, has a convincing argument. According to Solms and Turnbull (2015), Freud was a neuroscientist and a neurologist for the first two decades of his professional life (Solms, 2002; Solms and Saling, 1986; Sulloway, 1979). Freud planned to locate the construction and functions of the mind, and he understood that these were closely connected to the structure and functions of the brain. He knew that brain research did not have the proper methods to explore these relationships at his time. He, therefore, shifted to a purely psychological method – a shift that he reluctantly saw as a necessary compromise.

Freud wrote:

> Biology is a land of unlimited possibilities. We cannot guess what answers it will return in a few dozen years. They may be of a kind that will blow away the whole artificial structure of our hypotheses.
>
> (1920, 60)

Solms and Turnbull (2015) write:

> There are many such statements throughout Freud's work. All reveal, first, that he viewed the separation of psychoanalysis from neuroscience as a *pragmatic* decision. Second, he was always at pains to clarify that progress in neuroscience would have the inevitable result that *at some time in the future* the neurosciences will advance sufficiently to make the gap bridgeable. As one of the quotes above suggests, his rough estimate was that this might happen in a "few dozen years." That was in 1920.
>
> (15)

In the post-Freudian world, we see a split in psychoanalysis. Alongside single-approach communities whose source of knowledge rests solely on the clinical situation (such as Klein. Winnicott, Kohut), troubled scientific communities (Govrin, 2016, 27–28) engage in laboratory research for research aimed at validating and investigating psychoanalytic conceptualizations. Despite its small scope and limited sphere of influence, the scientific community has never ceased to be active in universities and research centers. Its prominent representatives were Luborsky and the Penn Psychotherapy Project, The Menninger Project and Robert Wallerstein process research at Ulm of Kachele, The Mount Zion group, Sydney Blatt at Yale University, Otto Kernberg at Cornell University, and Loyd Silverman at The Research Center for Mental Health at New York University.

Therefore, the empiricist-positivist tradition has never disappeared, and neuropsychoanalysis is an offshoot.

Neuropsychoanalysis has succeeded above and beyond these research successes for two reasons: It continued Freud's vision of bridging between brain research and psychoanalysis. Second, brain research is psychology's most intriguing, prestigious, and appreciated research activity. Therefore, it has given many therapists the feeling that what they are doing is related to another activity at the forefront of science.

Neuropsychoanalysis simply asserts that a subject (person) is connected to an object (body/brain). To be a sceintific psychology, psychoanalysis needs to "link the findings of the science of the mind as an object with those of the mind as a subject" (Solms and Turnbull, 2015, 3). The discipline acknowledges this dualistic mind-body realization:

> If we accept this philosophical approach, it follows naturally that we would want to make use of *both* points of view on our object of study, as perceived externally and internally. Why would we want to exclude, *a priori*, a full half of what we can learn about the part of nature that we are studying?
>
> (Solms and Turnbull, 2015, 22)

The Intricate Relations between Neuropsychoanalysis from Orthodox Psychoanalysis

Despite the movement's international success and popularity, many hard-core analysts remain uninterested in its discoveries.

Because orthodox psychoanalysis shares with neuropsychoanalysis the world views of positivism, realism, and scientism, one would expect that they would collaborate, especially when neuropsychoanalysis returns to Freud's vision of the importance of brain research to understand the human mind. However, the opposite became true. Orthodox psychoanalysis (Clarke, 2018; Blass and Carmeli, 2007) became its fiercest critics.

As I wrote elsewhere:

> The most highly charged controversies in psychoanalysis occur between an existing fascinated community with a canonical tradition and a troubled community that offers a new theory of the human psyche and that ultimately becomes a fascinated community itself. As we will see, the two communities share a similar perception of images of knowledge and agree on a hierarchy of legitimate sources of knowledge. The charged discussions in these cases are about "the facts."
>
> (Govrin, 2016)

Thus, although orthodox psychoanalysis and neurophysioanalysis share the same worldview, they strongly disagree on the question of the **source of knowledge**. The only source of knowledge of classical psychoanalysis is the clinical situation, and they wish to exclude any external source of knowledge.

The critics claim that neuropsychoanalysis

> diminish the role of psychic meaningfulness in ways that allow for the neuroscientific findings to have some relevance for psychoanalysis.
>
> (Blass and Carmeli, 2007, 35)

Between 2015 and 2020, neuropsychoanalysis was indicated as a keyword 84 times in various scientific journals. Only ten were psychoanalytic journals (not including "Neuropsychoanalysis" journal).

Another example is the notion of trauma. Psychoanalysts put trauma at the center of their thinking. The classical psychoanalytic theory of repression maintains that a patient who experiences amnesia following a traumatic event is dynamically repressing the memory of that event because it is intolerable. But Yovell et al. (2015) cite neuroscientific studies, according to which, during times of overwhelming fear, it is possible that declarative memories would not be *encoded* at all because a critical neural structure necessary for their formation, the hippocampus, can be partially or entirely shut down by the high levels of adrenal steroids. If this is true, as it probably is, it would mean that there is no repression, at least not in some cases.

Analysts from all schools could have greeted this finding as a precious gift. However, in all likelihood, many analysts do not know about it. I suspect that, if we were to tell analysts that traumatic events are not repressed because they were never encoded in memory, many of them would raise their eyebrows and react with apparent indifference. Many other essential findings from brain research relevant and highly significant are unknown to the psychoanalytic mainstream community.

How can rational people, devotees of Western culture with an education based on the scientific ethos, dismiss findings relevant to their work? Can the fact that mainstream analysts show so little interest in scientific research like brain research be logically explained?

Those who oppose neuropsychoanalysis usually tell us that it is not consistent with the specificity of psychoanalysis (Blass and Carmeli, 2007).

Those who try to explain why analysts dismiss these findings think that it is due to their arrogance, feelings of superiority, and indoctrination (Bornstein, 2002). But I believe such arguments will not take us very far. They do not reflect the way analysts perceive psychoanalytic knowledge, and they leave us a binary distinction between a community open to new knowledge (scientists) and a zealous and indoctrinated community (hard-core analysts).

I will attempt to answer this question from a different perspective: how established scientific communities resist change. My central thesis is that a) the resistance of mainstream psychoanalysis to neuropsychoanalysis is a private case of a much broader and documented phenomenon in the history of science when seemingly unassailable evidence is refused and called anomalous by a scientific community; b) only if we could "get into the heads", so to speak, of loyal orthodox analysts, understand their fears and suspicions, we would have a good chance to overcome their resistance and encourage the incorporation of relevant parts of neuropsychoanalysis into clinical work.

These have been good decades for neuropsychoanalysis, but there is now considerable evidence that the empirical findings that contributed so much to the field's current visibility are not being adequately attended to by mainstream psychoanalysis. To flourish, the field must grow, and to grow in a strong and enduring manner, it must have a greater impact and instigate a dramatic change in psychoanalytic theory. It cannot do it without understanding the deep reasons for the resistance to accept its findings.

I will show mainstream psychoanalysts have two worries: They experience difficulties in relying on findings that are not related to the clinical situation, and they find it challenging and even impossible to use findings that are not neatly tied to the all-encompassing psychoanalytic narratives that they believe in and use with their patients.

Fascinated and Troubled Analysts

I have written elsewhere (Govrin, 2016) that psychoanalysis has successfully embraced an amalgam of what I have chosen to term fascinated and troubled communities throughout its history. A *fascinated community* is a group that adopts a psychoanalytic theory (such as Bion's, Klein's, Winnicott's, or the like) to represent their worldview. A *troubled community* is not satisfied with the state of psychoanalytic knowledge and seeks to generate a fundamental change that does not square with existing traditions.[1]

One of the troubled communities is neuropsychoanalysis, which is a scientifically troubled community – a community that uses empirically based research to support psychoanalytic findings (the other two are new psychoanalytic schools and culturally, philosophically troubled communities).

Post-positivist philosophers of science, such as Larry Lauden, Thomas Kuhn, Imre Lakatos, and Yehuda Elkana, demonstrate using countless examples that what I term here as fascinated and troubled communities are quite common in the scientific world. A theory's survival depends upon a loyal community of followers who strongly believe in its truth and enthusiastically engage in its development. Once advanced, the theory will inevitably come under fire and be confronted by critics with its inadequacies, inherent contradictions, and lack of practical success. Sometimes, as a consequence of such objections, the idea is refuted and replaced by an alternative theory; in other instances, the theory advances and broadens its scope, becoming more vibrant and varied. The tension between the original set of ideas and the criticism leveled at it, between the loyal followers and the skeptics, occasionally triggers a change in the theory and cajoles its adherents to further develop and reinforce its intellectual depth. Thus, this tension is a source of dynamism and a key to survival. Thanks to it, the idea is not abandoned. However, the communities grouped around it, far from resting on their laurels, engage in updating it and preventing it from becoming obsolete or irrelevant. The tension, therefore, is a source of new creativity and innovation in the face of criticism, hatred, and scorn.

Part of the difficulty in convincing analysts of the relevance of brain research to psychoanalytic therapy is, thus, linked to the inherent tension between fascinated and troubled communities. As I will show, fascinated communities have their own sources of generating knowledge, and they are unwilling to combine these with novel methods of validation easily.

Resistance to Change in Science according to Post-Positivist Philosophy of Science

Beginning in the early 1960s, several new philosophies of science were developed as alternatives to positivism (Lauden et al., 1986). These contributions effectively terminated the hegemony of positivism by revealing its key doctrines (such as the cumulative of science, the reducibility of theoretical to observational language) to be radically at odds with the actual practice of science. Post-positivist philosophers of science developed models of scientific change and progress, which, they insisted, were based upon and supported by empirical study of the workings of actual science, as against the logical or philosophical ideals of epistemic warrant emphasized by the positivist tradition.

Change in science was a central question. The notion that scientific change was simply the result of a direct competition of facts was critically disputed (Makari, 2000). Philosophers such as Paul Feyerabend, Thomas Kuhn, and others posited that the traditional epistemological theories of philosophers of science had insufficient explanatory power to how science actually progress. Kuhn's perceived change in science fluctuates among relatively quiet non-progressive periods ("normal science") and periods of revolutionary break. The normal stages entailed the "group loyalties" of a "disciplinary matrix" to a "paradigm." These theoretical loyalties create a socially authorized agenda. For this reason, Kuhn's theory of scientific change could illuminate the frequent cases in the history of science when indisputable confirmation is rejected and called anomalous by a scientific community (Makari, 2000).

Many of the post-positivist philosophers have described resistance to change in various ways. In his account of revolutions in science, Cohen (1985) states:

> The desire to be an active part of a revolutionary movement is often in conflict with the natural reluctance of any scientist to jettison the set of accepted ideas on which he has made his way in the profession. New and revolutionary systems of science tend to be resisted rather than welcomed with open arms because every successful scientist has a vested intellectual, social, and even financial interest in maintaining the status quo.
>
> (35)

In *The Origins of Modern Science*, Herbert Butterfield argued, "The most difficult mental act of all is to rearrange a familiar bundle of data, to look at it differently and escape from prevailing doctrine" (106). He also writes that

> of all forms of mental activity, the most difficult to induce even in the minds of the young, who may be presumed not to have lost their flexibility, is the art of handling the same bundle of data as before but placing them in a new system of relations with one another by giving them a different framework.
>
> (13)

Throughout the course of their careers, scientists develop experimental skills, accumulate data, and formulate theories that

> enable them to perform their work, but, paradoxically, may constrain their ability to innovate. According to Kuhn (1962), there is nothing unusual about scientists' inability to reorient themselves to a newly emerging paradigm. Lifelong resistance, particularly from those whose productive careers have committed them to an older tradition of normal science, is not a violation of scientific standards but an index to the nature of scientific research itself.
>
> (151)

According to Laudan et al. (1986), here are some of the common themes that different post-positivist philosophies of science agree upon:

> The most important units for understanding scientific change are large-scale, relatively long-lived conceptual structures which different modelers refer to as

"paradigms," "global theories," "research programs" or "research traditions, and which, for neutrality, we term 'guiding assumptions.'"

(154)

Guiding assumptions, once accepted, are rarely, if ever, abandoned simply because they face empirical difficulties. They tend to endure despite negative experimental or observational tests. In short, negative evidence is less critical in assessing large-scale theories than is commonly thought. This conclusion is obviously at odds with the older Popperian insistence on the centrality of refutation and the commonsense assumption of most working scientists and historians that counterevidence strikes at the heart of any theoretical structure under test.

Data do not fully determine theory choice – i.e., observations and experiments do not provide a sufficient base for clear choices between sets of guiding assumptions or between rival theories. The technical machinery of confirmation theory and deductive logic has little to shed on theory appraisal. Theories are constantly confronted with apparent empirical difficulties and are never abandoned simply because of those difficulties. The solutions given to problems by a scientific theory are often recognized as approximate only when a new theory has replaced that theory.

How does change occur despite resistance? Lauden et al. (1986) discuss and summarize various accounts in post-positivist philosophy that answer this question:

Acceptance of a dominant set of guiding assumptions begins to break down when: persistent empirical difficulties arise (Kuhn); a few scientists sense that the prevailing guiding assumptions are no longer functioning adequately (are failing to predict novel phenomena) (Kuhn); scientists are prepared to leave the difficulties unresolved for years (Kuhn); scientists often refuse to change those assumptions (Kuhn and Lakatos); scientists ignore the difficulties as long as the guiding assumptions continue to anticipate novel phenomena successfully (Lakatos); scientists believe that those difficulties become grounds for rejecting the guiding assumptions only if they persistently resist solution (Kuhn, Lakatos); scientists often introduce hypotheses which are not testable in order to save the guiding assumptions (Lakatos). Any set of guiding assumptions can be made to appear empirically successful, so long as enough clever scientists work on it (Lakatos, Feyerabend).

Scientists usually switch from one set of guiding assumptions to a new set: within a decade or so of the recognition of acute empirical difficulties with the older set (Kuhn); with a few community members shifting at first and then increasing allegiance by all but a few elderly hold outs (Kuhn, Toulmin); because of the propaganda of the advocates of the new set, not for good reasons (Feyerabend).

According to Cohen (1985), four successive stages can be distinguished: the formulation of the new set of guiding assumptions by a small group; the commitment to those assumptions; the dissemination to the wider scientific world; and the conversion of a significant number of scientists (Cohen, 1985, 28–32) (17).

To sum up, the reluctance of analysts to endorse the findings of a neuropsychoanalysis is part of a broad and well-documented phenomenon in science. Any

comprehensive narratives on the growth of scientific paradigms and research traditions include many instances of resistance to scientific change even in the face
of compelling and robust evidence. Psychoanalysis, like science, is vulnerable to
all the peculiarities characteristic of any social activity: group bias, resistance to
change, and a tendency to ignore shortcomings. Any attempt to enhance the incorporation of neuropsychoanalysis within psychoanalysis should, therefore, consider
the rich literature of the post-positivist philosophy of science. This literature can
inform us of the reasons for this refusal. From that, we can explore ways that might
help mainstream analysts take neuropsychoanalysis into account in their clinical
thinking.

The Exclusivity of the Clinical Situation

Whether findings outside the clinical situation are relevant to clinical psychoanalysis has been controversial from the very outset. Freud showed ambivalence toward
scientific findings that did not stem from the clinical situation.

In 1934, Saul Rosenzweig, a Harvard-educated psychologist and psychotherapy
researcher, sent several reprints of experimental investigations of psychoanalytic
propositions to Sigmund Freud. On February 28, 1934, Freud (as cited in Shakow
and Rapaport, 1964, 129) replied:

> My dear Sir: I have examined your experimental studies for the verification of
> the psychoanalytic assertions with interest. I cannot put much value on these
> confirmations because the wealth of reliable observations on which these asser-
> tions rest make them independent of experimental verification. Still, it can do
> no harm. Sincerely yours, Freud (as cited in Shakow and Rapaport, 1964, 129).
> Still, in The Question of Lay Analysis, Freud (on the occasion of defending
> Theodore Reik) argued that origin is not a criterion for judging the current sta-
> tus of a discipline. The theory of electricity, he observed, had its beginnings in
> observations of nerve-muscle preparations, yet it I absurd today to regard it as
> a part of physiology, And, further, although radiology has a medical applica-
> tion, it is surely part of physics. In the course of these arguments Freud noted
> that, although in their treatment of patients all psychoanalysts must conform
> to the rules laid down for all therapies, psychoanalysis is nevertheless more
> than a therapy. He argued that an exclusive concentration on the therapy diverts
> attention from the scientific aspects of analysis and thus narrows its purview, its
> cadre, and its generativity. "I only want to feel assured that the therapy will not
> destroy the science;" he wrote. The true line of division is not between medical
> and applied psychoanalysis but] between *scientific* analysis and its *applications*
> alike in medical and nonmedical fields.

(Freud, 1926, 256–257)

According to Holzman (1985), This passage implies that separation needs to
be made among three arenas of psychoanalysis: those of therapy, of a source of

hypotheses, and of a collection of premises, generalizations, and commentaries on the human condition. To recognize the third of these arenas demands a fourth: a program of systematic confirmation and disconfirmation of those generalizations (1985, 726).

Likewise, Donald Spence (1993) represented an apparent position according to which psychoanalysis needs to base itself on extra clinical evidence if it aspires to be a serious science:

> We have no fundamental knowledge of underlying patterns and structures. We are at the same point as the medical establishment found itself at the turn of the century: we need to develop a basic science of psychoanalysis that can be used as a foundation for our clinical wisdom. When wisdom is turned into knowledge in this manner, it stands apart from the clinical moment. It carries a truth that is not conditioned by the specific needs of the patient and analyst in the midst of a particular clinical encounter. Just as medicine now rests on hundreds of chemical and biological facts that apply equally to all forms of life, so we need to ground psychoanalysis on a set of principles that go beyond the specific clinical happening.
>
> (131)

Still, mainstream psychoanalysis showed relatively indifferent to extra-clinical findings, which can be demonstrated by the limited space it occupies in both psychoanalytic training programs and journals. Furthermore, several prominent classical and relational analysts heavily criticized such tendencies (Blass and Carmeli, 2007; Green, 2000; Spezzano, 1993).

How can we understand such refusal that seems to be irrational and sources of knowledge? Yehuda Elkana's (1981) account of images of knowledge might help us understand this oddity as a perfectly rational phenomenon.

According to Elkana (1981), every scientific community shares socially determined views about knowledge (as opposed to views about nature or about society). Occasionally, several parallel sub-communities may hold differing or contradictory images of knowledge even within the same body of knowledge. Some images of knowledge are apparent and conscious; others are concealed and non-conscious. The ranking of the possible areas of research in their order of importance is also decided by socially determined criteria, thus settling what will and what will not be at the frontier of scientific research.

A very important aspect of each scientific community's images of knowledge are the sources of knowledge. These are the sources upon which a particular field of research is based. The theory itself does not decide upon the legitimate sources of knowledge; instead, such sources are determined by images of knowledge.

Sources of knowledge are hierarchically organized, and they range from those that have gained the broadest levels of acceptance within a large community to sources associated with smaller and more marginal communities, including sources linked to specific research institutes. These last images of knowledge hold sway for much shorter periods.

Among knowledge's multiple sources are experimentation, sensory experiences, clear and coherent ideas, tradition, authority, discovery, innovation, beauty, intuition, and analogy.

From this, it transpires that the main difference between mainstream analysts and the neuropsychoanalytic community is found in their sources of knowledge. Whereas the neuropsychoanalytic community believes that a non-analytic source such as neuroscience is relevant to psychoanalytic knowledge, the mainstream communities almost always rely solely on the clinical situation. I wrote "almost always" because, in the beginning, when psychoanalytic theory was first construed, it allows the originators of the various schools to use non-analytic sources on which to base their approach. Thus, at first, Freud's "project" was to create a scientifically based psychology that would enable him to develop a theory of the brain's functioning by applying a quantitative method. He termed this approach "psychology for neurologists," through which he wanted to show how the psychic machine works, how it responds to stimuli, controls, and emits them. Freud's mechanical images and his technical vocabulary – "neurons," "quantity," "biological principles of attention and protection" constituted the language used in Freud's world in his medical studies (Freud, 1895/1950). Freud merged these terms in his attempt to establish psychology as one of the natural sciences basing it on neurology's sound foundation. Arguments linked to brain research also appeared in the controversies during the 1940s in the British psychoanalytic society between Melanie Klein supporters and Anna Freud supporters (King and Steiner, 1991).

However, Sigmund Freud was by no means the only one who used non–analytic sources to develop his thinking. It was also done by Melanie Klein, Donald Winnicott, Anna Freud, and even Jacques Lacan, all of whom were influenced by observations of infant development. The dependence of thinkers on non-analytic disciplines was more critical in the first stage of the theory's development than in later stages by which time the theory had already been institutionalized and completed (Steiner, 2000). The fresh conceptualizations that began accumulating in the minds of the canonical thinkers on developmental psychology and transference relations require every possible assistance in being broadened and further developed. However, they became independent once the theories had been consolidated and stood on firm clinical ground. From then on, they are treated as real entities, and the sources that nurtured them in the past are no longer required.

To conclude this point, the vast majority of psychoanalytic theories did not emerge from either the laboratory or any other form of controlled experimentation. Most psychoanalytic theories were the product of just one source of knowledge: the clinical situation, the most common and accepted source of knowledge for mainstream communities. The knowledge gained in the clinic was passed on to community members through written case histories. Every one of Freud's major conceptualizations – which, for many years after his death, constituted the infrastructure of psychoanalytic knowledge – were derived from the clinical situation; the Oedipus complex, castration anxiety, his theory of the unconscious as well as the topographic structure of the mind – all were founded on knowledge deduced from clinical material (for details of Freud's investigative methods see, Hinshel-wood, 2013, 73–77).

Many analysts believe that the clinical setting is the only real place from which psychoanalysis can really derive its knowledge about psychic reality. This reality is only accessible through the free associations and interpretation of the patient and the analyst (Steiner, 2000).

It's almost impossible to convince a scientist (or an analyst) to change his or her images of knowledge (or sources of knowledge). The sources of knowledge are not determined in a calculated or planned way. They are more comparable to moral positions, emanating from intuitions, gut feelings, emotions. Like ethical stands, they are often immutable and non-negotiable. For example, those who oppose abortions are incapable of persuading supporters of abortion to change their minds. Since rational arguments do not determine the ethical stance, such evidence will not change it. A therapist belonging to the movement that believes in empirically supported treatments (EST) will never be convinced that descriptions of cases are a reliable source of knowledge in psychotherapy. A psychoanalyst will never be convinced that knowledge of a person's psyche must be based on empirical research. The discourse between them resembles a dialogue of the deaf. Images of knowledge and sources of knowledge are determined by different factors such as education, training, the therapeutic orientation of the therapist/supervisee, and so on. For example, many analysts inclined toward neuropsychoanalysis studied neuroscience early in their training and fell in love with the subject. This is exemplified by Mortimer Ostow (Turnbull, 2004), a New York psychoanalyst, psychiatrist, neurologist, and one of the founders of neuropsychoanalysis. Here is how Mortimer relates to his choice to integrate the domains:

> I was interested in the relationship to start with. It was not something I came to. As you saw, I was focusing on it from both directions, spontaneously. And then came applied neuroscience, in the form of psychopharmacology, so that was just a natural for me. And my analyst, Hermann Nunberg, who was a very distinguished analyst and a student of Freud's, encouraged me. And he encouraged my neurophysiologic fantasies at the time.
>
> (210)

Apart from the clinical situation, Ostow's relevant sources of knowledge also include neuroscience. His choice was not necessarily due only to a rational, ordered thought or an investigation of various sources of knowledge. His studies and close connection with his supervisors (Lawrence Kubie) are clear. Rationality and argumentation have a role in questioning psychoanalytic methods and sources of knowledge and revealing its limitations. However, the process of engaging with a psychotherapeutic school (and its images and sources of knowledge) is heavily influenced by one's own therapists and supervisors. Katz et al. (2012) found that personal therapist/psychoanalyst, supervisory experiences had an enormous influence on the decision to pursue psychoanalytic training and particular school.

Many fascinated analysts were part of psychoanalytic training institutes. Their supervisors and analysts believed in a close link between therapeutic work and knowledge creation. They considered a therapeutic case to be a kind of small laboratory from which knowledge about treatment, psychopathology, and development emerges. Non-analytic sources may interest them, but such sources do not rank highly in their hierarchy of sources of knowledge, even if they are empirically based and are founded on accepted research methods. From this point of view, fascinated analysts are no different from any other scientific community. As is the case for all scientists, their hierarchy of sources of knowledge is determined by education, training, and emotional ties to people they know who supervised and analyzed them, shaping their therapeutic world.

Psychoanalytic Narratives

There is yet another essential reason for the indifference of fascinated analysts toward brain research findings – a compelling narrative that fascinates them and which they use in their clinical work.

Spence (1983) spoke a great deal about the enormous rhetorical influence that the psychoanalytic narrative exerted over the patient – but it is also important to note the power that this narrative has over the therapist. Psychoanalytic narratives are astonishingly productive. They can create meaning for infinite clinical phenomena, and the analysts who learn to use them are exceptionally skilled in finding a hidden thematic link between the adult patient and his early experiences.

A rich, complex, and overarching narrative is available to the analyst. This overarching narrative offers a coherent scene in the form of a story that unfolds over time. The overriding narrative's central hero is the human infant and his complex storyline. It is a narrative that makes sense of the experiences the infants have with their self and their immediate environment as they mature; in other words, as they turn into adult patient. In the course of doing so, the infant passes through different and significant developmental turning points: the Oedipus complex, the good breast, and the bad breast, the transitional object, or the empathetic failure are phases central to the plot. The overarching narrative of each school endows the therapist with endless story-telling options to gain an understanding of the patient. This narrative directs the therapist's listening, determines what is central and marginal to the conversation, helps him to decide between different interventions, and even defines the objectives of the ultimately chosen treatment. At the same time, a psychoanalytic narrative also limits the range of possible interpretations because it confines them to a single, coherent plot.

The overarching narrative (conceivably more than one) that the analyst follows is rich, nuanced, overly complex, highly detailed, and offers many options for giving meaning to clinical material. In the face of this richness, it's hard to see how a strong desire for non-psychoanalytical finding might evolve within the therapist's minds.

The overarching narrative creates in the analyst a sense of coherent wholeness. The analyst had become used to thinking – an idea supported by experience – that all the spaces and gaps, the contradictions and complexities, in the patient's life could be dealt with by one theory or by several closely related theories. A fascinated analyst can live through an entire professional life without feeling, even once, that he needs anything other than the psychoanalytic formulations with which he or she is so familiar. The analyst derives pleasure from the game of psychoanalytic possibilities, interpretations, language games, and the abundance of options it offers. Furthermore, the narrative itself might have a therapeutic effect. Many believe (see Hinshelwood, 2013) that the rationale for psychoanalytic treatment is to help the patient create a more coherent, meaningful narrative of their lives and that the aim of knowledge-generation should be converted to meaning-generation (80).

One can regard psychoanalytic narratives as a genre with its own rules and one that does not readily integrate many additions inconsistent with the narrative's essential storyline. This is somewhat like writing a screenplay for a James Bond film. James Bond novels and movies are an admixture of realism and science fiction and are frequently shot in spectacular locations worldwide allowing for infinite number of possible plots. At the same time, the Bond movies represent a certain genre that imposes a limitation on the screenwriters. It is hard to imagine that they could incorporate a text from Shakespeare, Byron, or a children's cartoon into the screenplay.

Many analysts do not take an interest in neuropsychoanalysis because such research is not an integral part of the main narrative they use; rather, it is an alien component to the understanding of the patient in precisely the same way that a Greek tragedy is alien to a James Bond plot.

Therapeutic failures do not cause the therapist to feel dissatisfied with the theory he is using. The narrative already contains the possibility of failure, which means that the narrative explains the failure itself. Furthermore, the narrative suggests numerous ways to take action in the case of an impasse or failure. When therapists are overcome by confusion and uncertainty in those many cases where they do not understand some facets of their patients, they will tend to look for answers in the overarching narrative they believe in. If the therapist is still dissatisfied with the ongoing process, he or she is likely to turn to a supervisor who works with a similar narrative.

It is conceivable that therapeutic failures will lead the therapist to conclude that a minority of patients do not respond well to his method or that, for various reasons, he erred in implementing the method's principles (Govrin, 2016).

So, even failures will not lead most analysts to look for answers elsewhere.

Let me demonstrate this point by referring again to the neuroscientific data that can fail to be encoded in declarative form under certain stressful conditions. Yovell et al. (2015) demonstrate the relevance of neuroscience to clinical analytic practice by bringing up the case of Ms. A.

Ms. A, they write, was repeatedly abused as a child by the adolescent son of friends of the family. During the first year in therapy, "she communicated isolated memory fragments" (1532) of this to the therapist. Her mother and the mother of the adolescent boy denied that abuse took place; her brother remembered that there was abuse but was unsure of the details. Ms. A herself was in doubt regarding the integrity of her account, at times blaming herself for making up a story to excuse her difficulties with men. Ms. A affirmed her belief that if the events happened, she would have been able to recall them in detail. Yovell, Solms, and Fotopoulou then provide the following very crucial few lines:

> Indeed, after a few weeks in treatment, she revealed that one of her main reasons for entering psychoanalytic therapy was her hope and expectation that more detailed and complete memories of the events would emerge, concomitant with the lifting of her repression in the course of the treatment. Should this not occur, she would be inclined to believe that the abuse never took place. She felt that it was essential for her to know what had actually happened to her, and was not prepared to accept the view that how she remembered and understood her past, and what meanings she ascribed to it and the vicissitudes of her relationship with the analyst, were just as important as finding out whether she had actually been abused. She stressed that a lot lay in the balance for her – on an interpersonal level, her relationship with her mother, who flatly denied the abuse, and on an intrapsychic level, her extremely negative view of herself as someone who propagates false accusations to explain and justify her emotional difficulties. Ms. A expected psychotherapy to provide her with keys to her missing memories, which, she believed, might still lie within her, waiting to emerge. No new memories of her past emerged during her first two years in treatment, and Ms. A saw this as growing proof of the fallacy of her accusations of abuse, and as evidence of her inherent "badness."
>
> (1532)

Neuroscience shows that, conceivably, the patient's failure to remember is not the result of dynamic unconscious reasons at all, just biological ones. The analyst can relieve the patient's distress by informing her of this. Yovell et al. note that:

> Telling her that she *might* never be able to remember her abuse, although she is still affected by it, and explaining to her why this might be the case, as Ms. A's analyst ultimately did, relieved her anxiety and sense of shame and guilt to a significant degree. More importantly, it freed her and the analyst to pursue the complicated task of coming to terms with her damaged internal past so that she could stop repeating it.
>
> (Yovell et al., 2015, 1537)

But, this intervention cannot be combined with any one of the essential narratives believed in by psychoanalysts. To use such a response, analysts would be forced to stray from their own narratives and be assisted by a narrative external to it. So, for example, the narrative of many analysts does not accept the idea of calming the patient through information, however useful it may be. Thus, for example, a Bionian therapist can work with a therapist based on the absence of knowledge being something absolute in life and accordingly change her view so that she accepts her "not knowing." A therapist in self-psychology can validate her feelings toward the event rely on her fragmented memories and view them as valid. A Kleinian therapist can regard her fragmented memories as a powerful phantasy in the patient's life and lessen the importance of the actual event. In all these cases, it would be challenging to incorporate external neuropsychoanalytic intervention.

It is important to note that even if a psychoanalyst seriously takes neuropsychoanalysis findings, he might not know how to use it. In the case of trauma, it might be easier: The analyst will not expect to recover an explicit memory and will focus more on the difficulties processing experience when traumatic emotional memories are involuntarily evoked. However, it might be more difficult to work with in other neuroscience research, such as repression or dreams or the structure of the id.

To conclude, a narrative is a very productive tool for many analysts. However, it might restrict many alternatives and possibilities to generate meaning that does not fall within the narrative's coherence, especially from extra-clinical sources. Therefore, it is less susceptible to external influences.

An Outline of a Solution

Considering these two obstacles, how can neuropsychoanalysis have more influence on fascinated analysts and become even more prominent in the field of psychoanalysis?

One possibility is that the neuropsychoanalytic community keeps doing what it already does. In 2019, neuropsychoanalysis celebrated the 20th annual Congress of the International Neuropsychoanalysis Society. The highly creative community has established a substantial international presence with local chapters in many countries. It is active and vibrant, publishes a journal, and conducts annual conferences. It maintains regional groups that have been studying neuroscience and psychoanalysis for several decades and are very productive. It has undoubtedly stamped its mark on the map! From this perspective, it does not need the recognition of hard-core analysts. It is well established and can continue to follow its independent path.

However, if the neuropsychoanalytic community does want to exert a more significant influence on the psychoanalytic community, it needs to engage with loyal analysts. To be successful in this mission, the community has to be minded of several things:

> Firstly, fascinated analysts are most unlikely, to say the least, to change their ranking of sources of knowledge. I doubt if experienced fascinated analysts will ever regard brain research as an essential source for their narratives. It is better to lower expectations than to fight à lost battle.
>
> Second, I recommend that neuropsychoanalysts should demonstrate the relevancy of neuropsychoanalysis to analysts' narratives. Let me give you an example.

William Singletary (2015) wrote a highly informative paper in the journal neuropsychoanalysis about ASD. His account provided a context for his model of allostatic overload as a central drive in the disorder. He included psychoanalytic theories that take the inner mental experience of the autistic child seriously.

A year later, Ann Alvarez (2016) commented on the paper. Although Ann Alvarez is a devoted psychoanalyst, she also likes to integrate psychoanalytic theory with new findings in infant development and infant psychiatry. This is what she wrote about William Singletary's account:

> What a relief and even thrill it is to see someone tackling the probable complexity both of the etiology of autism and of the types of treatment needed to address the condition. I have often wondered if the psychoanalytic theory could ever catch up with either the complexity addressed by the great clinician/thinkers in the field and whether it could ever match the complexity with which our medical colleagues try to teach us about molecular, cellular, and physiological processes in the body. Our simple model of defenses against fear or pain can sometimes seem terribly one-dimensional, even when used in the context of object-relations theory.
>
> (3)

As can be seen, she has engaged with Singletary's findings, and if one reads her commentary, it is evident that neuroscience's findings inspired her concerning autism. Now, Alvarez is an exceptionally open-minded analyst. Hopefully, this can be followed by other analysts who are closed-locked within their respective narratives to become similarly engaged with such findings. This is why I think Singletary's testimony is such a brilliant example. First of all, his account is about a clinical phenomenon – autism. Autism is not a psychoanalytic word; it is a clinical syndrome independent of a specific theory. But psychoanalysis has a lot to say about autism, as, indeed, does neuroscience. And so, while acknowledging some psychoanalytic insights as necessary, neuroscience can add something that analysts need to know. The new information is added, and Alvarez can now use it with her patients incorporate it into her narrative, which is what she has done.

So, I think the best thing for neuropsychoanalysis to do is to engage experienced loyal analysts with their findings. Perhaps it would be helpful to establish an ongoing study group with leaders from both fields to consider the creation of new psychoanalytic theories that would be consistent with discoveries in neuroscience.

There is yet another community like neuropsychoanalysis that has ound another source of knowledge for psychoanalysis – infant research. They often ask hard-core analysts to write chapters in their books commenting on infant research findings and to write how infant research helped them in their work (Beebe et al., 2005).

Engaging analysts with the findings of brain research will not only provide clinicians with new ways of thinking about clinical psychoanalysis but also let them make a unique blend from the findings. Let the key figures themselves work on the findings and find the relevancy of brain research to their narratives. It will not be easy. It will probably be confronted with a great deal of resistance. Still, I think the key is finding clinical phenomena at the center of psychoanalytic clinical work, like autism, trauma, borderline patients, psychosis. These are all practical diagnostic fields (as opposed to more theoretical fields about mental structures or various functions). The neuropsychoanalysis community has already done a significant job in these areas.

At the same time, one must admit that Ann Alverez's approach, characterized by an openness to non–analytic sources of knowledge and an awareness of the shortcomings of the psychoanalytic approach, does not typify the community of experienced analysts. Therefore, yet another way to make neuropsychoanalysis more influential is to focus on the training of the up-and-coming younger generation. Everyone for whom neuropsychoanalysis is important must admit that the battle over the current generation of mainstream analysts has not been successful. Most of the old generation of psychoanalysts now are not medically trained and need refresher courses in neurology to absorb and understand neuropsychoanalytic data. But, within the younger generation, through education, special courses, and training, there is a chance that brain research will become relevant for the therapeutic work of those at the beginning of their way. Young therapists starting their university studies arrive with a healthy dose of skepticism, criticism, and open-mindedness. They do not yet have much experience in their work based on one particular theory, and they consider no single approach to be self-evident. Brain research fascinates them, and they are thirsty for external validation of the psychoanalytic theory. The objective of the training of these therapists will also be to develop a powerful curiosity about the workings of the human brain. The supervision has to combine clinical psychoanalytic knowledge with neurological knowledge so that the knowledge gained from brain research will be relevant to understanding clinical knowledge.

The hope must be that such instruction will lead to a new generation of therapists who, alongside their enthusiasm for and devotion to the psychodynamic approach, will also be involved in neuropsychoanalysis. Only a massive effort of supervision and clinical courses by the neuropsychoanalytic community can develop a new generation of analysts who combine brain research alongside their fascination with psychoanalytic theory.

Conclusion

This chapter shows that positivism is not just an external philosophy. It expresses a human psychological need to find evidence for the conceptualizations we believe in through objective research. The great success of neuropsychoanalysis expresses, first of all, a response to this need. If psychoanalysis is inextricably linked to the forefront of brain research, it connects it to one of the most prestigious fields of science and raises its prestige and value. Many psychodynamic psychotherapists feel they are standing on solid ground if the therapy they believe can be incorporated with brain research. Most importantly, it interests them and helps them to be sensitive to their patients in aspects to which neuropsychoanalysis is relevant.

However, most of the psychoanalytic community does not share the yearning to connect science and psychoanalysis. Most psychodynamic therapists simply do not need scientific evidence to know what they already know from their training from their patients, colleagues, and professional literature. It is nice to know that brain research has revealed what one already knows and what one has always believed. Nice, but not required.

The best chance for neuropsychoanalysis to be incorporated within psychoanalysis, including the orthodox one, is through clinical problem-solving. A clinical problem is anything intriguing and unusual about humans without satisfactory explanations in existing theories, such as dreams. Psychoanalysis has specialized precisely in solving clinical problems and does it better than any other theory. The next chapter on innovations in psychoanalysis will be devoted to how psychoanalysis innovates exciting and groundbreaking new explanations. Also, how did analysts make innovations in the past, and how do they innovate today?

Note

1 To read more about the reasons of why analysts become fascinated or troubled with their psychoanalytic theories, see Govrin, ch. 1, 14–37, 2016.

References

Alvarez, A. (2016). Impaired Interactions Triggering Defense or Exposing Deficit: Exploring the Difference between the Withdrawn and the "Undrawn" Autistic Child. Commentary on "An Integrative Model of Autism Spectrum Disorder: ASD as a Neurobiological Disorder of Experienced Environmental Deprivation, Early Life Stress, and Allostatic Overload" by William M. Singletary, M.D. *Neuro-Psychoanalysis*, 18(1), 3–7.

Axmacher, N. and Heinemann, A. (2012). Toward a Neural Understanding of Emotional Oscillation and Affect Regulation: Investigating the Dynamic Unconscious and Transference. An Interdisciplinary Study. *Neuro-Psychoanalysis*, 14(2), 141–155.

Beebe, B., Knoblauch, S., Rustin, J. and Sorter, D. (Eds.) (2005). *Forms of Intersubjectivity in Infant Research and Adult Treatment*. New York: Other Press.

Blass, R.B. and Carmeli, Z. (2007). The Case Against Neuropsychoanalysis. *The International Journal of Psychoanalysis*, 88(1), 19–40.

Bornstein, R.F. (2002). The Impending Death of Psychoanalysis. *Psychoanalytic Psychology*, 19(3), 580–590.

Clarke, B.H. (2018). A Cat is Not a Battleship: Thoughts on the Meaning of "Neuropsychoanalysis". *International Journal of Psychoanalysis*, 99, 425–449.

Cohen, I.B. (1985). *Revolution in Science*. Cambridge, MA: Harvard University Press.

Elkana, Y. (1981). A Programmatic Attempt at an Anthropology of Science. In E. Mendelson and Y. Elkana (Eds.) *Science and Cultures*. Dordrecht, Germany: Reidel, 1–76.

Freud, S. (1920). Beyond the Pleasure Principle. *Standard Edition*, 18, 7–64.

Freud, S. (1926). The Question of Law Analysis. Conversations with an Impartial Person. *Standard Edition*, 20.

Freud, S. (1950). Project for a Scientific Psychology (1895). In J. Strachey (Ed. and trans.) *The Standard Edition of the Complete Psychological Works of Sigmund Freud*. Vol. 1. London: Hogarth Press, 281–391.

Govrin, A. (2016). *Conservative and Radical Perspectives on Psychoanalytic Knowledge: The Fascinated and the Disenchanted*. London: Routledge.

Green, A. (2000). "Science and Science Fiction in Infant Research" in Clinical and Observational Psychoanalytic Research: Roots of a Controversy. In J. Sandler and R. Davies (Eds.) *Clinical and Observational Psychoanalytic Research: Roots of a Controversy*. Madison, CT: International Universities Press, 41–72.

Hinshelwood, R.D. (2013). *Research on the Couch – Single-Case Studies, Subjectivity and Psychoanalytic Knowledge*. London: Routledge.

Holzman, P.S. (1985). Psychoanalysis: Is the Therapy Destroying the Science. *Journal of the American Psychoanalytic*, 33, 725–770.

Katz, D.A., Kaplan, M. and Stromberg, S.E. (2012). A National Survey of Candidates: II. Motivations, Obstacles, and Ideas on Increasing Interest in Psychoanalytic Training. *Journal of the American Psychoanalytic Association*, 60(5), 1015–1055.

Kessler, L. (2013). Conscious Id or Unconscious Id or Both: An Attempt at "Self"-Help. *Neuro-Psychoanalysis*, 15(1), 48–51.

King, P. and Steiner, R. (1991). *The Freud-Klein Controversies 1941–1945*. London, UK: Tavistock/Routledge.

Kuhn, T.S. (1962). *The Structure of Scientific Revolutions*. Chicago: University of Chicago Press.

Laudan, L., Donovan, A., Laudan, R., Barker, P., Brown, B., Leplin, J., Thagard, P. and Wykstra, S. (1986). Scientific Change: Philosophical Models and Historical Research. *Synthese*, 69(2), 141–223. Testing Theories of Scientific Change (November 1986).

Makari, G.J. (2000). Change in Psychoanalysis. In J. Sandler, R. Michels and P. Fonagy (Eds.) *Changing Ideas in a Changing World: The Revolution in Psychoanalysis. Essays in Honour of Arnold Cooper*. London: Karnac, 255–262.

Panksepp, J. (2013). Toward an Understanding of the Constitution of Consciousness through the Laws of Affect. *Neuro-Psychoanalysis*, 15(1), 62–65.

Saporta, J. (2003). Synthesizing Psychoanalytic and Biological Approaches to Trauma. *Neuro-Psychoanalysis*, 5(1), 97–110.

Shakow, D. and Rapaport, D. (1964). The Influence of Freud on American Psychology. *Psychological Issues, Monograph*, 13.

Singletary, W.M. (2015). An Integrative Model of Autism Spectrum Disorder: ASD as a Neurobiological Disorder of Experienced Environmental Deprivation, Early Life Stress and Allostatic Overload. *Neuro-Psychoanalysis*, 17(2), 81–119.

Solms, M. (1997). *The Neuropsychology of Dreams: A Clinic-anatomical Study*. Mahwah, NJ: Erlbaum.

Solms, M. (2002). An Introduction to the Neuroscientific Works of Sigmund Freud. In G. van de Vijver and F. Geerardyn (Eds.) *The Pre-Psychoanalytic Writings of Sigmund Freud*. London: Karnac.

Solms, M. (2013). The Conscious Id. *Neuro-Psychoanalysis*, 15(1), 5–19.

Solms, M. and Saling, M. (1986). On Psychoanalysis and Neuroscience: Freud's Attitude to the Localizationist Tradition. *International Journal of Psychoanalysis*, 67, 397–416.

Solms, M. and Turnbull, O.H. (2015). Chapter 1: What is Neuropsychoanalysis? In M. Solms (Ed.) *The Feeling Brain – Selected Papers on Neuropsychoanalysis*. London: Routledge, 13–34.

Spence, D.P. (1983). Narrative Persuasion. *Psychoanalysis and Contemporary Thought*, 6(3), 457–481.

Spence, D.P. (1993). Discussion: New Understandings of Psychoanalytic Process. *The American Psychoanalytic*, 41S(Supplement), 131–141.

Spezzano, C. (1993). A Relational Model of Inquiry and Truth: The Place of Psychoanalysis in Human Conversation. *Psychoanalytic Dialogues*, 3(2), 177–208.

Steiner, R. (2000). Introduction. In J. Sandler, A. Sandler and R. Davies (Eds.) *Clinical and Observational Psychoanalytic Research: Roots of a Controversy*. Madison, CT: International Universities Press, 1–20.

Sulloway, F.J. (1979). *Freud: Biologist of the Mind. Beyond the Psychoanalytic Legend*. London: Burnett Books.

Turnbull, O. (2004). Founders of Neuro-Psychoanalysis. *Neuro-Psychoanalysis*, 6(2), 209–216.

Westen, D. and Gabbard, G.O. (2002). Development in Cognitive Neuroscience: I. Conflict, Compromise and Connectionism. *Journal of the American Psychoanalytic Association*, 50, 53–98.

Yadlin-Gadot, S. (2017). Truth Axes and the Transformation of Self. *Psychoanalytic Review*, 104, 163–201.

Yovell, Y. (2000). From Hysteria to Posttraumatic Stress Disorder: Psychoanalysis and the Neurobiology of Traumatic Memories. *Neuro-Psychoanalysis*, 2, 171–81.

Yovell, Y., Solms, M. and Fotopoulou, A. (2015). The Case for Neuropsychoanalysis: Why a Dialogue with Neuroscience is Necessary but Not Sufficient for Psychoanalysis. *The International Journal of Psychoanalysis*, 96(6), 1515–1555.

Chapter 7

Facts and Sensibilities

What Is a Psychoanalytic Innovation?

From the previous chapters, the reader can get the false impression that analysts read philosophy books before deciding what to write and how to innovate. However, the truth is far from it. Most analysts have no background or training in philosophy. Philosophy is always in the background. Philosophy influences the images of knowledge of the period. According to Elkana (1981), images of knowledge are socially determined views about knowledge (as opposed to views about nature or society). These ideas touch on questions such as the validation concept of each theory. As we have seen in the book's first part, classical psychoanalysts believed that the psychoanalytic theory corresponds to the psychic reality in the world. In contrast, relational and intersubjective analysts are much less inclined to accept this fact.

However, psychoanalysis is not just about incorporating philosophies or adapting to contemporary images of knowledge. Its primary motivation is to solve clinical problems and conceptualize human phenomena using psychoanalytic tools. Social, cultural, and political changes also lead to new human phenomena that must be conceptualized using psychoanalytic accounts. Hysteria and neurosis became less common and were replaced by eating disorders, disorders of the self, loneliness, and self-alienation that characterize the technological age. This chapter complements the previous chapters by trying to define what a psychoanalytic innovation is. The development of psychoanalytic theory is described not as being influenced by philosophy but as trying to conceptualize a new phenomenon with new tools and, at the same time, remain faithful to the core of psychoanalytic theory.

This chapter explores what it means to innovate psychoanalytically.

Psychoanalytic innovation is easy to recognize but difficult to define. There is a dearth of literature exploring the nature of innovation in our field. My central thesis is that psychoanalytic innovation can be of two types. Psychoanalytic innovation of the first order concerns discoveries concerning facts related to the psyche, development, transference relations, or psychopathology. It usually emerges as a development of insights from canonical psychoanalytic theory; offers an original explanation for a choice of empirical psychic phenomena hitherto unexamined; is perceived as creative and useful when it succeeds in reconceptualizing the relations between the patient's past, unconscious dynamics, and the transference relations;

DOI: 10.4324/9781003498162-11

often resembles poetic expression; and registers a truth we knew but did not yet put into words. When it is of the second order, psychoanalytic innovation challenges either methodological or philosophical assumptions held by psychoanalysis without pretending to replace existing theories. It constitutes a "sensibility" that its adherents strive to incorporate into the existing corpus. I distinguish between two types of sensibilities: cultural-philosophical sensibility, represented by the relational approach and methodological sensibility represented by infant research and neuropsychoanalysis. In the last part of the paper, I analyze psychoanalytic progress, pointing to its merits and shortcomings.

The Problem

Does psychoanalysis progress? And, if so, what does progress mean in our field? Can we find regularities in the last decades of this progress?

Understanding innovation in our field is challenging. On the one hand, psychoanalysis is in constant flux: Those who currently understand their patients according to Freud's original topographic and structural model are few and far between; members of the professional communities inspired by Klein or Kohut do not work the same way as their predecessors. Even our understanding of fundamental psychoanalytic concepts such as the unconscious, interpretation, object relations, transference, and countertransference has grown extremely varied.

On the other hand, the past remains highly influential: The 20th century's grand theories are more dominant than any current development. No new school of thinking, including a novel developmental theory, therapy, or psychopathology, has emerged since the 1980s (for definition of a psychoanalytic school, see Govrin, 2006). Most current innovations are reinterpretations of old canonical texts.

The most-read and -cited papers are written by psychoanalysts who are no longer alive. Psychoanalysts representing different approaches continue to work in a way that does not stray far from Freud's method: Together with the patient, they create a narrative hinging on the latter's early development and transference relations. It is, therefore, practically impossible to distinguish between old and new.

First-Order and Second-Order Questions

Freud represents the **Golden Age** of psychoanalysis. During this period, the infrastructure of mental life is formed, including its structure, the conflictual dynamics that activate it, the relations between different mental structures within the psyche, sexual development, and much more. Here were the great and exciting discoveries of the unconscious, the topographic model, the psychosexual theory of sexuality, the interpretation of dreams, the etiology of mental disorders, and the importance of transference relationships. Freud the Conqueror discovered an entire continent. Everywhere he goes, he sticks a peg. But he cannot encompass this mighty continent alone. Freud sets psychoanalysis on three axes: development, psychopathology, and treatment. These three axes will become the basis of the psychoanalytic canon.

After Freud died in 1939 and until the late 1970s, a period began that I call The **Silver Age**. In these 40 years, the post-Freud psychoanalytic canon was formed. During these years, all psychoanalytic schools of thought were created: Klein Kernberg, Mahler, Horny, Masterson, Kohut, Winnicott, Lacan, and others (several of these thinkers already operating in Freud's time). All these schools of thought begin with clinical questions that occupy the founder. Each founder points to a group of phenomena he or she feels other theories do not address appropriately.

In 40 years, psychoanalysis has produced new and exciting maps of the human psyche with dazzling speed. Behind most founders grow fascinated psychoanalytic communities or schools that continue to develop the theory after the founder's death. Communities are characterized by one conception of truth and indoctrination.

The 40 years after Freud's death were the most creative period. Here, the most critical conceptualizations developed and the most significant texts written.

Psychoanalysis has never experienced, nor will it ever since, made such spectacular, prodigious, and creative progress as it did in those 40 years. All this great deed is the fruit of the work of only one generation.

During the Silver Age, there is no declared change in philosophical assumptions. Clinical practice is revolutionary and boiling with debate, but the methodological foundation stays positivist and orthodox: It relies on clinical psychoanalytic observation to develop and construct psychoanalytic theory. The prevailing truth is correspondence with reality and naïve realism. The therapist is the authority; the distinction between subject and object remains in place, and developmental theories and psychic structures are considered mental realities rather than useful metaphors.

In this domain, debates are like those between scientists: Are the assumptions underlying the innovation valid, or can they be refuted?

The arrival of postmodernism signals a breaking point and ushers in the third era. In the 1980s, self-psychology is the last major psychoanalytic school, or Grand theory, a mega narrative encompassing all mental phenomena.

From this point onward, there are two types of questions that analysts deal with second and first order. The already existing schools of Lacan, Bion, Klein, and Winnicott continue to find explanations to first-order questions. They develop within the existing schools the meaning of psychic phenomena such as envy, anxiety, sexuality, the unconscious, psychopathology, and transference phenomena (for a description of innovations of each school, see Govrin and Mills, 2019).

Second-order claims are made about knowledge itself. If psychic phenomena involve first-order empirical questions about the substantive entities of the "mental," second-order questions concern the internal consistency, the methodology, or the epistemology on which first-order questions rely (Laudan, 1977). Why there are slips of the tongue is a first-order empirical question and the "fact" that it reveals an unconscious thought is a first-order explanation. However, what is the best way to validate our explanation about slips of the tongue is a second-order question. Note that the first-order question, such as "Why are there slips of the tongue?" is independent of its explanation. It does not need to be phrased in psychoanalytic jargon. It is inseparable from Freud's repression theory, and therefore, it is not theory-laden. The importance of the difference between first-order questions and theories (explanations) that attempt to solve them will be elaborated later (Laudan, 1977, 139–146).

During the last decade, a few psychoanalytic communities have incorporated other fields of knowledge to create new sensibilities that deal with second-order questions. There are two kinds of sensibilities: Methodological sensibilities, which are scientifically oriented and present a new source of information and methodology. There are at least two methodological sensibilities: Neuropsychoanalysis derives from brain research and infant research that incorporates findings from infant studies to the psychoanalytic encounter (mentalization-based therapy is also a methodological sensibility). The other type is a cultural-philosophical sensibility. It is influenced by changes in society, culture, and philosophy. It adapts psychoanalysis to the changing world. Since the 1990s, this sensibility can be observed in the relational approach, which was inspired by postmodernism, contemporary feminist thinking, and intersubjectivity. Neither of the three sensibilities is meant to be new psychoanalytic schools or alternative psychoanalytic theories. Nevertheless, they want analysts to be sensitive to aspects of the psychoanalytic encounter that they argue were overlooked. Of the three sensibilities, the relational approach was the most influential, with thousands of practitioners joining and establishing a worldwide organization that supported a transformation in how analysts perceive the analytic encounter and the analyst's subjectivity.

In this paper, I investigate innovations in first- and second-order questions. But let us begin with some preliminary remarks.

I discuss psychoanalysis in general, even though it is far from being monolithic (English-speaking psychoanalysis is quite different from French or Latin-American psychoanalysis, not to speak about the variety of schools – Freudians, Lacanians, Millerians, Winnicottians, Kleinians, Jungians, etc.). However, discussing the innovative aspects of each of these branches would require another paper. This paper does not present a historical description of innovations in psychoanalysis. Its focus is instead on particular revolutionary developments to illuminate what novelty in psychoanalysis involves.

Theoretical Innovations in Psychoanalysis

The Merriam-Webster Dictionary offers two definitions for innovation: (1) the introduction of something new and (2) a new idea, method, or device.

For a theoretical innovation to be valuable, it can be expected to improve something that already exists creatively. Therefore, I will include this sense of usefulness in my notion of innovation as a particular type of thinking outside the box.

How do psychoanalysts decide that something is innovative? Following the previously mentioned definition, psychoanalysts are not likely to agree on what counts as innovative in their profession. When Klein presented her new ideas in the field of infant development at the London Institute of Psychoanalysis in the

1940s, she met with the opposition of Anna Freud and her colleagues who considered them as anything but an innovation: They saw them as a foreign body in psychoanalysis and did all they could to keep them out (King and Steiner, 1991). When Kohut introduced empathy as a central concept at a conference in the USA, some major establishment figures left the auditorium (Strozier, 2001). Both Klein and Kohut, however, created impressive and innovative theories that eventually changed psychoanalysis,

While certain innovations were embraced by most of the psychoanalytic community, others were ignored and forgotten. Here are two examples.

First is Klein's concept of projective identification, which was developed by analysts such as Bion (1959) and Casement (1985).

It hits the psychoanalytic world like a meteor, leading to substantial changes in the perception of the psychoanalytic encounter. Projective identification prompted a wealth of publications and conferences elaborating it from various perspectives. Its brilliance lies in the same stroke of genius that produced Freud's notion of transference: Something hitherto regarded an obstacle to treatment transforms overnight into a resource, diagnostic as well as therapeutic. The notion of projective identification enables a new reading of therapeutic processes.

Second, there is innovative psychoanalytic knowledge that has not been well-received by the community and has been rejected and forgotten. An example is the fascinating experimental work of Loyd Silverman (Silverman, 1982, 1985) on subliminal psychodynamic activation (see preface). Silverman attempted to identify the unconscious conflicts associated with specific symptomatic behaviors through this method. Findings indicate that when participants are shown a subliminal message – "Mommy and I are one" – this leads to improved behavior and reduction of a variety of symptoms, from psychotic ones in schizophrenic patients through nicotine addiction and academic underachievement all the way to phobias. The results of this research impressed psychoanalysts when they came out.

But, in spite of its promising reception, the method was not eventually embraced by psychoanalysts and they did not seek to equip their clinics with a tachistoscope. No matter how innovative, subliminal psychodynamic activation never became a psychoanalytic practice and fell into oblivion.

We may conclude that for an idea to be regarded as innovative, it takes a community to consider it as such. Truly innovative psychoanalysts never worked in isolation: Their innovation was the product of an entire network. Obviously, it took genius and profound theoretical knowledge to invent notions like a transitional object, schizoid-paranoid positions, and reverie. But it was even more fundamentally necessary for a tight network of psychoanalysts who were writing about the new conceptualization, elaborating it, employing it in the clinic, discussing it with their supervisees, and lecturing on it in psychoanalytic meetings.

This is why my preferred definition of psychoanalytic innovation crucially refers to the psychoanalytic community: Psychoanalytic innovation is a conceptualization found effective by the psychoanalytic community in yielding a new insight into psychoanalytic technique, clinical, or mental phenomena. An accepted innovation is where a psychoanalytic community finds something that so far eluded its understanding. This innovation must respect psychoanalytic specificity. It cannot be merely effective. Psychoanalysis, to begin with, is a special type of response to a special type of appeal. It rests on an ethics whose products are the results of the patient's psychic search into their self with as their main tool the therapeutic relationship and the centrality of the unconscious. Psychoanalysis aims not only to relieve suffering or to get rid of symptoms; it holds the fundamental principle of "Know Thyself" – a knowledge that every psychoanalytic approach conceptualizes in its own way.

Now, we are in a better position to understand why we do not find tachistoscopes in analysts' clinics, but we do find a preoccupation with projective identification, transitional objects, and self-object needs. Silverman's subliminal psychodynamic activation was not taken up in psychoanalysis precisely because it is very remote from the specificity of psychoanalysis, which aims to find where transference intersects with the patient's needs and conflicts. It is much closer to hypnosis and suggestion, which impose conscious, explicit, and deliberate suggestion on the analysand. This is anti-psychoanalytical, "useful" as it may be. It is a short way to alleviate symptoms. It is not the psychoanalytic way.

Is Psychoanalysis Obsolete?

Critics of psychoanalysis argue that the discipline does not move with the times: Psychoanalysts often refer to texts originally published a century, 80, or 50 years back. In this, they argue, psychoanalysis resembles religion, which refers to a static canon. This is factually undebatable. The Psychoanalytic Electronic Publishing (PEP) online archive has two statistics: the most cited and most viewed papers. We may assume that most frequently read and cited papers reflect what is most influential among contemporary psychoanalysts, what has left most marks on the community, and the authors on whom psychoanalysts rely when they write their own papers. In PEP statistics for the past five years, the most frequently quoted paper is by Klein, initially published in 1946: "Notes on Some Schizoid Mechanisms" (Klein, 1946). The list of the most frequently accessed papers is headed by an paper by Winnicott from 1953: "Transitional Objects and Transitional Phenomena – A Study of the First Not-me Possession" (Winnicott, 1953).

Most papers on the list of the most popular articles were published between 1935 and 1992, and only two of them are from the early 2000s: Ogden and Benjamin. Most of the best-read psychoanalysts are no longer alive: Klein, Ferenczi, Bion, Rosenfeld, Winnicott, Strachey, and Joseph.

This state of affairs suggests two things: First, postmodernism's great insight into the nature of truth seems hardly to have penetrated the community. A considerable proportion of the 30 most accessed and most cited papers are by authors who wrote before the advent of postmodernism (Winnicott, Klein, Joseph, Bick, Sandler, Kohut, Rosenfeld, and Heiman) and represent what relational psychotherapy has come to call a "one person psychology." This, arguably, signals a triumph of the old school over postmodern approaches.

Second, this list of dead authors might tempt one to draw the sad conclusion that psychoanalysis is grinding to a standstill, that the community goes on celebrating the achievements of the past, and that none of the articles written since have had a comparable impact to the cherished canonical texts written up to roughly the mid-1980s[1].

As mentioned, critics of psychoanalysis comment negatively on its tendency to dwell on the past.

As Bornstein and Masling (1998) noted, "A geneticist of 1900 could not sustain a conversation with a contemporary geneticist, but Freud would have no trouble recognizing the psychoanalysis of 1997 or reading a modern psychoanalytic journal" (xviii–xix).

According to Bornstein (2001), psychoanalysis lacks any innovative quality. Uncurious about the extra-analytical scientific world and communicating only with each other, psychoanalysts do not expose themselves to alternative theories that might enrich their knowledge.

But this criticism mistakes the essence of psychoanalysis when it expects that, like scientific discovery, it will reveal new facts that then replace earlier, superannuated ones. It fails to consider the fact that psychoanalysis is a language that deciphers meaning and yields insights about the psyche – insights that can be used again and again.

Psychoanalysis is more like philosophy and literature than like science. While scientific theories in use decades ago will have given way to more novel theories, philosophical theories going back to antiquity, for instance, still continue to inspire, drawing interest among contemporary philosophers. University departments of philosophy around the world teach ancient Greek philosophy all the way to the philosophy of Modernity – Spinoza, Kant, Mill, Hume, Hegel, and Nietzsche, to mention but a few. These philosophers continue being read because the depth of their insights transcends historical periods, and their relevance does not diminish. If the type of statistics we found on PEP were to be done on periodicals in philosophy, they would also reveal a high percentage of quotations and viewings of no longer living authors.

The same goes for literature. Netz (2016) provides an illustration from the field of papyrology: In 1896, in Egypt, thousands of decaying papyrus scrolls were discovered. Scholars were excited: New texts and new books in the literature of ancient Greece were about to be discovered, they believed, and the study of antiquity was about to undergo a great upheaval. Here and there, indeed, an ancient papyrus carrying a hitherto unknown text was found (a poem by Sappho, for instance). But such incidents were rare. By far, the most discovered scrolls were manuscripts of texts we already knew: the same Plato, again, and the same Homer. The scholars' hope that our ancient forefathers knew other writers than the ones who were copied onto parchment in the Middle Ages proved vain. Monks in medieval Constantinople chose to copy the very same texts that had been copied on papyrus in Egypt, a millennium earlier. It transpired that literary taste does not tend to change and renew. Sophocles, Aeschylus, and Euripides were Athens' most popular playwrights, even in their own life times. They remained so for the next 2,500 years.

Conceptualizations concerning the psyche, likewise, do not lose their relevance rapidly. Truths of this type continue to be discovered by one generation after another. This innovation might be captured by the notion of wisdom, which casts a new light on mental life. Much like in the case of philosophy, these ideas become the source of inspiration for new ideas, which in turn will multiply.

Analysts reread classical references and adapt Freudian or, Kleinian or Winnicottian methods to contemporary clinical fields. Innovation comes through interpretive extension.

Three citations from a philosopher of science, a philosopher of aesthetics, and a poet illustrate the connection between tradition and innovation in non-psychoanalytic fields.

Kuhn writes that scientific revolution "requires a thoroughgoing commitment to the tradition," with which the fully successful innovator eventually breaks (Kuhn, 1977, 235).

In referring to art, Cavell also maintains that radical innovations occur in significant dialogue with the past. Here, he describes radical breaks in the music of the 20th century:

> What looks like 'breaking with tradition' in the succession of art is not really that; or is that only after the fact, looking historically or critically; or is that only as a result not as motive: the unheard of appearance of the modern in art is an effort not to break, but to keep faith with tradition.
>
> (Cavell, 1976, 206–207)

Eliot wrote: "The poem which is absolutely original is absolutely bad; it is, in the bad sense, 'subjective', with no relation to the world to which it appeals" (Pound, 1934, 9–10).

Four Characteristics of Psychoanalytic Innovations of the First Order

Psychoanalytic innovation of the first order (new discoveries concerning facts) has four characteristics.

First, most innovations concern new psychic dynamics linking between transference, psychopathology, and infants' mental life.

The 30 most cited and viewed papers written by Klein, Winnicott, Bion, and other prominent figures, the psychoanalytic canon, go on to inspire new work, and these prompt us to consider what it is about these inspirational sources that lead to innovative production.

While the innovative production represents different approaches (object relations, self-psychology, and relational psychotherapy), we can observe a common pattern: Almost without exception, they tie together the following domains:

development, psychopathology, and therapy. Hardly any one of them addresses only one of these topics in isolation. Psychoanalysts adhering to the various approaches find such narratives the most useful to their therapeutic work.

The specific psychoanalytic approach of the article in question does not seem to matter: Whether it is self-psychology, Klein, Winnicott, or Ferenczi, the patient's psychopathology appears in relation to the transference, and the transference is related to early interactions with the caregiver. It appears that canonical articles all present the regularities at work between these same components. So tightly interlinked are these three components that it is enough to ask any psychoanalyst to describe the key stations in an infant's life to gain a revealing insight into his approach and how he perceives transference. Once we know how a psychoanalyst defines transference, we can tell with reasonable accuracy what her ideas about infant development are.

So, if a novel idea in psychoanalysis is to have an impact, it should be tied to infantile mental life on the basis of both transference relations and mental distress and to the ability to give new meaning to transference relations on the basis of infantile mental life. Just as a problem in biology is solved in terms of biology, not in those of chemistry, a psychic fact is understood in this particular psychoanalytic way. This way of thinking has not altered since Freud and is in fact a variation on the transference neurosis; namely, the idea that the patient's early childhood conflicts resurface in the transference relationship with the psychoanalyst.

That innovations feed off the tradition does by no means reduce their creativity and contribution. Some innovators adhered faithfully to one theory but were plentifully creative within that context, and their extension of it can be considered significant and very influential. This is the case, for instance, with Joseph's work on Klein, Ferro's work on Bion, and Goldberg's work on Kohut, to name just a few. Other authors do not follow one theoretician but refer playfully and creatively to the existing literature, dancing, as it were, between various theories and leaving their personal marks in the creative links they forge, together with their own personal additions. Examples of this type of work are, for instance, by Bollas, Eigen, Phillips, and Milner.

New theoretical development can consist of illustrating an existing psychoanalytic conceptualization (through, for instance, a case study in which the concept is employed for clarification); extensions of a psychoanalytic conceptualization to new populations (e.g., applying self-psychological principles to issues concerning eating disorders); elaborating an existing conceptualization (e.g., manifestations of the female castration complex); discovery of an interesting therapeutic process and illustrating a clinical phenomenon using it; and in-depth discussion of the work of a vital psychoanalyst or exposition of a hitherto neglected text by her or him.

Second, psychoanalytic innovation solves empirical problems.

Psychoanalysis is a psychology. It addresses clinical phenomena and first-order facts, independent of theory: Patients suffering from hysterical symptoms visited Freud's clinic, and he had no idea what might be wrong with them. Having identified hysteria as a clinical phenomenon, Freud was then able to discover the unconscious and the various other mental structures and eventually, to develop his overarching theory.

The philosopher of science Laudan (1977) argues that science fundamentally aims at the solution of problems. He proposes that theories should be evaluated based on how adequately they solve significant problems. It is much less relevant to ask whether they are "true," "corroborated," or "well-confirmed." He claims that one of the main kinds of problems scientific theories want to solve is empirical problem. An empirical problem, he argues, is "anything about the natural world which strikes us as odd or otherwise in need of explanation" (15).

Empirical problems in psychoanalysis may be parapraxes, a three-year-old's fixation on her doll, intense, destructive jealousy, and dreams. All these phenomena exist in the world as they are unrelated to psychoanalytic theory. In fact, human suffering in all its forms and variations constitutes an empirical problem and the ways of treating it.

Some of the most interesting innovations in psychoanalysis have to do with solving empirical problems and discovering the problems in the first place. Many psychoanalytic phenomena were first recognized as empirical problems or felt to require explanation or clarification prior to these descriptions. Slips of the tongue were well known before Freud but were not considered scientific or empirical problems. Another example is Winnicott's transitional object. The fact that a toddler clings to a teddy bear was well-known before Winnicott gave it an explanation.

Often, innovators focus on an existing (nonanalytic) phenomenon and show its relevance to psychoanalytic theory. Hence, I assume that psychoanalytic innovation will, more than anything, occur in the field of empirical problem solving. Regarding first-order questions, innovation means a new explanation ("solution") to psychic phenomenon ("empirical problem").

Psychoanalytic journals are simply bursting with such topics. Here are some examples: "The Role of the Nanny in Infant Observation" (Yakeley, 2017); "The Masculine Vaginal: Working With Queer Men's Embodiment at the Transgender Edge" (Hansbury, 2017); and "The Encounter Between Holocaust Survivors and Perpetrators" (Auerhahn and Laub, 2018).

Another type of problem that theory might address is conceptual in nature. Such problems emerge from the theory itself; they have no existence outside the theoretical field in which they arise. Here are some titles reflecting this:

"Projective Identification and Relatedness: A Kleinian Perspective" (Roth, 2017); "Comparative Assessment of and Bion and Winnicott's Clinical Theories" (Aguayo and Lundgren, 2018); "Truth Axes and the Transformation of Self" (Yadlin-Gadot, 2017).

Third, psychoanalytic innovations are formulated poetically.

The new knowledge, however, is not communicated as if it were, say, medical knowledge. Often, texts in this domain seem vague, open to interpretation, hard to understand, and more like poetry in their formulations.

In typical texts by Bion, Ogden, Winnicott, or Eigen, sentences are often ambiguous and labyrinthine; meaning is dense and layered, the opposite of the clear and simple style that scientists admire. Often, the reader, in addition to gaining new knowledge or discovering an interesting solution, has an aesthetic experience that involves powerful emotional intensities. They seem to resonate deep layers with which the reader makes contact for the first time. The echoes of the text, their links, the things they are attentive to, and all the other ways texts and objects can be tied begin to struggle in the reader's or listener's mind with the semantic content (Scruton, 2015).

Canonical texts, in this sense, offer an enigmatic, complex phenomenon demanding explanation in its own right, like poetry. Most major psychoanalysts are rather gifted writers, and their texts may resemble literary prose or poetry more than properly scientific texts.

As regards the beauty of Nature", writes Freud in On Transience (Freud, 1915/1942) when he was preoccupied with the losses of WWI, "each time it is destroyed by winter it comes again next year, so that in relation to the length of our lives it can in fact be regarded as eternal (Freud, 1915/1942). The beauty of the human form and face vanish forever in the course of our own lives, but their evanescence only lends them a fresh charm. A flower that blossoms only for a single night does not seem to us on that account less lovely.

(304–305)

But psychoanalytic thinking is not poetry and the poet has somewhat different motivations from that of the analyst who uses words to describe the psyche, although the two may at times overlap.

Scruton (2015) thinks that the aim of a poem is not to convince readers of the correspondence of words to reality. Rather, its purpose is to facilitate readers to imagine the world as the poet depicts it.

Now, although poetic truth of this kind is not alien to psychoanalytic writings, it does seem to differ from it in some important sense. Think about the authors of psychoanalytic texts. They all want first and foremost, to understand an unknown psychic fact (empirical problem). The innovative analyst has just met a patient. This patient suddenly behaves strangely. The analyst is puzzled. She feels that she cannot rely on current theories. She holds a curious, not-knowing position until she discovers an interesting, innovative explanation. She knows that her description must correspond to the psychic reality "out there" in the transference relations and that she cannot imagine it or make it up like a poet. The truth value of her innovative explanation depends not merely on how successfully it conveys experience (although this, too, is very important, see next section) but on how adequate her description is in convincing the community that it corresponds to psychic reality.

She is fully committed to something to which the poet is only loosely committed; namely, to understand what happened there – both in the past and in the present.

Despite their differences, psychoanalytic writing and poetic writing have much in common. When a psychic fact is put into words, the effect is sometimes emotionally powerful. Thus, psychoanalytic thinking, when it works well, can form a genre in its own right, representing psychic facts in a singular way through the symbolic. Often, psychoanalytic innovations will describe universal themes – but always in singular terms. It is precisely this combination between the universal and the singular that is so powerful.

Here, to illustrate, is a passage from Parsons, on creativity:

> If creativity is the discovery of what we had not thought of looking for, or the making of something which was, up till now, unimagined, it must call for a special sort of vulnerability. To open ourselves to the shock of creative discovery we must put ourselves at risk and be ready to give up, with no certainty about the future, ways of seeing which up till now have served us well.
>
> (Parsons, 1990, 420)

Parsons does not only present an answer to a question (What are the conditions under which creativity flourishes? Answer: The ability to take risks, to forfeit certainty, and in other words, to be vulnerable); his writing also includes a poetic element (the surprising and metaphoric association between creativity, the hitherto unthought – and, on the other hand, vulnerability as well as the musical-rhythmic effect of the juxtaposition of creativity-discovery-vulnerability-certainty).

The solution or answer and its psychoanalytic textual form, the scientific and poetic elements, cannot be seen in isolation. The emotional musical qualities of the language add validity to the conceptualization.

Parsons could have put the same idea in many forms, some more scientific and informative. But it is not clear whether it would have passed had he not used this poetic mode of expression.

All psychoanalytic writing displays this tension: Scientific writing aims at solving empirical problems. It is disciplined, clear-cut, and tells us how to think. It is systematic and aims at solving profound mysteries and riddles. Poetic writing is undisciplined, unpredictable, and full of subjectivity; but it is passionate and spontaneous, seeking, rather, what Bollas calls "psychic intensities" (Bollas, 1995, 60). We need both, as they seem to empower each other, creating a certain energy that outweighs their separate meaning and impact.

Fourth, psychoanalytic innovations conceptualize what we already know.

There is another sense in which innovation in science is unlike in psychoanalysis. While new knowledge concerning a scientific problem reveals what we did not know earlier, psychoanalysis, like art, adds meaning to what we already know. We can, in other words, regard psychoanalytic writing as a type of symbolic writing in so far as it takes an existing experience to which we had no verbal access and makes it accessible. Something we experience without being aware acquires articulate meaning.

Both Meltzer and Bion emphasize that psychoanalysis has not discovered any new ideas about its subject, the human mind, and that it is unlikely to do so. However, through the psychoanalytic method, old ideas can be rediscovered in a new context (Meltzer, 1983, 98).

And Freud writes:

I find myself for a moment in the interesting position of not knowing whether what I have to say should be regarded as something long familiar and obvious or as something entirely new and puzzling.

(Freud, 1940, 274)

The truth of Winnicott's notion of a transitional object as an object that is both real and also helps to maintain a connection to the absent mother is hence directly associated with the fact that a well-known and universal human experience here is formulated for the first time. When Klein spoke about manic defenses like contempt for the object and arrogance, she first put into words what we had known for a long time about our attitude to our closest objects. The psychic fact and the poetic are not two distinct modes of knowledge. The poetic supplies the esthetic experience to the real and rings with something of the mysterious truth we already know.

While the clinical experience or phenomenon (envy, transitional object, slips of the tongue, castration experience) is what it is, in line with reality, its description can take many forms. This may be what characterizes psychoanalysis' epistemology. Psychoanalytic innovation, from this perspective, occurs when new facts concerning a psychic phenomenon come to light, but our ability to perceive them as correct is based on the fact that we are already familiar with them. The poetic language in which a new description of a clinical phenomenon is couched functions like a muscle that supports its approach to the truth: It elicits a robust, emotional engagement with the newly discovered facts. We have experienced this knowledge, but it was unconceptualized so far. For the discovered facts to ring true, the poetic quality of the text is crucial. Should facts about the mind be communicated in terse scientific language, the reader would be unable to connect with the actually lived experience.

Loewald thought that language "ties together human beings and self and object world, and it binds abstract thought with the bodily concreteness and power of life" (Loewald, 1978, 204). This is because language, in the form of the sounds of the mother's speech, imbues the infant's lived experience from the beginning of life. The sounds of a mother's speech are part of the infant's experience of interacting with the mother, and over time, those sounds become differentiated from other sensations of the lived world as a special kind of sound; these special sounds grow into words. But the sounds also remain connected in memory to the rest of experience and, for that reason, a powerful way to recall one's inner experience and communicate it to another. Indeed, the lived feeling that language can create is a reflection of its experiential nature. Although the semantic possibilities of words expand over development, they do not overtake the experiential possibilities. A word is always an experiential memory.

Sensibilities: second-order innovations.

I first encountered the word "sensibility" in an article by Stolorow et al. (2001), authors who took a central role in developing the intersubjective approach. Inspired by postmodernism, this theory claimed that in the therapeutic encounter, an intersubjective domain arises in which two partners mutually constitute each other. This co-creation – and not the patient's isolated mind – is the therapy's heart. They call this theory a "sensibility" rather than a clinical theory: Their work, they claim, is informed by the clinician's attitude and the ensuing process rather than by any hard and fast procedure.

Psychoanalytic communities develop sensibilities when they turn outward: Methodological sensibilities absorb significant scientific changes (in brain science or in infant research); cultural-philosophical sensibilities incorporate changes in philosophy, culture, or society (e.g., constructivism, postmodernism, or feminism). Like a seismograph, they register these changes and bring them to bear in psychoanalysis. Introducing a foreign element to psychoanalytic discourse, texts of this kind are sometimes met with indifference or hostility. Studies based in brain or infant research seek to cast a different light on what exists, to change the approach to patients rather than to change theoretical models. Both neuropsychoanalysis and infant research believe they are actually restoring something to psychoanalysis. Thus, infant researchers claim to only deepen analysts' knowledge of the nature of early development, which is, after all, central to their theory. Similarly, neuropsychoanalysts think their findings expand the analyst's therapeutic possibilities. They remind us that Freud himself was a neurologist and that he sought to integrate the study of the brain and psychoanalysis (Johnson and Flores Mosri, 2016).

The Relational Sensibility – Truth, Knowledge, and Politics

The implications of the relational approach for the psychoanalytic encounter are far-reaching (see Chapter 5 for a detailed discussion). It assumes that the analytic relationship is systematically mutual and two-directional throughout. The notion of the therapist as an object of the patient's projected relations from the past is exchanged for one in which the therapist is a subject in the therapeutic relationship. Puget (2017) captures this difference in her use of "interference," a mutual process, with which she replaces "transference," which relies on notions of object-subject distinctness and wholeness.

The relational approach assumes that the therapist's personal involvement in the therapy is inevitable. It is a matter of mobilizing this involvement for the patient's benefit. Aron (1996), for instance, argued that Freud's elimination of the "subjective factor" in the therapeutic situation has been a damaging omission. In tune with the academic-scientific thinking of his times, Freud aimed to achieve an objective science of the psyche. Postmodernism, as said, questioned this approach, by arguing that any theoretical model is historically and linguistically mediated. Thus, Hoffman (1998), a major proponent of the relational approach, argued that the patient's experience in the therapy and the way it is subsequently made sense of, are understandings that emerge in the course of the encounter based on both the therapist's and patient's personal histories and their typical modes of organization. It would be inappropriate to judge these construals as simply wrong or right rather than consider them more or less applicable.

A similar shift also occurred on the epistemological plane, where the relational approach no longer assumes one monolithic truth, embodied in a grand theory. Instead, theories are seen as possibilities – narratives that help in framing the therapeutic relationship and the patient's psychic history and reality (Mills, 2005, 2017).

By redefining its boundaries of relevance, the relational approach has also come to include political issues that were outside the traditional scope of psychoanalysis. Clinical questions touching on gender and ethnicity are integral part of it as well as, for instance, a critical attitude to the therapist's unconscious racism. Altman writes:

> It should be taken for granted that none of us will be able to overcome our personal racist attitudes altogether. Thus, I am advocating that clinicians become familiar with their racism, not that they overcome their racist feelings and attitudes. The danger in implying that clinicians can and should overcome their racist feelings is that they will mistake their conscious goodwill and good intentions for a thoroughgoing nonracist attitude.
>
> (Altman, 2000, 601)

A Sensibility Related to Infant Research

Innovation also occurs when psychoanalysts are powerfully attracted to an extra-analytic domain of knowledge that while relating directly to psychoanalytic theory, uses a different language. This extraneous knowledge, they believe, has the potential to influence the conceptualization and understanding of the therapeutic situation; however, in this particular case, rather than by reference to the adult therapeutic situation, through the observation of real interactions between infants and their caregivers. Infant researchers consider the method whereby infant development is derived from the psychoanalysis of adults or older children as naive.

Fonagy writes:

> Melanie Klein's baby and Winnicott's baby were adultomorphic to a considerable degree. They seemed in some way put there to explain the conflicts and vicissitudes of the adult years rather than to genuinely map how the mind emerges from an early infant in many ways biologically and physically unprepared for the challenges of the external world. The infants of early psychoanalysis were retrofitted to the couch.
>
> (Fonagy, 2014, xx)

The infant in these studies is unlike those in Freud, Klein, Bion, Winnicott, and Kohut (Seligman, 2018). Traditional psychoanalytic theories present a baby with a primitive psychic organization which develops into an adaptive organization. Initially, this baby's mental life is chaotic, unintegrated, and in conflict with the social world. Psychopathology is understood in terms of distortions in this process. The traces of psychosis or borderline personality can be discerned in early infancy.

Infant research has revealed a very different baby: This observed infant is not fundamentally disorganized, chaotic, or primitive, spending most of its time in a dream state or fearing persecution. Nor is it undifferentiated from its environment. From the first moment, its life is organized around a relational matrix, continuously subject to reconstruction and change in line with experience (Stern, 1985). From day 1, the infant is already directed toward reality, influences and is influenced by its surroundings, is active and passive, dependent and independent, and possesses a variety of resources for organizing its behavior. One might have expected that anyone, once exposed to this research, would turn away from psychoanalysis – the chasm between these two conceptualizations is so enormous. But what actually happened was the opposite. The psychoanalytic infant research community, including researchers and practitioners who apply their insights in psychoanalytic psychotherapy, insists that its research is relevant to psychoanalysis and is bound to enrich it. They argue that their perspective is especially promising for work with adult patients who are more difficult to reach (Rustin, 2012).

In trying to understand the clinical distinction of this change in perspective, Stern observed that much of what occurs between people who are closely interacting involves an intersubjective consciousness. This implies that there is a realm of knowing that is implicit, outside awareness, and not requiring verbalization. The present moment, writes Stern (2004), rather than the past, becomes the focus. Stern (1985, 2004) extended this idea from everyday interaction to the patient/therapist encounter as crucial for an appreciation of how therapeutic change comes about. New ways of being and being with others are created through intersubjective processes of implicit relational knowing.

Rustin, who is identified with self-psychology, explains infant research's complementary role vis á vis existing psychoanalytic theories very well in her book Infant Research and Neuroscience at Work in Psychotherapy (Rustin, 2012).

Because new facts about human behavior emerge daily, psychoanalysts must integrate them into their practice. She writes, "These theories, and their accompanying principles and techniques, inform everything that I do. Through immersing myself in infant research, I found a way to expand and update self-psychology in my clinical practice" (171). She argues that infant research's focus on infant and caregiver relations underwrites Kohut's notion of empathic engagement. But it also contributes to self-psychology by demonstrating that "an interaction is always a bidirectional, co-constructed process, thereby bolstering my commitment to intersubjectivity as a two-person model of clinical practice" (172). Infant research, for Rustin, is not a substitute for any of the traditional theories or techniques, but it holds out opportunities for knowledge and intervention: "additional sources of fluidity and elasticity to the therapeutic relationship and clinical process" (172–173).

Infant research posited a challenge to psychoanalytic methodology. Green (2000), who was fiercely critical of infant research, noted that infant research deviates from psychoanalysis' investigation of the unconscious and the intrapsychic through the transference within the parameters set by the psychoanalytic setting. For analysts like him, empirical researchers ignore the unconscious and change the psychoanalytic account into a theory of interpersonal relations.

Green even suggests that some researchers harbor sinister motivations, even those purporting to be acting in the interests of psychoanalysis: They want to get rid of psychoanalytic theories, in favor of a so-called scientific psychology, which is simpler, easier to teach, and more amenable to experimental studies. Green's fears were exaggerated. In fact, researchers aspired to make analysts sensitive to empirical findings, not to replace existing theories.

A Sensibility Related to Neuropsychoanalysis

According to Johnson (2009), neuropsychoanalysis is concerned with the common ground between neuroscience and psychoanalysis. As said, neuropsychoanalysts claim that incorporating brain research into psychoanalysis is a continuation of Freud's project. The neuropsychoanalytic community is very active and vibrant. It has founded an organization for its members, a journal, an annual conference, and research study groups worldwide.

Kaplan-Solms and Solms (2000) described contemporary use of neuroscience in psychoanalysis:

> The aim of a depth neuropsychology is not to replace our psychic model of the mind with a physical one. Rather, our aim is to supplement the traditional viewpoints of metapsychology with a new, "physical point of view. The aim is to gain an additional perspective on something that can never be known directly.
> (251)

It is plausible to think that this was appealing for the neuropsychoanalysis community. Psychodynamic concepts such as cathexis, dreams, self, and ego may now appear in new light if we can trace their neurological underpinning.

For example, Northoff (2012), regarding the "self," suggests that, instead of searching for the self-region or self-network in the brain, searching for essential executive and operational regularities will be more productive. The spatiotemporal structure of the resting state may present the basis for such regularities. If it is linked with the self or the ego, one would assume the organization of the resting state's spatiotemporal structure to somehow establish self-specific and thus reveal the ego's structure.

According to Yovell et al. (2015), for example, brain researchers discovered fear conditioning, a potent kind of implicit emotional learning. A person may have an extreme fear of a situation or another person without any explicit memory of why they have this fear. The corresponding implicit memory here is not repressed as classical psychoanalysis suggested. The authors argue that findings like this shed new light on a problem of traumatic memories that has haunted psychoanalysis from its first days. It explains why people who went through severe trauma were incapable of accessing direct memories of the traumatic events despite experiencing powerful, anxiety-inducing implicit memories.

Members of the neuropsychoanalysis community have published many other examples of how brain research can enrich and help analysts (Ruby, 2011; Giacolini and Sabatello, 2019; Iyengar et al., 2019). Some even have coined a new term "neuropsychoanalytic interpretation" (Johnson, 2009, 182).

Johnson writes:

My definition of a 'neuropsychoanalytic' interpretation is a discussion of impingements on the patient's thinking that clearly had to do with known biological factors. These included drug dreams, craving, justifications of using (clearly influenced by craving such as, "No one will know"), and telling her that craving would diminish with abstinence.

(Johnson, 2009, 185).

His case study describes 28 "neuropsychoanalytic" interventions made in 60 h. These were the interpretations guided by his neurobiological knowledge regarding the patient's addiction to cocaine, such as identifying long-lasting transformations in brain structure and function that affected "the ventral tegmental-nucleus accumbens   shell/dopamine-glutamate/hippocampal-amygdalar-cingulate-frontal functioning. The foremost manifestation of this change is the drug dream" (186).

The "neuropsychoanalytic interpretation" also helped to ease shame. Johnson's patient is able to understand that her behavior is not the outcome of some flaw in her personality.

He writes:

There is nothing remarkable or special about this treatment. It follows the ordinary psychoanalytic approach of having the patient free-associate and the analyst interpret. Comments about medication are required because they are part of the effort to facilitate her being sober.

(191)

According to Yovell et al. (2015), "psychoanalysis needs to be in a position to consider developments in science, even if it ends up dismissing some of them as irrelevant, due to the criteria and findings of its own epistemology" (1528).

Like infant research and the relational approach, neuropsychoanalysis challenges traditional psychoanalysis' epistemology and methodology.

Johnson and Flores Mosri write:

Neuropsychoanalysis is a twenty-first century development that has at its core the concept of dual aspect monism. Whether phenomena are evaluated empathically, or through measurements and statistics, it introduces an artifact of perception. Empirical data is filtered through the means by which it is made. Therefore, we are in the delightful position of being able to make observations by psychoanalytic clinical means that can also, perhaps with some technical difficulties, be made with genetic testing, animal observation of homologous behaviors, fMRI scanning, or some other nomothetic approach.

(Johnson and Flores Mosri, 2016, x)

Can Sensibilities Address First-Order Questions?

I have portrayed the relational approach as a sensibility that poses second-order questions regarding existing theories, while the latter in turn discovers first-order psychoanalytic facts. Most relational analysts do of course have a keen interest in "facts" and "empirical problems" (see Govrin, 2006). Ghent (1990) explores what patients need and how this need unfolds in therapy; Davies and Frawley (1992) discovered new facts regarding patients who suffered from sexual abuse and Stern discovered a new component of the unconscious which he called "unformulated experiences" (Stern, 1983). There is no hard, binary division between these orders of questions: It is, rather, a matter of a tension between facts and sensibilities, and this exists not only between different psychoanalytic communities but also within each psychoanalytic orientation and within analysts themselves. This also is true for infant research and neuropsychoanalysis. They too are interested in how new facts can change the clinical practice.

And yet, there is a difference between sensibilities and first-order psychoanalytic facts. Postmodernists, especially the USA relational group, select what they consider valuable in existing theories, extricate it from its positivist moorings, and insert it into an intersubjective and constructivist model. Likewise, findings from neuropsychoanalysis and infant research offer a new and additional perspective, specifically, on nonverbal and nonconscious processes of clinical interaction. The newer perspectives have opened creative pathways for empathic immersion, interaction, clinical understanding, and intervention. As Rustin (2012) writes:

> What I do offer is a way to use these research findings as another lens through which to view or think about some nonverbal, nonconscious aspects of clinical data and to tailor interventions so that they more effectively lead to therapeutic action. I view these concepts as additions that increase the possibilities for spontaneous and imaginative ways of working with patients.
>
> (10)

Psychoanalytic sensibilities attempt to integrate new disciplines and world views into mainstream clinical practice. Psychoanalytic schools, by contrast, have more ambitiously presented fully-fledged alternatives to already existing schools and offered new psychic facts concerning the link between infancy, psychopathology, and transference.

Rather than posing themselves as alternatives to psychoanalytic theories, sensibilities try to engage in a dialogue. In neuropsychoanalysis, the conscious id is another good case in point. Solms cites evidence that the upper brainstem (together with associated limbic structures) performs the functions that Freud attributed to the id. In contrast, the cortex (and associated forebrain structures) performs the functions he attributed to the ego. This is a radical new fact. It reveals a stark contradiction between the current concepts of affective neuroscience and those of Freud. The realization that Freud's id is intrinsically conscious has implications for psychoanalysis, which Solms describes (for example, if the id is conscious what is unconscious is withdrawal of automatization processes).

Solms's paper is a wonderful dialogue between brain research and Freudian theory. Solms goes back and forth from Freud's writings to brain images and data to show where he was right, ahead of his time, and where he erred. These illustrations show how neuropsychoanalysis and infant research mainly aims to shift the relations with the enduring metapsychology of psychoanalysis into something more workable.

Whereas psychoanalytic schools are all-encompassing and need no additions, the relational approach, infant research, and neuropsychoanalysis do not stand alone. They depend on a constant dialogue with psychoanalytic schools.

Does psychoanalysis make progress?

Now, I want to return to the questions I posed at the beginning of this paper: Does psychoanalysis make progress?

Let us start with "first-order questions." If we accept Laudan's (1977) philosophy of science, we appraise a theory by one sole criterion: whether it provides acceptable answers to significant questions. According to Laudan, problem-solving activity has no direct connections with truth, but this does not deprive the problem-solving model of its explanatory force. Rationality, argues Laudan, consists of doing or believing things because we have good reasons for doing so. What counts as a sound reason for accepting a new explanation in psychoanalysis? How can we know if a suggested description of, say, the dynamic of analyst-patient relations is a sound one?

It is important to note that any assessment of the rationality of accepting a particular theory is relative: It is relative to other earlier and competing theories and to prevailing views on methodology, and in the case of psychoanalysis, it is relative to the therapist's own theoretical inclinations. So, a psychotherapist who prefers to base psychotherapeutic theory on evidence-based research will not find psychoanalytic solutions as effective. However, the solution can be satisfactory to a psychotherapist who perceives clinical observations and single case studies as valid sources of knowledge.

My own clinical experience demonstrates the power of psychoanalytic theory to solve puzzling empirical problems (see also Govrin, 2016). One of my patients, single and in his late thirties, presented significant progress. He had experienced years of harsh relations with people, periods of severe loneliness, and a lack of social relations. After several months in therapy, he seemed less guarded, his relations with his colleagues had improved, and for the first time, he had gained the approval of his directors. But the more he recovered, the more hostile he became to me and the more critical he grew of the therapy. He would joke at my lack of experience, mock my interventions, and complain about my inability to support him. When he was not in an aggressive mood, he would express his hopelessness, feeling that I could not possibly help him. When he mentioned the improvements he had made in his personal and professional life, he spoke with indifference, indicating that, as far as he was concerned, it had nothing to do with therapy. I was bewildered, ill at ease, and infuriated. It was odd: A person whose life had undoubtedly changed for the better because of therapy not only failed to acknowledge it as such but did everything he could to mock what had been attained. My patient's attitude toward me was a clinical/empirical fact. It was not a matter of interpretation. Many psychotherapists working in different orientations have reported similar reactions.

My Kleinian supervisor helped me understand my patient's inner dynamic and how it affected the transference relations. She explained how the Kleinian approach understands the phenomenon of the negative therapeutic reaction (NTR): Due to envy, which Klein maintained was the mental representation of the death instinct, the patient avoids any recognition of the goodness of the analyst to secure his omnipotent phantasy and deny his dependency. The libidinal force that directs him to love, show gratitude, and make amends – leading to steadily improving his condition – is overridden by envy, revenge, and contempt. My Kleinian supervisor added that the patient perceived "suffering" as the connection between us and could maintain contact with me only if he supposed we were both suffering.

I had no reason to doubt the accuracy of this "solution." It seemed right and appropriate to this regressive phenomenon.

The literature on NTR is simply enormous. Analysts from different orientations have tried to explain it starting from Freud in his Wolf Man case study. Because numerous analysts have shared their thoughts and clinical experience the community obviously knows more about NTR than it did 50 years ago. Of course, the problem-solving effectiveness of the theories that explain NTR is not scientifically experimentally backed. But, if a community of psychotherapists dealing with first-order questions use a strong set of psychological theories which they believe to be essential to the understanding of psychopathology, then it is perfectly rational to assess innovations – that is, "solutions" – in light of their capacity to be accommodated within that prior system of beliefs and assumptions. There is much more to say about the appraisal of effective "solutions" in psychoanalysis which is beyond the scope of this paper. With its strange reliance on poetic style and the analysts' subjectivity, this appraisal might seem odd for an outsider. Still, the psyche is "odd" so it is likely that the explanations will match its awkwardness. As Lear (1998) wrote:

> There is one way to refute psychoanalysis entirely: if from now on, every person would act rationally and clearly, it would be easy to dismiss psychoanalysis as idle chatter. However, since people often act in strange ways, causing pain to

themselves and others, raising questions even among the players themselves, psychoanalysis will draw us to it.

(25)

Overall, I think that regarding first-order questions we are in a good position. NTR is just one example out of numerous "solutions" that psychoanalysts have found to puzzling psychic phenomena. Some of those problems (such as NTR) lack solutions from other nonpsychoanalytic theories (and other nonpsychoanalytic theories propose excellent solutions to other psychic first-order questions, though, I believe, in terms of scope, range and relevancy to human's life psychoanalysis outnumber other theories).

Concerning second-order questions, we must distinguish between the cultural-philosophical sensibility of the relational approach and the methodological sensibilities of neuropsychoanalysis and infant research. The relational approach, even if one resists its worldview, is undoubtedly the most important recent innovation in psychoanalysis. It revolutionized psychoanalysis by embracing new approaches to knowledge, which led to a novel perception of therapeutic relations.

The relational approach first refers, rather, to a whole new worldview, according to which therapy is a genuine relationship between two persons and not merely some one-way internal relations that belong exclusively to the intrapsychic life of the patient's mind (Davies, 1994, 168). The new worldview had important implications for analytic work (for example, how analysts work with enactments or the role of self-disclosure). As a result of this new worldview or, as I have been calling it, sensibility, analysts have changed how they think about their own subjectivity in the psychoanalytic encounter. This put an end to therapists struggling to hide their personalities and blur their subjectivity in order to ensure patients' emotional issues would stay untouched by the countertransference. Of course, this has taken its toll in the form of indifference to theory (Govrin, 2006) or excessive use of analyst self-disclosure (Mills, 2017).

The epistemology of methodological sensibilities is very unlike that of the cultural-philosophical sensibilities of the relational approach. In fact, by relying on scientific research, the epistemology of both neuropsychoanalysis and infant research is strikingly similar to that of the "silver era" of psychoanalysis, where realism and the correspondence theory of truth prevailed. So, contrary to the revolutionary meta-psychology of the relational approach, methodological sensibilities offer a new source of knowledge with a traditional epistemology. They challenge psychoanalytic sources of knowledge by offering to extend these sources by relying on other fields of knowledge besides the clinical encounter.

I believe that their most significant challenge is addressing an external conceptual problem (Laudan, 1977, 50). External conceptual problems are generated by a theory when it conflicts with another theory or doctrine its supporters believe to be rationally well-founded. There is a difference between mainstream psychoanalysis and between infant research and neuropsychoanalysis. For example, many mainstream analysts still use the term "symbiotic phase," despite findings from infant research showing that the infant from the very beginning is aware that she is physically separate, conscious of her caregivers, and continuously relating to her surroundings. In science, the answer to a "tension" between a methodology and a scientific theory is often reached by changing the scientific theory as to adjust it to the methodological standards. In other instances, it is the methodology itself that is transformed. Neither of these had happened in psychoanalysis because of infant research and neuropsychoanalysis.

As a result, infant research and neuropsychoanalysis have not, so far, prompted a paradigm shift in psychoanalysis. Perhaps this is because neuropsychoanalysis has not yet reached a point of development that obliges mainstream analysts to consider it a serious contributor. It did not lead mainstream analysts to think that the inconsistency and correspondence between methodological sensibilities are convincing enough, probably, because they speak different languages and methodologies.

To the credit of researchers from infant research and neuropsychoanalysis, it must be said that they never thought that psychoanalysts should kneel before their own scientific findings because they are more grounded and evidence-based, nor have they expected analysts to abandon parts of mainstream psychoanalysis. I believe that psychoanalytic problem-solving effectiveness is improved by new insights from brain research and infant research through a process of inquiry, argument, and agreement within open-minded communities. The reputation of psychoanalysis as a serious body of knowledge is enhanced if it can show that it successfully incorporates current scientific findings or at least conducts a healthy dialogue with these findings.

Conclusion

We have realized that most psychoanalytic innovations do not stem from changes in philosophy but from the need to solve clinical problems. Most analysts of the Silver Age (Freud, Bion, and Kohut are exceptions) were not interested in philosophy. They did not understand how complicated it was to make claims about the human psyche from an epistemological perspective. In this respect, one must be grateful that they were naïve realists. They had the freedom to explore and imagine without a postmodern burden. They explained human phenomena such as dreams, envy, and eating disorders with the same confidence as an astronomer explains about the solar system.

The real challenge they were wrestling with was innovating within the psychoanalytic framework. Any attempt to outline innovations in psychoanalysis will have to tread a narrow dialectic line between two opposing directions. On the one hand, we can point out a dynamic change in therapeutic approaches, the rise and fall of theoretical models, and the development of new therapeutic understandings of numerous psychic phenomena such as transference and psychopathology. On the other hand, there is the fact that there has not been much change in the influence of the main psychoanalytic theory (Freud, Bion, Klein, Winnicott, Kohut, and others).

In science, we witness the same duality (Laudan, 1977). Some philosophers of science emphasize the radical shifts in scientific thought. Others stress the outstanding continuities that mark its evolution. I think we can learn from Laudan's work on scientific progress and combine the two perspectives within psychoanalysis when we think in terms of first and second-order questions. Freud used a mechanistic-biological drive model to describe mental structures, object relations theories believe in self-object representations, whereas contemporary psychoanalysts perceive the analytic situation as shaped as a dynamic between two subjectivities. No doubt, this represents a movement of change in psychoanalysis. On the other hand, taking a "gradual" perspective, we may stress that psychoanalytic theory still champions Freud's original profound link between psychopathology, past experience, and transference. We still listen to our patients' unconscious, encourage them to free associate, interpret their dreams, consider unconscious transference dynamics as a decisive factor, and make the best interpretations that we think might help the patient to grow or improve his understanding of his inner motives.

The chief element of continuity in psychoanalysis (and in other sciences, see Laudan, 1977) is represented by the fundamental empirical problems or first-order questions. Ever since Freud, every psychoanalytic school has addressed anxiety, psychosis, narcissism, perversions, regressions, dreams, and other psychic phenomena. Although the empirical problem domain varies (we see less hysterics and more personality disorders) as a result of cultural and social changes, psychic phenomena within the psychoanalytic encounter tend to endure.

Where radical shifts occur, it is not so much at the level of the formulation or identification of first-order problems as at the level of explanation or problem solution. There are, for example, radical differences between how Kohut explains the parent-child relations and how Freud did. However, parent-child relations as such remain an essential problem for psychoanalysts. Of course, besides shared interest in the same psychic phenomena, there are often important common conceptualizations that persist through time (the central concept of transference, for example).

I assume this might seem strange to a contemporary relational analyst who perceives little if any, contiguity between Freud's drive theory, with its quasi-mechanistic and biological language, and the relational approach. A postmodernist would add that psychoanalytic theories also leave their imprint on the first-order questions. Hence, if the relational approach differs from Freud's drive theory, all the terms within these theories must have different meanings.

However, even with using different epistemologies and methodologies, we still use different theories to explain the same problem (such as agoraphobia or psychosis), even when we describe the problem in different languages.

In fact, I believe psychoanalysis' merit is precisely in its ability to find adequate explanations to significant psychic phenomena and clinical facts that differ from the psychoanalytic theories which attempt to solve them.

Psychic phenomena are, therefore, the "engine" behind psychoanalytic progress. In fact, this was the reason psychoanalytic schools have emerged from the first place. Each school defined a different set of clinical phenomena that previous theories overlooked or proposed an unsatisfactory explanation. Self-psychology covered empathy in development and clinical encounters; Klein covered paranoia and destructiveness; Kernberg covered borderline patients; Sullivan, the interpersonal cultural dimension; and so on.

This merit compensates for a methodology that relies on clinical observation and on subjective theorizing, which was thought by many as "crippling epistemological defect uncharacteristic of other science in that its theories are not subject to verification but must rely upon the point of view and basic assumptions of groups of analysts" (Hanly, 1983, 402). One promising solution of how we can test our subjective theories, at least in the clinical encounter, was proposed by Hinshelwood (2013) which offered a "testing process" (130) between different psychoanalytic theories based on occurrences that happen before and after interpretation.

Further inquiry is needed to determine how we distinguish between far-fetched and appropriate therapeutic solutions. We need to consider psychoanalytic schools in terms of their weakness and strength in finding effective "solutions" to psychic phenomena. Such inquiry can guide us to use different theories to understand different facts.

References

Aguayo, J. and Lundgren, J. (2018). Introduction to a Comparative Assessment of W.R. Bion and D.W. Winnicott's Clinical Theories. *British Journal of Psychotherapy*, 34, 194–197. https://doi.org/10.1111/bjp.12360.

Altman, N. (2000). Black and White Thinking. *Psychoanalytic Dialogues*, 10, 589–605. https://doi.org/10.1080/10481881009348569.

Aron, L. (1996). Relational Perspectives Book Series. In *A Meeting of Minds: Mutuality in Psychoanalysis*. Vol. 4. Hillsdale, NJ: Analytic Press, Inc.

Auerhahn, N.C. and Laub, D. (2018). Against Forgiving: The Encounter that Cannot Happen between Holocaust Survivors and Perpetrators. *The Psychoanalytic Quarterly*, 87, 39–72. https://doi.org/10.1080/00332828.2018.1430401.

Bion, W.R. (1959). Attacks on Linking. *The International Journal of Psychoanalysis*, 40, 308–315.

Bollas, C. (1995). *Cracking Up: The Work of Unconscious Experience*. New York, NY: Hill & Wang.

Bornstein, R.F. (2001). The Impending Death of Psychoanalysis. *Psychoanalytic Psychology*, 18, 3–20. https://doi.org/10.1037/0736-9735.18.1.2.

Bornstein, R.F. and Masling, J.M. (1998). Empirical Investigations of Events within the Analytic Hour. In R.F. Bornstein and J.M. Masling (Eds.) *Empirical Studies of the Therapeutic Hour*. Washington, DC: American Psychological Association, xv–xxxiv.

Casement, P. (1985). *On Learning from the Patient*. London: Tavistock Publications.

Cavell, S. (1976). *Must We Mean What We Say?* Cambridge: Cambridge University Press.

Davies, J.M. (1994). Desire and Dread in the Analyst: Reply to Glen Gabbard's Commentary on "Love in the Afternoon". *Psychoanalytic Dialogues*, 4, 503–508.

Davies, J.M. and Frawley, M.G. (1992). Dissociative Processes and Transference-Countertransference Paradigms in the Psychoanalytically Oriented Treatment of Adult Survivors of Childhood Sexual Abuse. *Psychoanalytic Dialogues*, 2, 5–36.

Fonagy, P. (2014). Introduction. In R.N. Emde and M. Leuzinger-Bohleber (Eds.) *Early Parenting and Prevention of Disorder: Psychoanalytic Research at Interdisciplinary Frontiers*. London, England: Karnac.

Freud, S. (1915/1942). On Transience. *The International Journal of Psychoanalysis*, 23, 84–85.

Freud, S. (1940). *Standard Edition: Splitting of the Ego in the Process of Defence*. Vol. 23. London: Hogarth Press, 275–278.

Giacolini, T. and Sabatello, U. (2019). Psychoanalysis and Affective Neuroscience. The Motivational/Emotional System of Aggression in Human Relations. *Frontiers in Psychology*, 9, 2475.

Ghent, E. (1990). Masochism, Submission, Surrender – Masochism as a Perversion of Surrender 1. *Contemporary Psychoanalysis*, 26, 108–136.

Govrin, A. (2006). The Dilemma of Contemporary Psychoanalysis: Toward a "Knowing" Post-Postmodernism. *Journal of the American Psychoanalytic Association*, 54, 507–535. https://doi.org/10.1177/00030651060540020801.

Govrin, A. (2016). *Conservative and Radical Perspectives on Psychoanalytic Knowledge: The Fascinated and the Disenchanted*. New York, NY: Routledge/Taylor & Francis Group.

Govrin, A. and Mills, J. (Eds.) (2019). *Innovations in Psychoanalysis: Originality, Development and Progress*. London: Routledge (forthcoming).

Hanly, C. (1983). A Problem of Theory Testing. *International Review of Psychoanalysis*, 71, 375–383.

Hansbury, G. (2017). The Masculine Vaginal: Working with Queer Men's Embodiment at the Transgender Edge. *Journal of the American Psychoanalytic Association*, 65, 1009–1031. https://doi.org/10.1177/0003065117742409.

Hinshelwood, R.D. (2013). *Research on the Couch – Single-Case Studies, Subjectivity and Psychoanalytic Knowledge*. London: Routledge.

Hoffman, I. (1998). *Ritual and Spontaneity in Psychoanalytic Process: A Dialectical-Constructivist View*. Hillsdale, NJ: The Analytic Press.

Iyengar, U., Rajhans, P., Fonagy, P., Strathearn, L. and Kim, S. (2019). Unresolved Trauma and Reorganization in Mothers: Attachment and Neuroscience Perspectives. *Frontiers in Psychology*, 10, 110. https://doi.org/10.3389/fpsyg.2019.00110.

Johnson, B. (2009). A "Neuropsychoanalytic" Treatment of a Patient with Cocaine Dependence. *Neuropsychoanalysis*, 11, 181–196. https://doi.org/10.1080/15294145.2009.10773612.

Johnson, B. and Flores Mosri, D. (2016). The Neuropsychoanalytic Approach: Using Neuroscience as the Basic Science of Psychoanalysis. *Frontiers in Psychology*, 7, 1459. https://doi.org/10.3389/fpsyg.2016.01459.

Kaplan-Solms, K. and Solms, M. (2000). *Clinical Studies in Neuro-Psychoanalysis: Introduction to a Depth Neuropsychology*. London, UK: Karnac.

King, P. and Steiner, R. (Eds.) (1991). *The Freud-Klein Controversies: 1941–45*. New York, NY: Tavistock/Routledge.

Klein, M. (1946). Notes on Some Schizoid Mechanisms. *The International Journal of Psychoanalysis*, 27, 99–110.

Kuhn, T. (1977). *The Essential Tension – Selected Studies in Scientific Tradition and Change*. Chicago: The University of Chicago Press.

Laudan, L. (1977). *Progress and Its Problems: Towards a Theory of Scientific Growth*. Berkeley, CA: University of California Press.

Lear, J. (1998). *Open Minded: Working Out the Logic of the Soul*. Cambridge, MA: Harvard University Press.

Loewald, H.W. (1978). *Primary Process, Secondary Process, and Language. In Papers on Psychoanalysis*. Vol. 1980. New Haven: Yale University Press, 178–206.

Meltzer, D. (1983). *Dream-Life. A Re-Examination of the Psychoanalytical Theory and Technique*. London: Clinic Press, for the Roland Harris Trust Library.

Mills, J. (2005). A Critique of Relational Psychoanalysis. *Psychoanalytic Psychology*, 22, 155–188. https://doi.org/10.1037/0736-9735.22.2.155.

Mills, J. (2017). Challenging Relational Psychoanalysis: A Critique of Postmodernism and Analyst Self-Disclosure. *Psychoanalytic Perspectives*, 14, 313–335. https://doi.org/10.1080/1551806X.2017.1342312.

Netz, R. (2016). Some Reflections on the Illusion of Literary Fame, Ho! *Literary Magazines*, 14, 191–203.

Northoff, G. (2012). Psychoanalysis and the Brain – Why Did Freud Abandon Neuroscience? *Frontiers in Psychology*, 3, 71. https://doi.org/10.3389/fpsyg.2012.00071.

Parsons, M. (1990). Marion Milner's "Answering Activity" and the Question of Psychoanalytic Creativity. *International Review of Psychoanalysis*, 17, 413–424.

Pound, E. (1934). *Selected Poems. Edited with an Introduction by T.S. Eliot.* London: Faber & Faber Ltd.

Puget, J. (2017). Discussion of Dominique Scarfone's Paper, "On 'That Is Not Psychoanalysis': Ethics as the Main Tool for Psychoanalytic Knowledge and Discussion": Terminable and Interminable Discussion. *Psychoanalytic Dialogues*, 27, 401–405.

Roth, M. (2017). Projective Identification and Relatedness: A Kleinian Perspective. *Psychoanalytic Perspectives*, 14, 350–355. https://doi.org/10.1080/1551806X.2017.1342416.

Ruby, P.M. (2011). Experimental Research on Dreaming: State of the Art and Neuropsychoanalytic Perspectives. *Frontiers in Psychology*, 2, 286. https://doi.org/10.3389/fpsyg.2011.00286.

Rustin, J. (2012). *Infant Research & Neuroscience at Work in Psychotherapy: Expanding the Clinical Repertoire (Norton Professional Books).* Kindle edn. New York: W.W. Norton & Company, 9.

Scruton, R. (2015). Chapter 7: Poetry and Truth. In J. Gibsons (Ed.) *The Philosophy of Poetry.* London: Oxford, 149–161.

Seligman, S. (2018). *Relationships in Development – Infancy, Intersubjectivity and Attachment.* London: Routledge.

Silverman, L.H. (1982). A Comment on Two Subliminal Psychodynamic Activation Studies. *Journal of Abnormal Psychology*, 91, 126–130. https://doi.org/10.1037/0021-843X.91.2.126.

Silverman, L.H. (1985). Comments on Three Recent Subliminal Psychodynamic Activation Investigations. *Journal of Abnormal Psychology*, 94, 640–643. https://doi.org/10.1037/0021-843X.94.4.640.

Stern, D.B. (1983). Unformulated Experience, from Familiar Chaos to Creative Disorder 1. *Contemporary Psychoanalysis*, 19, 71–99.

Stern, D.N. (1985). *The Interpersonal World of the Infant.* New York: Basic Books.

Stern, D.N. (2004). *The Present Moment in Psychotherapy and Everyday Life.* New York: Basic Books.

Stolorow, R.D., Orange, D.M. and Atwood, G.E. (2001). Psychoanalysis – a Contextual Psychology: Essay in Memory of Merton M. Gill. *The Psychoanalytic Review*, 88, 15–28. https://doi.org/10.1521/prev.88.1.15.17545.

Strozier, C.B. (2001). *Heinz Kohut: The Making of a Psychoanalyst.* New York: Ferrar & Straus.

Winnicott, D.W. (1953). Transitional Objects and Transitional Phenomena; a Study of the First Not-Me Possession. *The International Journal of Psychoanalysis*, 34, 89–97.

Yadlin-Gadot, S. (2017). Truth Axes and the Transformation of Self. *Psychoanalytic Review*, 104, 163–201. https://doi.org/10.1521/prev.2017.104.2.163.

Yakeley, J. (2017). Mind the Baby: The Role of the Nanny in Infant Observation. *The International Journal of Psychoanalysis*, 98, 1577–1595.

Yovell, Y., Solms, M. and Fotopoulou, A. (2015). The Case for Neuropsychoanalysis: Why a Dialogue with Neuroscience is Necessary But Not Sufficient for Psychoanalysis. *The International Journal of Psychoanalysis*, 96, 1515–1553. https://doi.org/10.1111/1745-8315.12332.

Concluding Remarks

Let us return briefly to Dr. Loyd Silverman, the New York psychoanalyst who, according to his daughter Gillian Silverman, explained everything through a Freudian perspective (Silverman, 2023). He was undoubtedly a naïve realist. But aren't we all in some way? When we construct the patient's past, telling her that her tormented relationship with her boyfriend is an expression of the repetition compulsion of her traumatic relations with her father, do we not believe strongly or faintly that it is a true construct? Of course, we do not possess tremendous self-conviction like our predecessors. However, pushed to the wall, with a promise that we would not be prey for a shrewd analytic philosopher, we would not hesitate to say that we believe it to be true. The argument for naïve realism resides simply in our psychology: Our understanding of the patient's past is useful. Psychoanalytic constructs simply make our thinking more efficient. As William James wrote:

> Any idea upon which we can ride, so to speak; any idea that will carry us prosperously from any one part of our experience to any other part, linking things satisfactorily, working securely, simplifying, saving labor; is true for just so much, true in so far forth, true *instrumentally*. This is the "instrumental" view of truth.
>
> (1907/1975, 34)

More than anything else, we intuitively work with a pragmatic theory of truth, even without knowing how James, Pierce, and Dewey back up our intuition. Indeed, throughout this book, I have shown how psychoanalysis incorporates philosophical influences. The incorporation exists not just in side details we randomly encountered but in the heart of the central themes that psychoanalytic theory deals with, such as infant development, transference relationships, and psychopathology. It is no coincidence that the opening sentences of *Civilization and Its Discontents* (1930), when Freud writes about the values that man pursues, such as honor and possessions, are almost identical to the first sentences of *On The Improvement of the Understanding* (1677) by Spinoza. The same inquiry of the dark and mysterious to illuminate or decipher it, with the seeking of truth, are undoubtedly central subjects in both Freud's fundamental approach and philosophical heritage.

DOI: 10.4324/9781003498162-12

From the description obtained, psychoanalysis seems reminiscent of the character "Zelig" from Woody Allen's 1983 film. Like Zelig, psychoanalysis appears to be an enigmatic figure who, out of his desire to integrate and be liked by the world, unwittingly acquires characteristics of popular philosophies from its surroundings. Thus, when the scientific ethos was dominant, psychoanalysis was "scientific." When modern hermeneutics became popular, it became "hermeneutic," when the influence of postmodernism was evident, psychoanalysis became "postmodern." Psychoanalysis has a flexible and varied foundation that allows it to change and adapt to different worldviews. As we saw in the last chapter, various and contrasting philosophies have existed in dialectical tension since psychoanalysis was founded. The dominant philosophy changes and transforms the field, but its roots can be detected long before it becomes central. Ferenczi was the forerunner of the relational approach, but only in the second millennium did psychoanalysis incorporate postmodern ideas that provided Ferenczi with philosophical theorizing.

Is the Zelig quality of psychoanalysis a sign of weakness and an "anything goes" stance that might lead to irresponsible relativism, or is it a sign of intellectual strength?

Stepansky (2009) argues that embracing theoretical pluralism through psychoanalysis is inconsistent with the structure of a mature science. According to Stepansky, maturing sciences do not allow such pluralism: No astrophysicist would dream of moving playfully between Ptolemaic and Copernican cosmologies or between Aristotelian and Newtonian physics. Hence, he claims that accepting pluralism is why psychoanalysis did not evolve into a mature science. Stepnsky likes to see psychoanalysis evolve like medicine: Medicine matured from a craft into a science by refining its methods.

Stepansky is, no doubt, a positivist. He perceives psychoanalysis as part of medicine, not philosophy or humanities. He calls for a single hegemonic truth instead of epistemic multiplicity.

However, anyone who believes, like I do, that a multiplicity of contradictions and definitions characterizes psychoanalysis and that it is at the same time both scientific and interpretive, both a science and a philosophy, both part of medicine and the humanities, cannot help but endorse its multiplicity of voices and its "Zelig" characteristic. Due to its complex and contradictory nature, psychoanalysis contains different and contradictory worldviews that maintain great tension between them.

While in Freud's writings, one can find a complex dialectical position of different worldviews, post-Freudian psychoanalysis was split between different communities, each identified with a different epistemological position. This diversity is essential for the continued development and growth of psychoanalysis. I would not want psychoanalysis to consist only of scholars in a research laboratory. I also would not like the entire community to turn relational and endorse two-person psychology. I believe the ideal situation is to have different psychoanalytic communities with different images of knowledge working side by side. For too long, the scientific worldview of classical psychoanalysis reigned supreme, and hermeneutic epistemology, or the importance of the therapist's subjectivity, was marginal and sideways.

Scientific ideology, realism, and the correspondence theory of truth no longer retain their once-pivotal role in the control and subtle disciplining of new ideas in psychoanalysis. Scientism, as a sole force, has seemingly never really existed other than as an ideal image of knowledge. We now live in much more fragmented, disparate, and highly complex society, which has been profoundly affected by post-modernism hermeneutics, feminism, and post-structuralism. Consequentially, ever more complex social relationships and forms of knowledge and communication continue to change. Once preserved through psychoanalytic institutes and journals, hegemony and institutionally produced discourse can no longer sustain and repro-duce the established orders of the past.

On the other hand, despite the difficulties in empirically validating psycho-analytic assumptions, scientific communities, even in the postmodern era, have not given up on the connection between empirical research and psychoanalysis. Neuropsychoanalysis represents this line most prominently. It chose an organ in our body – the brain – that could be measured, scanned, compared, and conducted in proven experiments. It is not alone and is joined by the community of infant researchers, the community of psychotherapy researchers, and the community of researchers of therapeutic efficacy. These communities are connected to research centers and universities and continue to engage in vital and vigorous scientific activity.

Alongside this scientific activity, which is carried out in a limited and not always known to mainstream psychoanalysis, the masses of analysts continue to be busy in therapeutic relations, perceiving the clinical encounter as placed in contexts of meaning. They are continually informed by unconscious fantasy and the vicissi-tudes of desire subjectively experienced.

Their case studies (and theories) will continue to be read like short stories and will continue to suffer from a of "the serious stamp of science" (Breuer and Freud, 1895, 160). Paraphrasing Freud in this most cited paragraph, we must console our-selves with the reflection that the nature of the subject is evidently responsible for this, rather than any preference of our own.

References

Breuer, J. & Freud, S. (1895). *Studies on Hysteria*. Standard Edition 2.
Freud, S. (1930). *Standard Edition: Civilization and its Discontents*. Vol. 21. Hogarth Press.
Silverman, G. (2023). Growing Up in the House of Freud. *The New Yorker*, July 15.
James, W. (1907/1975). *Pragmatism: A New Name for Some Old Ways of Thinking*. New York and London: Longmans, Green & Co. [Reprinted Cambridge, MA: Harvard University Press.]
Spinoza, B. (1677). *On the Improvement of the Understanding*, trans. R.H.M. Elwes. South Carolina: CreateSpace Independent Publishing Platform.
Stepansky, P. (2009). *Psychoanalysis at the Margins*. New York: The Other Press.

Index

Admas, Jane 119
Allen, Woody 192
Altman, Neil 116, 136, 178
Alvarez, Ann 159
American Association of Psychoanalysis 38
American psychoanalysis, xii–xiii
American Psychoanalytic Association
    41, 63
A, Ms. 156–157
anaclitic relation 20
Analysis of the Self, The (Kohut) 75, 77, 79
anti-positivists 64–66, 93
anxiety xi, 72, 83, 153, 157, 166, 181, 187
archaic narcissistic configurations 72
archeological truth xiii
archeologist 77–78
Arendt, Hannah 91
Arlow, Jacob 38
Aron, Louis 93, 116
Atlas, Galit 116
Atwood, George xiv, 97–113
authenticity 63, 116, 127, 128, 130, 131,
    134–135, 136
authoritarianism 90, 131
authority xii, 29, 32, 37, 90, 91, 92, 94, 95,
    101, 109, 111, 112, 123, 126, 129–133,
    136–137, 153, 166
autism 159
autonomous objectives 46–47
Avenarium, Richard 12

Bacon, Francis 42
bad breast 155
Baker, Ronald 57
Bass, Anthony 116
Becker, Ernest 125
Beebe, Beatrice 104
behaviorism 44–45

Being and Time (Heidegger) 98
Benjamin, Jessica 65, 116
Bergmann, Martin 47, 54, 117
Berman, Emanuel 93
Bernstein, Richard 93, 101–102
Berthold-Bond, D. 7
Binswanger, Ludwig 5–6
Bion, Wilfred 116, 120, 166, 171, 174,
    176, 179
Blanton, S. 32, 33
Blatt, Sydney 145
Blum, H.P. 39
Bohr, Niels 56
Bollas, C. 172
Bornstein, Robert 14
Brandchaft, Bernard 97
Brenner, Charles 38, 41, 66–67
Brentano, Franz 5, 16
British Independent Group 119
British psychoanalysis xiii
Bromberg, James 116
Buber, Martin 91
Busch, Fred 44, 58–59
Butterfield, Herbert 149

Carnap, Rudolph 12
castration anxiety 153
castration fear 14
catharsis 29
chess 55, 82
Chicago Psychoanalytic Institute 69
Civilization and Its Discontents (Freud) 191
classical psychoanalysis: definition
    38–39; development theory 112; ego
    psychology xiii, 34, 37–38, 41–48,
    56, 57, 63, 65–66, 75–76, 86, 109;
    epistemological position 40, 41;
    instrumentalism 49, 51–56; limitations

For Product Safety Concerns and Information please contact our EU
representative GPSR@taylorandfrancis.com
Taylor & Francis Verlag GmbH, Kaufingerstraße 24, 80331 München, Germany

www.ingramcontent.com/pod-product-compliance
Lightning Source LLC
Chambersburg PA
CBHW050648280326
41932CB00015B/2819

9 781032 806990